AFTER THE ASYLUMS

Elaine Murphy is Professor of Psychogeriatrics at the United
Medical Schools at Guy's Hospital, London, and Vice Chairman of
the Mental Health Act Commission. She was formerly a consultant
psychiatrist with Redbridge and Newham Health Authorities. She
has a special interest in the planning, management and evaluation of
community care services as a result of some years spent in health
service management. She is also founder editor of the *International
Journal of Geriatric Psychiatry* and UK adviser to the World Health
Organization on the health of elderly people. She has published
extensively in her own clinical research fields of depression and the
epidemiology of mental disorder in the community and also on
community care services. Her published books include *Affective
Disorders in the Elderly* (Churchill Livingstone, 1986) and *Dementia
and Mental Illness in the Old* (Papermac, 1986).

AFTER THE ASYLUMS
Community Care for
People with Mental Illness

Elaine Murphy

faber and faber
LONDON · BOSTON

First published in 1991
by Faber and Faber Limited
3 Queen Square London WC1N 3AU

Photoset by Parker Typesetting Service, Leicester
Printed in England by Clays Ltd, St Ives plc

A CIP record for this book
is available from the British Library

ISBN 0–571–16357–2

Contents

Acknowledgements

I owe thanks to the many people who gave me their time to discuss the issues this book addresses. I wish to mention in particular Dr David Abrahamson, James Collier CB, the Rt Hon. Lord Ennals, Ros Hepplewhite, Tessa Jowell, Dr Niall Moore, Isobel Morris, Dr Felix Post, the Rt Hon. Enoch Powell MBE, Dr John Reed, Dr Sandy Robertson and Professor John Wing.

I must also acknowledge the influence on me of the work of Professor George Brown, Dr David Challis, Paul Clifford, Professor John Gunn, Professor Julian Leff, Dr Frank Holloway, Dr Roy Porter, Dr Anthony Thorley, Fraser Watts and their many co-workers.

Special thanks go to colleagues William Bingley and Professor Tom Craig who commented very constructively on earlier drafts, and also to my editor at Faber and Faber, Roger Osborne, for his continuing, painstaking interest. Finally I must mention my unofficial, ruthlessly helpful editor, my husband John Murphy, and Chris Thomas, who indefatigably typed a dozen redrafts.

The views expressed in this book are personal ones and may not reflect the views of statutory and voluntary bodies with which I am associated.

Elaine Murphy
February 1991

1 A Vision of Community Care: Introduction to the Themes

Introduction

The No. 4 bus I took home from school in Nottingham stopped at the Old Market Square Terminus right alongside the No. 31 for Mapperley. Mapperley – the very name was awesome to me. It meant the asylum, the 'loony bin', the 'nut-house', a massive, gloomy red-brick institution where crazy, peculiar people lived secret, mysterious lives. Perhaps the maniacs, the loonies, the 'fruit and nut cases' inside the walls were violent, possibly chained up? How old were they? Were they there for life?

All of us schoolchildren speculated and joked about Mapperley in an anxious kind of way. We used to examine the bus queue for tell-tale signs of craziness but everyone looked disappointingly normal. None of us knew anyone who was 'mad', or at least thought we didn't, and no one ever talked about mental disorder or told us what went on inside the hospital. As a child I never met anyone who had been inside its walls, or at least who admitted to it, and the stigma of the asylum was such that ordinary families never mentioned relatives who were cared for there.

But, looking back, I knew a fair number of 'normal' people with mental problems. There was poor Mrs Shipley next door, who put her head in the gas oven when her husband deserted her and their two children. There was my friend Anita's father who was living permanently in a hospital somewhere for unexplained reasons; Anita's older brother also had a series of 'nervous breakdowns' in his late teens. There was senile, frail Miss East who rarely emerged from behind the filthy net curtains of her squalid house opposite and who was the focus of endless gossip and concern until the day she broke her hip and was miraculously removed permanently to hospital, to the neighbours' relief. And then there was my aunt, unpredictably cold and withdrawn, who took against people for no apparent reason and from time to time suspected, ridiculously, that neighbours were stealing her prize garden plants. As a child I never made any connection between the familiar problems of neighbours, friends and relatives and the work of the forbidding old hospital.

Fear of mental hospitals may have lessened to a degree in the last thirty years but children today make the same old jokes and still, as I did, fail to comprehend the everyday nature of mental health problems. The general public's understanding of the function of a mental hospital has changed very little, and perceptions about mental disorder and attitudes towards sufferers stem in part from the historical role played by these large institutions where generations of people with mental disorder lived their whole lives in physically impoverished, socially isolating environments, cut off from their fellow men and stigmatized by their disorder and their environment.

Ironically, at the time I describe, the 1950s and 1960s, Mapperley Hospital was nationally renowned amongst professionals in the field for the quality and innovativeness of its rehabilitation services. The medical superintendent, Duncan MacMillan, pioneered policies of early discharge and social aftercare, and Mapperley was a very good mental hospital compared with most. Since then local services have remained in the vanguard of developments and Nottingham now has one of the most highly developed community mental health services in the country. But Mapperley still stands as a forbidding symbol of the old asylum system, and no matter how much money is spent on upgrading wards to make them more welcoming and homely, the main drawback to its acceptability by the general public is its history. Every large mental hospital in the country carries the same unforgettable, unforgivable legacy of its past.

The struggle to create better mental health services in the community, as an alternative to the large asylum system of care, began well over half a century ago, but in the past decade there have been strident protests about the continued rundown and closure of the old hospitals. Members of the public and professionals point to the disastrous manner in which community care policies have been implemented, and inevitably the philosophy underlying the policies has been questioned. As a result, throughout the 1980s the government vacillated in its support for 'community care', unwilling to commit itself wholeheartedly to the policy, although never actually reversing it or stopping the closures.

The opponents of the policy argue along these lines: doing away with the asylums does not do away with the tragedy of mental disorder; people do not miraculously get cured by living 'in the community'; at least patients in the cocoon of an institution are safe, warm, clean, clothed and fed; furthermore, the 'community' is not a real place, only a fictional ideal; the community is, in reality, over-burdened families who have little choice; perhaps, therefore, we should reassess the asylums and realize that they were not so bad after all, and certainly better than no service at all. The dissenters, when illustrating the failure of community care, point to the homeless, destitute, crazy people sleeping rough in every town in Britain; the numbers of unsupported, isolated families trying to cope with a disturbed relative; and the desperate plight of mentally ill people discharged to bed and breakfast hostels from acute psychiatric wards only a day or two after admission in order to make room for even more urgent cases.

It cannot be denied that current 'community care' services are frequently severely inadequate and fail many thousands of vulnerable people. But it is the thesis of this book that there is nothing wrong with the concept of community care, nor is there a lack of knowledge about how to implement it effectively. Rather, for a variety of reasons, we are simply making a hash of doing it properly. In fact Britain is now in a position to create an excellent community mental health service, but it will take government leadership, the proper organizational structures, professional determination and a public better educated about mental health problems to achieve the necessary standards of care.

The community care and mental health failures of the last half-century are the results of a combination of political, economic, bureaucratic and professional factors which together conspired to allow the rundown of the admittedly imperfect asylums before better, more suitable alternative facilities and services were available in the community. Clearly there is no merit in closing down one system, however, inadequate, unless it is replaced by something better.

But what is done is done. Huge numbers of mental hospital beds have now been closed and it is simply too late for these large hospitals ever again to assume a major role in the services. The most important reason, however, for not returning to the old asylum system is that people with mental disorder do not wish to remain in hospital for long periods of time and should not and will not be compelled to do so: people have a much clearer concept of their rights to liberty and choice than even a few decades ago. Twenty years ago reluctant patients were often shifted out of general hospital psychiatric admission wards into long-stay back wards in remote hospitals against their wishes, sometimes under legal orders if they would not go quietly. Involuntary removal to long-stay wards still happens today to old people with dementia who cannot protest effectively; although relatives sometimes complain on their behalf, they do so quietly, knowing they can offer no realistic alternative. But younger mentally disordered people, who can object to being treated in this way, do object; the majority simply do not want to go into long-stay wards, a view which is usually shared by their relatives. Relatives, however, for their part, are often ambivalent; they hate the idea of a spouse, mother, son or daughter going in to a long-stay ward and they support the individual's right to free choice; but they are often put-upon, over-stressed and unable to cope and a system which somehow removes the individual elsewhere has its appeal at times.

It has been suggested that the remaining hospital places, at least, should be kept open so that no further people are released on to an unwelcoming community – the idea is that this would provide some respite for services to tackle the existing problems. This notion is wholly wrong. The 60,000 people who remain behind are mostly old or very disabled, and not since the mid-1980s have the hospitals contained more than a few people who could be so discharged. There are now no random discharges of patients from old long-stay beds and it is a misconception to believe that stopping the closure of the old hospitals would have any impact at all on the community problem. The issues are now, quite simply, unrelated. Furthermore, half-deserted, decaying hospitals are uneconomic to run and soak up resources which could benefit people in the community.

And the community is where most of the 'problem' now lies. Schizophrenia, the mental disorder which is most likely to produce long-term serious disabilities, affects some 300,000 people in Britain, but only 20,000 or so, less than 7 per cent of the total, are still cared for permanently in old hospitals. The vast majority are living in 'the community', so we have 'community care' of a sort, whether we like it or not. Keeping the asylums open would do nothing for the care of the overwhelming majority of people with schizophrenia. Even in the early twentieth century, the point of greatest expansion of the asylums, they did not provide care for everyone with long-term, serious mental disabilities. There was always a large number of such people looked after by their families or living alone, managing as best they could. The asylums were always, therefore, only a partial solution as well as a very unsatisfactory one.

There is overwhelming evidence that, given a choice, people with long-term mental disorders wish to live in ordinary homes of their own, doing the normal everyday things that other people do. *The purpose of community care is to help individuals achieve and sustain a fulfilling and rewarding 'normal' life when this has become difficult through mental disability.* The challenge of community care is how to provide an integrated network of services, including physical facilities, adequate, trained personnel and appropriate organizational structures, to enable the system to work effectively for every individual who requires assistance.

The need for a vision of community care
The word 'asylum' acquired unpalatable connotations in the late nineteenth and twentieth centuries, but the asylum movement was the outcome of a fifty-year campaign by humane men of conscience who felt that they had found a solution both to providing care for people and to curing them. The Lunacy Act of 1845 was the

culmination of their efforts and there was almost universal agreement at the time about what needed to be done – a shared vision which fuelled the enthusiasm of politicians, social reformers, doctors, clergymen and other influential people.

In the twentieth century we have abandoned the old vision, having recognized its limitations, but we have created no new vision to replace it. We must now develop a vision of community mental health care which can provide inspiration for everyone concerned with mental disorder and which will serve to drive political action to turn vision into reality. At present in Britain, government is confronted by seemingly widely divergent opinions about the best route to successful community care. It responds to opposing factions by cautious appeasement of the various interest groups, giving a small grant here, a minor change in welfare benefit there. Government is unlikely to make significant changes or agree increased financial investment in the services until professional bodies, voluntary organizations and public authorities responsible for running the services unite with the service users and their families to demand with one voice the same things.

Moreover, the current much-publicized differences of opinion between the various opposing pressure groups are more apparent than real. Conflicts are not about the fundamental objective of an improved local community-based service but about the speed and energy with which hospital closures should be pursued, the best use of old buildings and land, and the real costs and affordability of good community alternatives. Unseemly interprofessional squabbles also hamper progress; these are about the appropriate roles that doctors, nurses, psychologists, social workers and the new 'care managers' should play. Interagency rivalries, too, lead to fights about which statutory authority should hold sovereignty over funds and take the leading responsibility for service planning. But underlying all this there is remarkable unanimity about the principles of community care.

This book is about the principles and essential components of a community-based mental health service. It is also about the historical cycle of events from the pre-asylum days of community neglect, through the rise and fall of the asylums to the emergence of the community care ideal and the reasons for the current failure of implementation of community care policies. It is written in the hope that an understanding of past and present influences on the process of change within the mental health system will help us to pursue a new vision with the insight to avoid the failures of the past.

The rise and fall of the asylums

The nineteenth-century lunatic asylums were built as places of refuge, shelter and sanctuary, as havens where reparation and restoration of troubled minds could take place. The concept was of a therapeutic, curative environment, based on the well-aired principles of the 'moral treatment', a notion that by treating mad people humanely, improvements could be brought about in the mental and physical health of the sufferers. Asylums were also meant to put paid for ever to the scandalous neglect of mentally disturbed people which had become a feature of the small private madhouses, parish workhouses and bridewells of the eighteenth century. Asylums would protect vulnerable people from cruelty, exploitation and destitution.

Some small local asylums developed in the eighteenth and early nineteenth centuries, but the 1845 Act commanded all county councils to build their own lunatic asylums. The building programme expanded rapidly to cater for ever-increasing numbers. Asylums quickly filled up, not only with pauper lunatics but also with an array of social and psychological derelicts who could not be conveniently dealt with elsewhere in workhouses or prisons. The asylums grew as a result of increased demand brought about by general population growth but also because of the continuing poverty of the labouring classes which led many people into destitution. The growth of the asylums was assisted by funding arrangements which encouraged local parishes to move the parish poor into asylums because asylums were funded by the county council, not the parish.

By the late 1860s the asylums were already too large and overcrowded; they were also inadequately resourced and badly staffed. Enthusiasm for the idea of asylums as a place of cure rapidly waned and an ethos of custodial care came to dominate the services and continued throughout the nineteenth century and right up until after the First World War. The numbers of people resident in mental hospitals grew steadily until 1954 (see Figure 1) when the resident population reached a peak of 148,000. Since then there has been a dramatic reversal of the trend and by 1990 the numbers had fallen back to about 59,000, the level of the 1880s.

The decline in the asylums was in part due to changes in public attitudes to mental health problems but also to the rising influence of psychiatry as a branch of medicine. Psychiatrists successfully consolidated the notion that mental disorder was simply medical disease in a different guise. Medical methods of managing mental disorder assumed pre-eminence over other approaches and were given particular credence by some spectacular new physical treat- ments developed in continental Europe in the 1930s – especially electroconvulsive therapy, lobotomy and insulin coma treatment. Meanwhile, a few pioneering, socially orientated psychiatrists had begun to develop rehabilitation and aftercare schemes for less seriously disturbed long-term patients. By the late 1930s there was growing optimism that new episodes of mental disorder could be treated effectively by vigorous medical treatments and a growing belief that there would be less need for continuing long-term care in the future because people treated with the new methods would not develop long-term handicaps. The apparent effectiveness of vigorous early intervention in the treatment of the psychiatric casualties of the Second World War gave impressive new support to this notion. Although many of these treatments were subsequently shown to be ineffective, the swing towards a medical approach to care was firmly established.

By the late 1940s the best, most innovative hospitals had begun to encourage an 'open door' policy of rapid admission, vigorous treat- ment and early discharge. They had developed rudimentary day care services, new outpatient clinics in general hospitals and closer links with the local community.

The introduction of effective psychotropic drugs in the 1950s gave even further influence to psychiatrists, who now possessed treatments of demonstrable efficacy. The therapeutic impact of

Figure 1 The Rise and Fall in Residents of Lunatic Asylums / Mental Hospitals, 1830–1990

INSERT Fig I

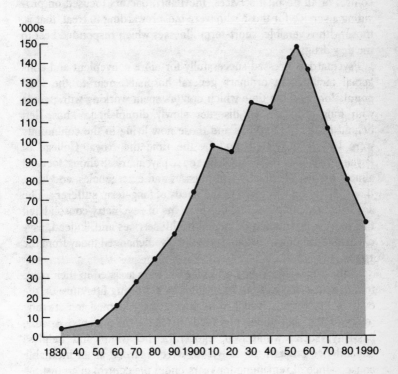

Asylum / Mental Hospital
Resident Population, England and Wales

Source : Annual Reports of Lunacy Commissioners and Board of Control, 1850–1930 and DHSS, 1930–1990 HMSO.

these new drugs on long-term patients has been far less significant than was believed at the time, but such drugs certainly helped to shorten new admissions and gave doctors confidence that fewer hospital beds would be needed in the future. They also encouraged the discharge of the more socially competent long-term patients back into the community. Drugs therefore hastened the rundown of the asylums, although they did not cause them to close.

After the introduction of the National Health Service in 1948, the profession of medicine dominated mental health services almost to the exclusion of other approaches to care, as it in effect assumed control of all hospital services. Inevitably, doctors focused on providing a service for those who were most rewarding to treat, that is, those with reversible, short-term illnesses which responded best to the new drugs.

Psychiatrists pressed successfully for more convenient and congenial facilities in ordinary general hospitals, near to the local population, and the time which doctors spent working with people with long-term mental disorder slowly diminished. Those left behind in the old asylums and those now living in the community were largely neglected, and by the time the Royal College of Psychiatrists was established in 1971, psychiatric training focused almost exclusively on short-term cases and emergencies, and little, if any, attention was given to the needs of long-term sufferers. The academic teaching hospital departments of psychiatry consolidated this narrow orientation of mental health services and, indeed, psychiatrists' training in Britain is essentially unchanged today from the 1940s.

In the 1950s and 1960s, psychiatrists were assisted in their drive to move their services out of asylums by a growing literature on the evils of institutions, which were increasingly blamed for creating many of the disabilities observed in long-term patients. Apathy, passivity, social withdrawal, egocentric behaviour and helpless dependence on staff for daily care were regarded as an inevitable consequence of remaining for years under the control of an institutionalized, repressive regime where social conformity and acquiescence to the rules were rigidly imposed. Although it was clear that bad institutions did have many detrimental effects, and research had demonstrated that less restrictive regimes promoted improvements in patients' social behaviour, many of the disabilities observed in long-term patients were later shown to be symptoms of mental disorder itself, not a consequence of the institution. These symptoms are not miraculously prevented by keeping people out of institutions. However, the literature on 'institutionalization' served the purpose of encouraging staff in the services to consider alternative ways of managing mental health problems.

The decline of the asylums was also helped, indirectly, by the 'antipsychiatry' movement of the 1960s, which sprang up to protest at the all-pervading power of conventional psychiatry over the lives of people with mental disorder. People with differing views and a collection of disparate theories found a champion in R. D. Laing whose writings also served as a rallying point for disaffected former patients who had suffered from over-enthusiastic treatment, for those who resented being labelled as 'ill', and also for civil libertarians pursuing patients' rights to reject unwanted treatment and seeking better safeguards for those legally detained against their wishes. 'Antipsychiatry' grew out of the widespread anti-authoritarian feelings of the 1960s and was an important precipitant of the movement which eventually led to the liberalizing Mental Health Act of 1983.

Government adoption of the community care policy
By 1960 there was a clear reversal in the trend of resident numbers in the old hospitals. These statistics, coupled with the ascendancy of psychiatric treatments and the obvious deteriorating physical conditions in the overcrowded asylums, resulted in the 1962 Hospital Plan which enshrined government support for the development of community-based mental health services and the closure of the old mental hospitals. The plan called for the NHS to provide a service based in general hospital psychiatric units and for local government social services departments to provide social support in the community in the form of day care and residential services.

By 1974 there were 60,000 or so fewer residents in the old hospitals than in 1954, but very few services had been provided in the community. The decline in numbers partly came about because old patients died and were not replaced by new ones, but many patients were discharged, a few lucky ones to new 'group' homes outside the hospital, some to relatives, but many to unsatisfactory lodgings. Discharged patients were rarely followed up by the hospital services beyond a few months.

Concerned by the lack of progress in community care, the government tried to stimulate the growth of community services by restating in a White Paper, *Better Services for the Mentally Ill*, published in 1975, what facilities were required, and by setting down numerical targets. This exhortation to do better came at a time of economic recession and pessimism about public services; it had little impact on the continuing haphazard dissolution of the hospitals and the almost total failure of statutory and local authorities to provide proper community-based long-term care.

Why the community care policy failed

Between 1975 and 1990 successive governments have taken little interest in mental health issues. Numerous reorganizations of the NHS have taken place but have been concerned mainly with improving the efficiency of the administration of the voraciously expensive general hospitals service and with improving GP-based primary care. Any effect on mental health services was largely accidental and consisted mainly of the services becoming submerged under a weight of management tiers and thus largely invisible to senior managers. The vital close links with local authorities which are necessary to develop the social infrastructure of housing and support services became increasingly difficult to sustain and develop. At the same time, local authority social services were themselves subjected to structural changes designed to improve the administration and professionalism of social work services, but which effectively destroyed mental health services as an indentifiable entity within local authorities.

In the last twenty years central government has also imposed a series of measures designed to curb local government spending. Local government, like central government, has never regarded mental health as an electorally sensitive issue and although some authorities have been willing to fund developments as long as it was possible to raise the required money from local taxation, the curbs on local government spending had a disproportionately serious effect on mental health services. Overall, the erosion of local government power has been catastrophic for mental health services. Even though a small fund, Joint Finance, was introduced in the mid-1970s to encourage the transfer of services from the NHS to local authorities to foster community-based developments, it has made no major impact on service developments apart from a few small demonstration projects which serve as useful examples of service innovation.

An extraordinary, unplanned, almost accidental and massively expensive incentive to shift people out of long-stay hospitals into private sector residential facilities in boarding-houses, care homes and nursing homes came about in the late 1970s and early 1980s. This was the new availability of social security welfare benefit to individual claimants for payment of board and lodging charges. Huge numbers of long-stay patients who were formerly a charge on the NHS, and were originally to become the responsibility of local authorities, suddenly became a charge on a totally separate government department, the Department of Social Security. Unfortunately the services provided to these former hospital patients in their new homes were often markedly inferior in terms of physical, psychological and social care than the care they had received in hospital. The NHS, in effect, shuffled off thousands of high-cost in-patients to low-cost care funded by social security benefits.

As long-stay patients moved out of hospitals, the cost of the reducing numbers of remaining patients rocketed. Huge deteriorating institutions soaked up money in maintenance and became less and less efficient to run and, though numbers of patients declined, the wage bill for staff remained much the same or even grew. Until an institution was closed in its entirety, it proved impossible to make much of a dent in running costs. In spite of the steep decline in resident patients, the overall cost of the mental health service remained more or less static (see Figure 2 below) due to the rising costs of inefficient, old hospitals and to the fact that a good deal of money needed to be invested in new general

2 Mental Illness In-patient Costs

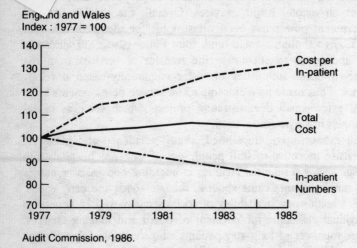

England and Wales
Index : 1977 = 100

Audit Commission, 1986.

hospital units and other 'acute' mental health services. Money has, therefore, remained 'locked in' to hospital beds and has not become available, as originally envisaged, for developing community services.

Money from the sale of old hospital sites, once it is available, is reckoned broadly to cover both the capital costs of new community services and many of the revenue costs of running new services. However, large sums of bridging capital and 'double-running' revenue, that is money to run the old and new services together for a while, are required to build up the services in the community in advance of the final closure and this bridging money has not been forthcoming. In the early 1980s Regional Health Authorities each targeted one or two hospitals for closure and produced some bridging funds, but it was too little, too late; although services developed for the lucky few being discharged from the targeted hospitals, the haphazard transfer of patients out of other hospitals continued. Furthermore, no new money was made available for the many thousands of long-term sufferers living in the community without adequate help.

The NHS and Community Care Act of 1990 imposes a

Figure 3 Population Trends, 1974–98

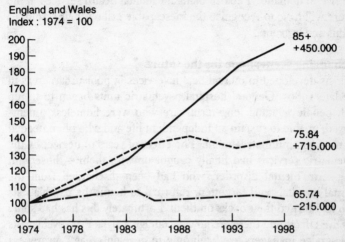

England and Wales
Index : 1974 = 100

Source : OPCS figures to 1984 and Government Actuary's Department 1983-
based forecasts

'gate-keeping' role on local authorities who, from April 1993, will control access to all state funds for residential and domiciliary care outside the hospitals. This should lead to a more rational allocation of resources for care in the community but will not solve the lack of bridging capital, an issue which requires further imaginative short-term solutions by government.

The final important factor which has slowed down the development of community care is the increasing needs of Britain's rapidly ageing population, a factor which has had an enormous impact on all health services. The rise in the number of over 75- and over 85-year-olds has created a staggering increase in new cases of senile dementia such that by 1990, half of all long-stay psychiatric beds were occupied by old people with dementia. Resources to provide community-based mental health services for the elderly population and their families have inevitably been carved in part out of resources which would formerly have provided care for lifelong chronic sufferers of mental disorder. Profound demographic changes will, however, continue to have a significant impact on all health and social services and it is estimated that a 2 per cent increase in funding above inflation is needed simply to keep up with the rise in demand. Thus all plans for mental health services in the future will have to recognize the inescapable call on their resources of this needy group.

A changing scene: hope for the future

A crisis developed in mental health services in poor urban areas in the late 1980s. General hospital psychiatric units began to fill up with people needing long-term care who were homeless, unemployed, unable to sustain an independent life and who often needed years of continuing treatment. The effect of years of neglect by the psychiatric services had finally caught up with them – those with long-term mental disorder, who had been discharged from the mental hospitals and forgotten, returned to haunt the psychiatrists who had turned their backs on them. Fortunately this has had some positive effects and there are now encouraging signs that psychiatrists and service managers are beginning to develop greater awareness and interest in the needs of people with long-term disorders. The crisis has also encouraged other professions, notably psychologists, to play an increasingly important role in service development for those with long-term needs.

But mental disorder creates special problems for those planning services. Service users and their families are rarely demanding consumers and are easily ignored. Also the stigma of mental disorder creates fears and anxiety in an ill-educated general public embarrassed by people who sound or look different from normal. A further problem is that people with mental disorder do not always share the views of those around them about what is wrong with them and often reject help and refuse treatment. There are wide philosophical differences in society about how such people should be treated. There are those who hold to the paternalistic view that we owe it as a duty of care to people who have impaired reasoning and judgment as a result of mental disorder to treat them, if it is in the best interests of their health and safety, even when the individual concerned disagrees. And there are those who feel that individuals have a right to determine their own future, even if their choice will not be in their best long-term interests. The arguments are often about the degree of control and style of treatment which it is justifiable to impose on unwilling recipients of care, and society has been unable as yet satisfactorily to resolve the dilemma. The Mental Health Act of 1983 provided a legal framework for decision-making but did not solve the day-to-day dilemmas which crop up in community work. The Act has wrongly been accused of tying psychiatrists' hands; it does in fact allow early intervention to protect relatives and to promote the health of the individual but it needs to be much better understood by all professionals.

Practical problems of community care

Community services are disorganized and fragmented and face numerous operational, practical problems. One major problem that service users and their relatives complain about is having insufficient personal income to make realistic choices for themselves. Welfare benefits, both for individuals and their supporting families, are small and tiresomely difficult to winkle out of the social security system.

There is also tremendous variation in the commitment to, and funding of, mental health services between different geographical areas, both by District Health Authorities and by social services authorities. Nor is there any correlation between local health and social services spending; one does not appear to compensate if the other is a low spender and neither authority ever seems to base its spending on a realistic local assessment of need. Private sector homes have developed mainly in prosperous suburban, rural and coastal areas where there are cheap, large properties available for conversion, thus adding to geographical disparities in services.

A further problem has been the lack, until the 1990 Act, of a community-based professional member of staff identified as responsible for ensuring that an individual's needs for care and treatment are properly assessed and adequately met by a range of appropriate services. It has been a recurring cry that 'no one is in charge out there' in the community.

General practitioners have been much less closely involved in providing long-term care services than might be expected. This is because their training, like that of other doctors, has not focused on continuing care, and also because former patients have sometimes been thoughtlessly resettled out of hospital without local GPs being invited to participate in planning for their needs. GPs, like psychiatrists, generally have not perceived a role for themselves beyond undertaking specific medical interventions.

The final problem which needs to be addressed is the staffing of the services. A traditional asylum provided care for all the activities of daily life with an emphasis on 'hands-on' personal and domestic care round the clock. It thus provided shelter, food, clothing, occupation and opportunities for social interaction, much of it by unqualified nursing assistants and domestics. In the community there has been insufficient recognition of the need to provide people with long-term mental disorders with personal, domestic and social care. There is a need for a greater concentration of resources away from the traditional professional skills of medicine, nursing and therapy in favour of larger numbers of less highly qualified but properly trained mental health care staff working in the community to provide more supportive care at home focused on the practical tasks of daily life. This new workforce needs to be backed up by a skilled team of professional mental health workers supervising all aspects of care.

The problems of community care, then, are not just financial. They result from a gaping disunity between health and social services and are the outcome of a lack of thought about who should be responsible for delivering services and a consequent absence of the right sort of staff with appropriate training. But underlying all these problems is a careless and sustained neglect of people with chronic long-term mental disorder by central government, local government, the medical and other professions and the community at large.

What makes community care work?

A great deal is known about the characteristics of successful community care projects, and certain principles and characteristics can be readily translated to service-planning on a large scale. Projects work when:

- Services are underpinned by explicit, clear values and principles about what the project is trying to achieve
- The views of service users are taken into account in planning
- Professional skills of a wide range of health and social service staff contribute to plans
- Recipients of schemes are integrated into the local community and have access to ordinary community facilities

Successful schemes have other characteristics too:

- A driving project leader who steers the project through to completion
- A focus on action by a small group of people able to commit resources
- A collaboration by two or more organizations (for example, social services and a housing association or a voluntary organization and the NHS) to provide a new service
- A local neighbourhood focus on a geographical area where members of different statutory, voluntary and private sector organizations know each other personally
- Collaboration between many different professionals and voluntary workers in delivering the service

In the late 1980s a series of government reports reviewed the financing structure and organization of community care services and made recommendations to encourage better use of resources and foster good community care planning. The two most influential reports, the first by the Audit Commission in 1986, and the second by Sir Roy Griffiths in 1988, heavily influenced the new NHS and Community Care Act of 1990. The Act provided that local authority social services departments should take the leading responsibility for assessing the needs of individuals in their local population, setting local priorities and service objectives and arranging the required care by designing, organizing and purchasing a spectrum of services. To allow local authorities to do this, all social security benefit for board and lodging and other community care grant monies are to be channelled via local authorities from April 1993.

The government also recommended that social services should establish a 'care management' system, a network of staff taking specific, identified responsibility for assessing and arranging care for groups of people in need of community care. It is hoped that these new 'care managers' or 'case managers' will be the long-awaited people 'in charge out there' to whom those in receipt of care will look for ensuring the smooth coordination of the various services they need. The government also identified a small specific grant for spending on community developments, but one which can only be spent by the joint agreement of the local health authority and social services departments. This initiative is intended to promote joint planning across health and social services boundaries.

The new arrangements, if adequately funded, could foster the development of community services for people with long-term mental disorder, particularly those living in their own homes, and will encourage care at home rather than in institutions. It also seems clear that authorities could develop more effective joint strategies for delivering services if they combine their purchasing power in joint contracting schemes. Unfortunately the NHS Act omitted one of Sir Roy Griffiths' most important recommendations – that there should be a new Minister for Community Care to provide decisive central government leadership, establish clear objectives and national priorities, develop interdepartmental working at government level and set measurable targets for local authorities. The government also failed to 'ring-fence' community care grant money from the general allocation of local authority grants, enabling those local authorities, if they so wish, to spend community care grants on other services such as roads, schools or other local government priorities.

In spite of these problems the proposals have the potential for improving the balance of services for people with mental disorder, although to achieve lasting benefit they will need to be supplemented by short-term bridging finance prior to the closure of the many large hospitals. The government still needs, however, to play a more positive and forceful leadership role in developing community mental health services. Unless it does, the necessary joint working across health and social services is unlikely to happen very quickly.

The principles of community care

The philosophy that underpins community care is a belief that every individual has rights and entitlements and also responsibilities. Community care services aim to develop an individual's capabilities to live as normal a life as possible within the constraints of his or her disabilities. The general targets and principles for such services are:

- *Consultation and participation*. Service users should be involved in plans for their care
- Services should promote *self-determination and autonomy* by offering information on which choices can be made
- They should seek to create a *normal home environment*
- There should be minimal *segregation* from the general community
- *Protection from abuse* and harm and 'asylum' in the sense of a haven or retreat is essential
- Services should be organized on a *small, local neighbourhood* scale
- *Practical, everyday solutions* which the recipient can use for him- or herself are generally better than arranging a special service
- Services should try to *alleviate distress*

In order effectively to provide a service, the following criteria need to be met:

- There should be a mechanism for *identifying people in need* of the service
- It should offer *help with an individual's finances*
- It should offer *24-hour crisis help*
- It should offer *social rehabilitation* facilities
- The service should be *offered indefinitely*, if necessary for a lifetime
- Medical and *psychiatric treatment* should be available on a continuing basis
- It should provide *support for family, friends and the local community*
- The service should protect an *individual's legal rights*
- The service system should be organized to provide a *coordinated, 'seamless' service*

The components of a service

Every individual with mental disorder has the *ordinary needs* of all human beings for income, shelter, food, clothing, protection from harm, daily occupation and emotional, spiritual and social fulfilment. In addition he or she has *special needs* for specific treatment and care, which arise from his or her mental disorder; these are for medication, training, counselling and so forth. The component parts of a comprehensive service must therefore include:

- *Assistance with maximizing financial entitlements* to ensure adequate personal income
- *A range of housing options*, from individual ordinary flats and houses through a spectrum of staffed, supported housing such as group homes, sheltered flats and small hostels. The key elements of all schemes should be to offer security of tenure, a lockable, private room of one's own and personal bathroom and sanitation facilities, plus room for entertaining in private, all staffed to give adequate physical and emotional care
- *Day care services* which provide daily occupation, opportunities for social development and opportunities for participation in constructive long-term activities
- *Work opportunities* which provide genuinely rewarding opportunities for individuals to earn cash and achieve long-term goals
- Opportunities for *social activities and leisure* through social clubs, befriending schemes and schemes which promote the integration of individuals into normal community and leisure activities

The conditions and specialist services which are required in order to provide a full, overall service include:

- Ready access to a specialist multi-disciplinary mental health team of professionals operating twenty-four hours a day from the Community Mental Health Centre (CMHC) – see Chapter 8 – or equivalent facility, supplemented by outpatient clinics and emergency clinics
- A specialist Rehabilitation or Continuing Care Team of professionals specially identified to work only with long-term sufferers
- Sufficient in-patient beds to provide the acute treatment needs of

the locality and intensive care for seriously disturbed people for short periods of time

- A facility which provides close supervision of people who require 'slow-stream' but active treatment for several years

Services should be organized in such a way that both users and their relatives can play a full participating role in planning them. 'Tokenism' must be replaced by a real commitment to practical schemes which foster the involvement of users and relatives.

The new Act focuses on the purchasing, organizing role of health and social services authorities but it gives encouragement to a wide range of organizations, especially voluntary organizations and the private sector and 'not-for-profit' organizations such as charitable trusts and housing associations, to become 'providers of services'. This should stimulate a healthy diversity of service provision and a wide spectrum of services, though tight coordination is needed by the statutory services, as well as close monitoring of quality stand-ards, if services are not to become even further fragmented. Indeed, many more formal, structured programmes of quality assurance of mental health services, both hospital- and community-based, are required to ensure that individual components of a dispersed ser-vice do not deteriorate in the quality of care they give. We must avoid at all costs the scandals of the eighteenth-century madhouse. Local quality-assurance schemes implemented by authority man-agers should be supplemented by regular monitoring through a national quality-monitoring inspectorate, preferably one which covers all aspects of mental health services. These questions are addressed in detail in Chapter 8.

Some special problems in community care

There are some areas of mental health care which have, tradi-tionally, been largely neglected, but no successful community sys-tem can be set up without special thought being given to the needs of such groups as mentally abnormal offenders, single homeless people without a settled way of life, and people who misuse drugs or alcohol. Special thought, too, needs to be given to how best to provide services in a multi-ethnic society where racism, cultural barriers and social class barriers between the service providers and the service users conspire in some localities to create particular problems. These problems are given separate consideration in Chapter 9.

Community care works

Community care is by no means a cheap option, though it is now becoming clear from research evidence that a good, effective community service can be provided at broadly the same cost as keeping people in long-stay hospitals. The costs of a good service will, however, vary quite markedly from place to place; a poor urban area generates far greater needs for short-term treatment and long-term support and care than a more prosperous suburban or rural area. Government funding to the NHS and to local authorities needs to reflect those differences. Right now, it is possible to observe good community mental health services operating in localities that have received development funds or that have been fortunate in the commitment of the local statutory authorities. Such services are, however, disappointingly rare.

*

Even the best kinds of services can never take away the personal tragedy and disappointments of mental disorder – not, at least, until we find a cure for the disabling effects of such disorders. Sadly, we are little nearer a proper understanding of the root causes of serious mental disorder than were our Victorian forefathers, in spite of our vastly increased knowledge about genes, biochemistry and the psychology of interpersonal relationships. People still, therefore, have to come to an accommodation with distressing symptoms and blighted lives, although good services can provide a chance for people to live decent lives and gain fulfilment through meaningful occupation and friendships.

This book's purpose is to set out the key principles of community care and practical ways of implementing policies. The political, economic and professional factors which influence public mental health policy are considered in the historical context of the rise and fall of the asylums. The driving forces behind the community care ideal are outlined, together with the main reasons for the current failure of policies in this area. Finally, the book presents my views on the necessary organizational structure and the essential component parts of a mental health service for the 1990s.

2 The Rise of the Asylums: a Victorian Achievement

For 100 years, between 1850 and 1950, large numbers of people with severe or long-standing mental disorder were cared for in large institutions, away from their families and friends and usually at an inconvenient distance from the local town. In Britain the growth and expansion of large asylums was a uniquely Victorian achievement and the same powerful influences which generated the asylums also produced the municipal prisons and Union workhouses. To understand the difficulties we face now in providing good care for mentally disordered people living in the community, it is important to understand the problems which asylums were meant to solve, how the original humane vision was achieved and how its vision faded as the nineteenth century grew older. We can find early clues as to why the process of closure in the past forty years has been both inevitable and desirable and why the development of effective alternatives has been so difficult to achieve.

The early years

From the middle ages up until the seventeenth century the way in which people thought to be mad were dealt with largely depended on the means of the sufferer's family. There were, for example, a few small religious institutions which provided care; there was also one nationally known institution in London, the Bethlem Hospital, which specialized in short-term treatment for lunatics: Bethlem, or 'Bedlam', was founded as a priory in 1247 and began to provide care for the mad about a century later; it became a public secular institution on the dissolution of the monasteries in the reign of

Henry VIII. The great majority of mentally disordered people were, however, probably cared for by their families when they were able to do so, although it is likely that very many sufferers ended up in jails and small local workhouses or became drifting, destitute vagrants dependent on charitable handouts or begging, indistinguishable from other social derelicts living from hand to mouth. It should also be remembered that while there were few specific institutions for the treatment and care of mental disorder, there were very few general hospitals either for the treatment of physical illness. Indeed, only two general hospitals, St Thomas' and St Bartholomew's, both in London, existed in England at the end of the seventeenth century, and sick people were generally nursed at home, either by relatives or by paid attendants.

At the end of the seventeenth century a few physicians reckoned they were able to cure lunacy, although medical interest was in its infancy and the few small private madhouses which existed at that time were largely lay establishments. A few clergymen, too, claimed to have effective cures for lunacy – the provision of treatment and care did not become the exclusive province of doctors until the nineteenth and twentieth centuries.

The age of enlightenment

Mad people wandering the streets were a common enough sight in the seventeenth century and by the turn of the eighteenth century the increasing numbers of destitute poor were a highly visible public vexation. The Vagrancy Act of 1714 was designed to deter vagrancy by temporarily incarcerating the unfortunates in a local house of correction or bridewell. Lunatics got the same treatment as other vagrants but were specifically excluded from whipping, a sign of some human sympathy towards this group.

The amended Vagrancy Act of 1744 was a major step forward in distinguishing lunatics from other social outcasts. The statute provided for 'rogues, vagabonds, beggars and other idle and disorderly persons not having the wherewith to maintain themselves' to be committed by a Justice of the Peace to a house of correction for any time not exceeding one month. Section 20 went on:

Whereas there are sometimes persons who by lunacy or otherwise are furiously mad or so far disordered in their senses that they may be dangerous to be permitted to go abroad be it therefore enacted by the authority foresaid that it shall be lawful for any two or more Justices of the Peace to cause such a person to be apprehended and kept maintained and cared for, and this shall be for and during such time as the lunacy or illness shall continue.

This was the first attempt to provide *care* for mentally disordered people who had become a public nuisance 'to the great scandal, loss and annoyance of the Kingdom'. Responsibility for providing care was given to local parishes who were obliged to fund the care of lunatics out of the same meagre pool of money available for relief of all the poor of the parish. As the agricultural enclosure movement was in full swing at this time and large numbers of people were being thrown on the mercy of the parish, lunatics faced enormous competition from other deserving poor for whatever funds were available.

Parishes varied tremendously in what they could or would fund but some gave financial assistance to relatives to help them cope, funded home attendants or 'keepers', or on occasions placed sufferers in one of the growing number of madhouses. More usually, pauper lunatics would have remained in the parish workhouse if they were considered dangerous, or would have been allowed to roam the streets if not. Even at the end of the eighteenth century, Sir George Onesiphorus Paul, a philanthropist who investigated conditions in which village lunatics were held, found many villages where 'some unfortunate creature, if his ill treatment has made him frenetic, is chained in the cellar or the garret of a workhouse' or, worse, in a private house, 'fastened to the leg of a table, tied to a post in an outhouse or perhaps shut up in an uninhabited ruin, or if his lunacy be inoffensive, left to ramble half naked and half starved through the streets'.

In contrast, one Herman Tayler of Cheriton Fitzpaine in Devon, who was probably suffering from severe depression, received amazingly generous supervision and nursing care. In 1723 the parish paid for expensive medical treatment and when that failed sent him away to seek a second opinion which fortunately seems to have been successful. Meanwhile the parish supported his wife and children during the illness and even after he was better, and also funded a parish apprenticeship for his son. Over the two years of his illness the parish spent £49 11s 9d on his care, half the total annual poor rate for the parish. Although we have no comprehensive picture across the country, we must assume that few parishes were as generous as this Devon one. It is likely that very many mentally disordered people received little care at all due to lack of funds and vision.

The voluntary hospital movement in the first half of the eighteenth century produced a number of small specialist hospitals and early forms of asylum. The first hospital facility for 'incurable lunatics' was established by Thomas Guy, millionaire merchant, wheeler-dealer and philanthropist, in a wing of Guy's Hospital in 1726. He specified that it should care for 'such patients and persons who shall be discharged from The Hospital of St Thomas or Bethlehem or other hospitals, on account of the small hopes of their cure, or the great length of time for that purpose required or thought necessary'. Guy's example was, however, followed by few others; most philanthropists preferred to fund the more popular voluntary general hospitals and it was a quarter of a century before the first public asylums were established with charitable funding – St Luke's in London and St Patrick's in Dublin, the latter by the bequest of Jonathan Swift.

Wealthy families with mentally ill relatives consulted the growing number of physicians with an interest in insanity and hired attendants recommended by doctors to supervise the patient at home. Attendants were often little more than domestic servants, with no training in managing difficult or bizarre behaviours. Some doctors also opened their own small private hospitals or 'madhouses', and a large number of cheaper, smaller private madhouses, many with under a dozen inmates, were set up to cater for the long-term care of middle-class patients whose families could not cope at home. This completely unregulated 'trade in lunacy' flourished and expanded. Anyone so inclined could offer to take in a handful of lunatics in spare back rooms. Cheaper establishments catered for the parish pauper lunatic trade, funded by poor relief.

The appalling conditions and outright brutality which character-ized many private madhouses were well recognized and heavily criticized in repeated public exposés in the press. Social reformers pressed for statutory controls but had little impact until 1774 when institutions finally became subject to a modest level of monitoring, being obliged to be licensed and available for inspection.

As the eighteenth century ended, however, care at home remained the norm. Private madhouses and local parish work-houses and houses of correction contained, it is estimated, just under 5,000 lunatics nationwide, a relatively small number. Protests about conditions in madhouses were also growing throughout the country, though so too were examples of good asylum care.

When reviewing this haphazard, fragmented approach to care we must be careful not to make judgments based on twentieth-century attitudes. The belief that the state carried responsibility for creating social policy to improve the welfare of disadvantaged people came much later. The great success of the nineteenth-century reformers was in fixing social welfare policy firmly on the political agenda, a place where it has remained, sometimes rather precariously, until the present day.

The moral treatment

In the later years of the eighteenth century a new humane move-ment evolved in France and Britain. The doctrine of the 'moral treatment of insanity' focused not merely on 'care' but also on 'cure'. A French physician, Philippe Pinel, the doctrine's leading exponent, was unconvinced by the belief prevalent at that time that all insanity was caused by organic disease of the brain and therefore incurable. He thought that insanity was caused by psychological factors and that treatment must therefore be possible. He believed in the natural healing processes of nature, good nourishment, proper physical care and a conversational approach to patients using rational argument. Everything had to be done with firmness but kindness.

Pinel's genius was not simply in adopting these ideas, which were fairly commonly expressed by others before him, but in tenaciously overseeing their practical implementation through exceptional administrative talent. He is described as a shy, timid and self-conscious man and his writings have a modesty unusual for medical treatises of the period. He claimed no miracles but offered only descriptions of what he had witnessed for others to judge.

In 1794 he became medical superintendent of the Bicêtre asylum in Paris where 200 male patients were confined, many held permanently in chains. Convinced that fettering made lunatics more dangerous, Pinel courageously removed the chains. The widely predicted disaster did not occur and Pinel attributed his successful transformation of the Bicêtre to the support of the governor, Monsieur Pussin, an equally committed man whose determined rule over the attendants' behaviour and attitudes was judged by Pinel to be the key factor in maintaining a more therapeutic regime.

Word of Pinel's achievements spread rapidly and like-minded doctors in Britain adopted the phrase 'moral treatment' for this approach to the care of the mentally ill. William Tuke, for example, established The York Retreat in 1796, a Quaker-run charitable private asylum in York which impressed all its visitors with its family-like, homely environment, although the scandalous conditions in many other hospitals and madhouses continued.

The King's madness

The general public knew and cared little about mental disorder except in so far as the more visible sufferers living on the streets were a burdensome public nuisance. Then in 1788 the King went mad. George III suffered attacks of excitement, overactivity, agitation, severe insomnia and occasionally garrulous high spirits. At first he was merely irritating and confused but later became exhausting and quite clearly deranged. Dr Francis Willis was sent for after several other eminent physicians had failed to cure the King. Willis, a clergyman not a physician, had established a reputation for 'moral treatment' at his own small private asylum in Lincolnshire. Confident about his own healing powers, he espoused the use of Peruvian bark as the mainstay of his medical treatment, although his 'moral treatment' did not exclude the regular use of mechanical restraints, particularly the straitjacket. He also seems to have allowed attendants a free rein in handling his patients and one was observed to strike the King and 'knock him flat as a flounder'. Pinel did not share the general admiration for Willis and criticized his failure to train his attendants properly.

The management of the King's madness became a subject of national interest and great controversy until eventually the Lords appointed a committee of enquiry to look into his treatment. He recovered from his first two episodes but sank permanently into a pathetic state of dementia eleven years later. George III was a popular and well-loved monarch who took an interest in the lives of ordinary people; inevitably, therefore, public interest in the King's condition raised awareness of the plight of the thousands of common folk suffering from mental disorder and the lamentable state of medical ignorance on how to help the sufferers.

Reformers, pressing for a nationwide improvement in standards of care and a regulatory system to control the private trade, introduced a series of legislative proposals between the 1770s and 1844. However, the effects of these were largely nullified by amendments supported by madhouse proprietors and voluntary hospital boards, who naturally favoured as little state interference as possible. None the less, the Lunacy Asylum Enabling Act of 1808 encouraged counties to establish public asylums for the insane although few were moved to do so at that time.

The relaxed paternalism of the late eighteenth century was gradually superseded by the tougher social attitudes of a political economy dominated by the ideology of Free Trade. At the turn of the nineteenth century the economy was still predominantly agricultural, and the majority of the population lived in rural areas. The Land Enclosure Acts of the late eighteenth and early nineteenth centuries had a devastating effect on the lives of agricultural labourers. But while those who remained in employment on the efficient new large estates and farms fared well enough, many thousands of unemployed rural workers were thrown into poverty, unable to use the old common land for their own animals and disbarred from taking game on land which for generations had been available to everyone. Impoverished people were discouraged from migrating to towns to find employment because the Elizabethan settlement laws dictated that parish relief was available only to local parish residents. Destitute people were therefore liable to be forcibly removed back to their home parishes rather than become a burden on another. Nevertheless, the beginnings of the Industrial Revolution did create new jobs and gradually new industrial centres grew as the population was attracted from the countryside by higher wages.

Unemployment among the labouring classes continued, however, to rise, further exacerbated by the sudden influx on to the labour market of 400,000 men discharged from the armed forces at the end of the Napoleonic Wars. In the face of an apparently bottomless pit of unmet need, the social attitudes of the middle classes hardened. What the poor needed to do, they decided, was help themselves. Up until this time parish relief provided subsistence, called 'outdoor relief', to poor people living at home, to enable them to stay out of the local workhouse and remain as self-sufficient as possible. A notion grew that profligate handouts to the poor merely encouraged the indolent 'undeserving' among them to have larger families and remain dependent on charity. The logical answer was to make those in receipt of relief so uncomfortable and the receipt of relief so unpleasant that most poor people would be discouraged from seeking help.

The Poor Law Amendment Act of 1834 was largely successful in its aim of reducing claims on outdoor relief, although some local parishes continued to use discretion in making awards. But in most areas outdoor relief ceased altogether and to qualify for assistance the poor had to enter a workhouse. Local parishes combined forces with others and, as Unions, established one large workhouse for each area governed by a Board of Guardians. The great Victorian institution boom had begun.

The union workhouses

The story of the workhouses is well known and there is no need to repeat here the sad saga of the oppressive, regimented, prison-like existence led by the inmates of many of these establishments. But even though a comprehensive, truthful picture is hard to come by, some of these places were undoubtedly well run by kindly and humane people who did their best with the meagre resources allocated to them. The spirit of Monsieur Pussin must surely have flickered in a few beadles.

Union workhouses became receptacles for all types of social derelicts including chronically sick people and unsupported old folk: even though later in the nineteenth century workhouses were gradually transformed into warehouses for the growing numbers of frail, dependent old people, at the beginning of the century they took all-comers. Two groups quickly came to be regarded as a serious problem: those with infectious diseases, and lunatics. Infectious epidemics spread like wildfire through the malnourished and weakened inmates in crowded dormitories and so, in time, special fever hospitals were established. Lunatics, on the other hand, were simply regarded as unmanageable and their unpredictable, difficult and disruptive behaviour was a burden to both inmates and staff. Lunatics were also usually incapable of work and it was not long before the Guardians of the workhouses added their voices to those of others calling for lunatics to be removed elsewhere.

The asylum movement

The scene was almost set. Recurring madhouse scandals and the clamour of the workhouse Guardians to have lunatics removed created profound public unease and an opportunity for social reformers with a real commitment to improving the lot of the sufferers to take action. These social reformers seized with enthusiasm on the philosophy of 'moral treatment' and transformed a treatment ethos into a vision of a completely therapeutic lifestyle. The regenerated asylum would be a healthy, airy, peaceful, protective haven of spacious buildings in quiet countryside surroundings where the staff would be committed to effecting cures. Insanity, it was thought, might be healed by a gentle system of rewards and punishments, amusements, occupation and kindly but firm discipline.

Reformers pointed to where such theories seemed already to be working in practice. Dr E. P. Charlesworth, the medical director of

Lincoln asylum, and his successor, Dr Robert Gardiner Hill, were particularly innovative as well as staunch advocates of moral treatment. Hill dispensed altogether with straitjackets and other restraints in 1838. But the proselytizing St Paul of non-restraint and moral treatment was Dr John Connolly, one of the most impressive physicians of his generation. Connolly used techniques of non-restraint in the small asylum at Hanwell in West London where he worked. He gained influential support from *The Times*, the *Lancet* and, most important of all, from Lord Shaftesbury, the most active social reformer of the day.

The Lunacy Act of 1845 was the triumphant outcome of fifty years of agitation. Victorian men of influence were united in their vision: the Act directed the mandatory construction of lunatic asylums in every county and established the Lunacy Commission to regulate all asylums and hospitals, private, voluntary and public, where lunatics were liable to be cared for. There were, nevertheless, doubters and outright opponents. Many doctors, for example, were closely associated with the private madhouse system and opposed the reforms vigorously; Lord Shaftesbury never recovered his previous good opinion of the medical profession. There were others, like John Connolly himself, who felt that asylums should remain small and who were critical of the enormous monolithic institutions being created by statute. But the mood of the times was irresistibly in favour of the reforms, and the era of the asylums was established.

Inevitably, not all modern observers of the growth of the asylums see them as the products, in the main, of lofty motives. Asylums have sometimes been regarded as a creation of the prevailing contemporary middle-class culture: while feeling satisfied that they were doing their best for charitable reasons, the bourgeoisie had a convenient way of 'controlling the dangerous classes' by removing them from society to convenient warehouses. Yet no one can doubt the humanity and commitment of the instigators. Asylums were a serious attempt to manage a growing social problem in an enlightened way and those who founded them genuinely hoped that sufferers would benefit.

At the end of the eighteenth century there were approximately

2,000 residents of licensed madhouses and asylums and perhaps a further 3,000 in local parish houses of correction. By the end of the nineteenth century there were 100,000 inmates in public lunatic asylums and the numbers were rising.

The growth of the asylums

The county asylums prescribed in the Lunacy Act of 1845 were duly built all over England and Wales. Some of the early asylums were as much an architectural demonstration of civic pride as are town halls or even airports today. (My own favourites are the Italianate Gothic of Friern Hospital, formerly Colney Hatch Asylum, the neo-Carolean Dutch-gabled Cane Hill Hospital, and the pseudo-Jacobean Central Hospital, Warwick.) Behind the ornate façades, spacious wards, 'airing courts', work halls and communal dining halls were linked by miles of corridors. The phenomenal capital expenditure of the ambitious early projects soon gave way, however, to penny-pinching, drab, sad functionalism. The later asylums built between 1890 and 1910 were constructed particularly cheaply and with an eye to keeping running costs to a minimum. (Bexley Hospital in Kent had the distinction of being hailed in its day as the cheapest establishment to run, a mere 8 shillings per patient per week in 1898.)

Right from the moment of the 1845 Act there was a great sense of urgency to build, build, build. The Lunacy Commissioners pressed for more and more expansion, and additional asylums. In London, particularly, the need seemed limitless with more and more lunatics being moved into asylums. Several factors appear to have influenced this phenomenal growth.

First, the number of detained lunatics in 1801 – some 5,000 of them – was almost certainly substantially less than the number of people in need of such care. In addition, the population of England and Wales grew from 9 million in 1801 to over 32 million in 1900. But a low base figure in 1801, plus population growth, cannot account in full for the twenty-fold increase in detained lunatics over the period. The Victorians became gripped with a kind of custodial fever and all kinds of people who were not originally classed as 'curable lunatics' found their way into the institutions. People suffering from epilepsy, mental handicap, chronic alcohol abuse and simple senile dementia, plus an assorted flotsam of 'social inadequates' who did not seem best catered for in the prison system, all tumbled into the asylums. A growing national sense of prosperity, self-confidence and self-righteousness no doubt contributed to the growth of the asylums, but funding arrangements, too, favoured the committal of 'lunatics' to asylums rather than to workhouses. In many parts of the country asylums were actually cheaper than workhouses, but the major influencing factor was that workhouses were a charge on the parish while asylums were paid for by the county. In London, where a complex system of administration for poor law funds operated, the Metropolitan Asylums Board could cream funds off the top of parochial poor funds to spend at their discretion and a system of financial incentives encouraged local Unions to place as many people as possible in asylums rather than workhouses. Consequently between 1880 and 1910 the number of people in asylums in London was running at double the rate in the rest of the country. A suspicion was also voiced that certification fees, which inflated the income of some doctors, were encouraging the growth of committals. Clearly, even though social policy institutionalizes an idea, financial policy frequently dictates its execution!

As institutions became larger – 1,500, 2,000 even 3,000 inmates – therapeutic optimism waned. The 'moral treatment' did not deliver the expected cures and treating the insane well did not restore their reason. Even as early as the 1850s and 1860s, in the face of harsh criticism from the Lunacy Commissioners, mechanical restraints were being reintroduced and expectations of cure became more limited. Custodialism superseded the notion of asylum as therapy and asylum doctors found themselves more concerned with the administration of their remote 'island' communities than with treatment. They increasingly turned their medical training to the somewhat sterile task of observing and cataloguing the varieties of madness and peculiarity they witnessed rather than to therapy.

The early twentieth century brought further overcrowding in the asylums. Buildings became dilapidated as age, overuse, wartime stringencies and recession took their toll. Work opportunities for patients inside the asylums diminished. The Board of Control, the new name for the Lunacy Commissioners from 1913, complained in 1932 that 'it is distressing to go round wards and find scores of patients left to deteriorate in wearisome idleness.' By the time the Second World War was over the asylums were in apparently terminal decline.

Life in the Victorian asylum

In the early days asylum life probably offered a significantly better quality of life for pauper lunatics than either workhouses, common lodging-houses or living from hand to mouth on the streets. Henry Mayhew's eyewitness accounts of lice-ridden, rat-infested common lodging-houses in London in 1851, where rag-clad, impoverished people slept heaped up in overcrowded, stinking dormitories suggests that pauper life was horrific, even for those not suffering from mental illness.

Life in the asylum was governed by a rigid timetabled regime of sleep, work, eat, sleep. Whitewashed walls; plain brick, stone or wooden floors; deal benches and tables; and two WCs for thirty or forty patients provided a fairly cheerless though roomy environment. Windows were generally barred and many wards were locked, although the better asylums gave considerable internal freedom to the inmates. The pace and philosophy of daily life were determined largely by the medical superintendent who combined the roles of general manager and top doctor and whose resources were normally controlled by a Board of Guardians or, in London, the local asylum Committee of Visitors, lay committee of appointed local worthies.

Asylums had few doctors, perhaps three or four medical officers for 1,000 patients. Rigid divisions ensured that female patients were kept entirely separate from the males, and doctors, likewise, were employed specifically to care for one sex or the other.

Nursing attendants handled most of the day-to-day work and were also divided by sex. Their work was exceptionally arduous, they were untrained and their wages and conditions were far below what a domestic servant in a respectable household could earn. Many patients had to be hand-fed or tube-fed and some with 'dirty habits or destructive propensities' were kept in 'strong clothes' of canvas to prevent then stripping naked or tearing their garments. Many patients were heavily dependent on staff as a result of chronic neurological disease and physical illness. Typically, there might be a total staff of 170 for 1,500 patients, with attendants on duty from 6 am to 8 pm and working a ninety-hour week. Most were required to sleep near the wards in case they were needed in the night, while a couple of colleagues would stay up all night to walk the wards. Female staff were obliged to live in, though males could live out. Training for attendants was not introduced until 1891.

One positive aspect of asylum life was the opportunity for work, occupation having been regarded in the early days of the asylum movement as a valuable remedial agent. Asylums usually had their own farms, bakeries, cobblers, building maintenance workshops, tailors, sewing rooms and so forth. In some asylums over half the patients were employed in keeping the institution self-sufficient. It was, however, always a struggle to maintain the momentum of work, particularly as raw materials became more expensive and supervision of the workforce more costly. Many of the farms, however, were kept going until well into the twentieth century.

From time to time patients were provided with communal amusements such as outdoor fêtes and evening dances and the more docile were occasionally allowed out accompanied by an attendant. Visits from family and friends were encouraged, although the asylums were often in such remote locations and (in the case of asylums with city catchment areas) so far out of town that in practice such visits were quite rare for most patients.

While many patients stayed for life, some were admitted only for short periods during an episode of disturbance and were then returned home. The Victorian asylum was a more fluctuating community than is commonly thought, but discharge was hampered by a total lack of facilities outside in the community and little chance of extra help from poor funds. In practice only those with supportive relatives or friends could hope for a discharge.

The Lunacy Commissioners descended on the asylum at least once a year for a whole week, usually in groups of four. Their inspection was remarkably thorough, covering every aspect of asylum life from the fabric of the building to diet, clothing, occupation and treatment. Copious reports and statistics were produced for their perusal. They investigated patients' complaints, the most common one being of improper confinement. Their real powers were few, but they could be remarkably persuasive and in the early years, under Lord Shaftesbury's energetic chairmanship, they fought tirelessly for better physical conditions, a liberalizing of the regime and a more therapeutic approach.

The Commissioners were regarded by the Boards of Guardians with a mixture of irritation and respect. Not infrequently their suggestions were regarded as too fanciful or expensive. The Committee of Visitors at Colney Hatch Asylum, for example, responded angrily to the Commissioners' highly critical report of 1861: 'The Commissioners do not appear sufficiently to bear in mind the fact that Colney Hatch Asylum is established for Pauper Lunatics only, and that many luxuries and appliances suggested by them are quite unsuited to that class of patients . . .' Among the deficiencies listed by the Commissioners were 'a deficiency of ordinary domestic furniture, defective ventilation, cold dormitories, closeness and inconvenience of lavatories, the habit of bathing many patients in one lot of bath water, and bedsteads with sacking but no mattresses'. The Commissioners pressed on undaunted, however, and had the support of the majority of medical superintendents and a valuable ally in the *Journal of Mental Science* and the asylum doctors' journal.

Sadly, the Commissioners gradually lost some of their early revolutionary fervour and by the time they were superseded by the Board of Control their effectiveness had waned. The Board of Control was itself disbanded in 1959 but a new grandchild, the Mental Health Act Commission, was born out of the new Act of 1983; it has a restricted remit compared with the Lunacy Commission but has many of the same functions as its Victorian counterpart.

Each of the two world wars brought a temporary halt to the growth of in-patients but, as soon as peace was restored, the hospital population grew again, reaching its all-time peak of 148,000 in 1954. As I write, in 1991, the patient population has declined to the level recorded in the late 1880s, some 60,000, and we are quite clearly at a crossroads: any further substantial reduction in public care facilities for such patients will lead to an increase in private madhouses and bridewells, albeit in modern guise; indeed, some would say we are dangerously close to that point already. Alternatively, we can develop a new system of care. What we cannot do is return to the era of the asylums, for reasons I shall outline in the next chapter.

3 The Decline of the Asylum

From time to time during the nineteenth century some original thinker would suggest new ways of providing care outside the asylums. John Connolly, for example, suggested that specialist doctors might visit patients in their homes at an early stage in the illness to offer advice and, hopefully, to prevent admission. In the 1850s Devon County Asylum used two houses in its grounds as homes for 'tranquil patients'. In 1879 the Reverend Henry Hawkins, Chaplain at Colney Hatch Asylum, established the Mental After Care Association 'to facilitate the readmission of the poor friendless female convalescents from Lunatic Asylums into social life'. The Association still provides group homes and hostels for discharged patients. Alternative forms of care were quite clearly being explored from the early days of the asylums, sometimes with marked success.

In the 1920s the Royal Commission on Lunacy and Mental Disorder promoted the appointment of almoners (medical social workers) to asylums, introducing the notion that the welfare of patients was bound up with the welfare of their families and that it was vitally important for patients that external links should be preserved and fostered. The seeds of the community care idea were well established by 1930, when the Mental Treatment Act incorporated a request that local authorities should provide after-care for ex-patients. The Act also recognized for the first time that most patients could be treated voluntarily rather than by compulsion.

During the 1920s, too, the child guidance movement grew up on the hope, now recognized as misguided, that by seeking to create a generation of mentally healthy children many of the mental afflictions of later life could be avoided. Child guidance clinics sprang up all over Britain and the innovative idea grew that if children could be treated in clinics, why should it not be possible also to treat adults in clinics? Outpatient treatment of less severely afflicted patients first became commonplace in private practice, pioneered largely by psychoanalytic disciples of Freud. By the outbreak of the Second World War many were looking forward with optimism and confidence to the dissolution of the asylum system and its replacement by a system based on community treatment.

The Second World War

War produces psychiatric casualties in abundance. Military doctors in the Second World War remembered all too well the generation of shell-shocked, long-term mentally disabled soldiers created by World War I, and a concerted effort was made to prevent a similar disaster in World War II. It was soon established that at the first sign of 'acute battle neurosis' a man should be removed from the front line and sometimes temporarily sedated with barbiturate drugs. This gave the patient a good chance of reasonably rapid recovery, particularly if he could then be medically discharged to serve at home rather than sent back to active duty.

Medical enthusiasts for vigorous physical treatments were heartened by the response of war casualties and turned their therapeutic energies to other patients. Throughout the war new experimental treatments for the more severe and long-lived disorders were tried out on long-term patients in a spirit of hopeful enthusiasm. Belmont Hospital in Surrey, one of the Emergency Hospitals designated to take the psychiatric casualties of war, became a pioneering centre for treating not only these casualties but also local civilian patients. Insulin coma treatment, leucotomy (brain surgery), electroconvulsive therapy (ECT or electric shock treatment) and new drugs were all given an enthusiastic welcome. Most of these experimental treatments had originally been devised in continental Europe during the 1930s and were imported to Britain. For the first time, psychiatrists had a whole range of treatments at their disposal and a new sense of buoyant optimism pervaded the profession. Psychiatrists began to feel they could be 'proper' doctors engaged in diagnosis and treatment, perhaps even in cure.

Looking back now with the benefit of half a century of hindsight, it is easy to be disparaging about the lack of objective scientific thinking, the 'gung ho' disregard for the sometimes catastrophic failure of some of the procedures, especially leucotomy, and often the lack of concern for the safety of patients. Dr William Sargant, Deputy Clinical Director of Belmont and later a well-known consultant psychiatrist at St Thomas' Hospital, London, was perhaps the keenest exponent of physical interventions. His autobiography *The Unquiet Mind* reveals a single-minded, determined, perhaps even arrogant man eager to explore every possible option but always with the best of intentions on behalf of his patients. His case descriptions, and those of other eyewitnesses, tell at times of convincing, moving, even near-miraculous cures of individuals with severe disorders.

Electric shock treatment (electroconvulsive therapy, ECT), in particular, was seen to have a positive effect on people with severe depressions. Before the advent of ECT, patients sometimes remained in a state of near-motionless stupor or retardation for several years, often requiring hand-feeding, with all their other personal needs also carried out by nurses. Characteristically the illness lasted for anything from a few months to two to three years, after which patients would recover unpredictably over the course of some months. ECT had the surprising effect of producing an apparent rapid cure which, thought not always sustained, seemed sufficiently miraculous to become one of the mainstays of psychiatric treatment over the next half-century.

Other treatments fared less well over the succeeding years. Between 1942 and 1954 well over 10,000 leucotomy operations were performed, but by the beginning of the 1960s serious concerns about the damaging effects of such operations on the personality, combined with lack of evidence as to the efficacy of this drastic treatment, led to a rapid decline in enthusiasm. By the 1970s leucotomy was a rarity; now it is approaching extinction and is subject to stringent legal safeguards.

Another procedure which failed to stand the test of time was insulin coma treatment and a modified form of this treatment, in which patients were maintained in a semi-asleep state for some days or weeks and intermittently stimulated with insulin to improve appetite. Such procedures are difficult and risky to administer and required a complement of trained staff and close supervision. The treatment finally died out in the 1960s when it was shown to be ineffective.

Belief in the efficacy of many of the more bizarre treatments which were adopted nationwide during and after the war is understandable. Patients who had remained for years in an untreatable and hopeless state became the focus of interest and optimism by the new breed of psychiatrists and new patients were confronted with the possibility of rapid recovery and a return to normal life. It is not surprising that both doctors and patients responded favourably to possibilities afforded by the new therapies.

However, during the war the Ministry of Health and the London County Council, who administered the psychiatric hospitals in London, became seriously concerned about the introduction of these untried treatments, though whether this was due to natural bureaucratic conservatism, concern as to efficacy, a desire to protect the interests of patients, or concern about the costs, is unclear. Advocates of the new treatments, however, paid little heed to managerial injunctions and Sargant records with satisfaction that 'We generally got our own way in the end.'

While one school of psychiatrists was pioneering such physical treatments, another equally important psychiatric movement was developing around the concept of the 'therapeutic community'. Tom Main, a charismatic and colourful psychiatrist temporarily attached to the army, developed his own approach to the treatment and rehabilitation of sufferers of 'acute battle neurosis' and other breakdowns triggered by wartime service. At Northfield Military Hospital in Birmingham he fashioned an approach in which doctors, nurses, administrators, domestics and porters were engaged with the patients in developing a regime in which the rules of behaviour of the military system were relaxed and where recovery and rehabilitation took place through participation in group discussions and by focusing on the 'wellness' of individuals. Thus patients and staff came to share a joint culture based on common values and expectations. After the war, Main continued to develop his ideas on a carefully selected group of patients at the Cassel Hospital in surrey. The 'therapeutic community' idea also blossomed after the war in a number of 'ordinary' psychiatric hospitals, notably at Dingleton Hospital in Melrose under the direction of Maxwell Jones.

The advent in the 1950s of psychotropic drugs, and the shift away from the large hospitals as the main centres of acute treatment led to a lessening of interest in therapeutic communities, and nowadays the sole surviving relic of these is the weekly patients' meeting which is held in most psychiatric hospital wards. The efficacy of the therapeutic community in treating specific psychiatric disorders has never been demonstrated and few would now claim that social group 'milieu' alone can influence the course of serious mental disorder. However, the example of the therapeutic communities prompted many hospitals to recognize the important effects on the social behaviour of groups of patients on the emotional and behavioural state of individuals; it also led to a recognition of the important role played by ward-based nurses and other staff such as domestics with whom patients have daily contact.

The profession of psychiatry emerged from the Second World War rather satisfactorily. The therapeutic tool-box was well stocked with a range of new tools to suit all tastes. And patients really were getting better, particularly those who had suffered recent breakdowns – at least in the short term. Hospital admissions for psychiatric treatment continued to rise, but increasingly the expectation of those admitted was to be discharged within a few weeks, and the average length of stay in hospital began to fall. An open-door policy of easy admission and early discharge was gradually adopted by psychiatric hospitals up and down the country, and public acceptance grew that mentally disordered people required treatment and rehabilitation rather than incarceration.

But old habits die hard. While there were notable medical superintendents such as Duncan MacMillan at Mapperley in Nottingham and T. P. Rees at Warlingham Park, Croydon, who were actively seeking to rehabilitate and settle some of the long-term residents of the hospitals and create effective rehabilitation programmes for recently admitted patients, elsewhere in the country discharges still lagged far behind admissions and the total number of patients in mental hospitals continued to rise, reaching a peak of 148,000 in 1954. At Mapperley, Warlingham Park and other innovative hospitals, the numbers of residents had begun to decline by the late 1940s.

Antipsychotic drugs

The 1950s saw the introduction of drugs which were to prove of outstanding significance to mental health services. The new drugs revolutionized psychiatric practice, shifted the orientation of psychiatrists towards a general hospital model of care and had a major, largely adverse, impact on the focus of training and education of mental health professionals for a good thirty years. Of these new drugs, undoubtedly the one representing the most significant leap forward in the specific treatment of the symptoms of schizophrenias and other psychoses was chlorpromazine, introduced in 1953. This was followed some years later by imipramine, introduced in 1957 for treatment of depression.

A good deal of controversy frequently surrounds the introduction of new therapeutic compounds for the treatment of mental disorder and it is particularly difficult to evaluate the effectiveness of such drugs. There are no handy objective tools for measuring the state of an individual's emotions and thinking and researchers normally have to rely on their own observations, or on those of nurses and relatives. Over the last forty years complex research methods have been devised to assess the efficacy of new psychiatric drugs, using standardized schedules of questions and calibrated rating scales, but the natural history of newly introduced drugs seems to follow the same inevitable course. First the drug is hailed as a wonder cure by its manufacturers and by the doctors who first tried it. As time goes on it is cautiously adopted, provided clinical trials are convincing and it seems to have benefits over older tried and tested drugs. Inevitably, however, unwanted effects begin to emerge and there is a swing of disappointed opinion against the drug; it may then be many more years before a more measured view emerges and the drug assumes its appropriate place in treatment or is finally discarded as a troublesome failure.

Psychiatric patients have been subjected to more than their fair share of useless, addictive or dangerous medicines over the years, many of which have proved more trouble than they were worth. The amphetamines, bromides and minor tranquillizers such as Librium all fall into the 'addictive or dangerous' category. In the last twenty years a plethora of 'anti-dementia' drugs for the elderly have been launched which have been shown consistently to be clinically useless; this does not seem, however, to deter pharmaceutical manufacturers from launching new closely related compounds on to the market.

Chlorpromazine is neither useless, addictive nor dangerous but it does have unpleasant, unwanted side-effects which are most evident when it is taken over a period of many years. Chlorpromazine belongs to the class of drugs called 'major tranquillizers' or 'neuroleptics'. Although it has sedating properties when given in large doses, its major beneficial effects on psychiatric symptoms are not as a result of its tranquillizing qualities but of its ability to lessen phenomena such as delusional and persecutory ideas, hallucinations and incoherent speech and thinking. It works within a few days or weeks, releasing sufferers from an acute episode of schizophrenia so that they become less confused, more able to concentrate, more willing to care for themselves, and free of their preoccupation with voices and terrifying ideas. Chlorpromazine and drugs related to it can undoubtedly shorten an acute attack and bring under control subsequent episodes, and the effectiveness of antipsychotic medication has been well established by a large number of trials.

It is not surprising, therefore, that hospital doctors in the 1950s and later were keen to try out this new medication on members of the chronically disabled long-term hospital population, but while there were some successes, antipsychotic drugs proved to have less effect on unusual behaviour and on residual symptoms in longstanding disorders than on acutely disturbed patients. The distinction between those who would respond well and those unlikely to respond was not clearly understood in the 1950s, and soon after the introduction of chlorpromazine the manufacturers, Smith Kline and French, had a booming and profitable success story. Within a year of its launch in the United Stated chlorpromazine (called Thorazine in the US, Largactil in the UK) was being given to no fewer than 2 million people. The vast majority of inmates of mental hospitals who had at some stage in their lives been given a diagnosis of schizophrenia or paranoid illness were prescribed regular doses of the drug.

In the early 1960s it was widely believed that asylums could be run down due to the perceived success of antipsychotic drugs and, indeed, that the influence of such drugs was already manifest in the declining patient population. It is now clear that while drugs certainly facilitated early discharge of recently admitted patients and rendered some chronically ill patients less vulnerable to delusions and therefore more able to cope in the community, the rundown of the hospitals had very little to do with the introduction of such drugs. While the reduction in the numbers of inmates became apparent in national statistics in 1955, changes had already begun in a number of innovative hospitals in the late 1940s. The initiators of hospital reductions were medical reformers who wanted more out-patient care, day care and rehabilitation for employment and who wished to be able to treat acutely ill patients nearer home. They were tired of providing care in overcrowded, desolate, rundown institutions.

Real therapeutic advances have none the less been achieved with antipsychotic drugs and even though a later chapter considers the seriously adverse long-term unwanted effects of certain drugs, there can be no doubt that many thousands of individuals have benefited from them. But drugs do not influence the course of a mental disease, they merely control its most distressing manifest-ations. The availability of such drugs, however, became a con-venient rationale for government spokesmen to latch on to in order to justify closures. In 1971, the Minister of Health, Keith Joseph, confidently justified the government's policy of closing the mental hospitals as follows:

The treatment of psychosis, neurosis and schizophrenia have been entirely changed by the drug revolution. People go into hospital with mental disorders and they are cured, and that is why we want to bring this branch of medicine into the scope of the 230 district general hospitals that are planned for England and Wales.

With the benefit of hindsight it is clear that the major impact of the new drugs on health policy for the long-term mentally ill was not at a stroke to permit the wholesale closure of the mental hospitals but, rather, to provide doctors with a number of effective therapy options and thus to open up a new era for psychiatry.

The rise of psychiatry

The nineteenth-century asylum medical officers worked under considerable disadvantages compared with their counterparts in the general hospital system. For a start, the career prospects were appalling: their chances of rising to become a medical superintendent of an asylum were remote; once in the asylum system they were unlikely ever to get a job in a general hospital; and thus their chances of career advancement were poor. Second, as patients could not be removed from their designated place of detention, the asylum doctors were totally responsible for treating all the diseases and disorders of the patients under their care, including acute physical illnesses and trauma; thus asylum doctors acted as general practitioners, physicians and surgeons in addition to carrying out their work specific to mental disorder. They also had no control over admissions, which were arranged jointly by the parish doctor and a local magistrate who made arrangements with the asylum clerk; in many instances the clerk was not based at the asylum but in an office in the local town served by it. (The asylum clerk for Colney Hatch Asylum in North London, now Friern Hospital, used an office in Upper Street, Islington.) Nor could asylum doctors discharge people, although they gave advice on the timing of discharge to the Committee of Visitors who held that power. And to cap it all, they were poorly paid, of low status compared with other doctors, and frequently only two or three doctors were employed to provide care for 1,000 patients.

The need for doctors was decided according to the proportion of inmates judged to be 'curable'. Over the course of the nineteenth century, therapeutic optimism dwindled as 'moral treatments' failed to produce the cures first hoped for, and by 1876 even the Lunacy Commissioners pessimistically estimated that only seven in 100 lunatics were 'curable'. By then the dominating ethos was custodial. Consequently little was expected of the doctors and their status sank even lower. The more talented and ambitious often stayed for only short periods and then moved on in a search for greener pastures. Some moved to private asylums where pay and conditions were better, others like Henry Maudsley disassociated themselves from the public system and developed lucrative private practices in 'psychological medicine'. (Maudsley proved to be so successful that he was able to donate the major part of the capital cost of the famous psychiatric hospital in London named after him and intended only for curable short-term patients.)

The Association of Medical Officers of Asylums and Hospitals for the Insane, founded in 1841, suffered from the tensions between the doctors working in the public pauper lunatic asylums and those in the private sector asylums and in private office practice for the middle and upper classes. To their eternal credit it was the public asylum doctors who were the greater advocates of non-restraint of patients and the adoption of other humane practices. The Association published its own journal, the *Journal of Mental Science*, which survives today as the *British Journal of Psychiatry*. The original title reflects the yearning of asylum doctors to be accepted within the medical scientific community as real doctors, treating people with real illnesses.

Gradually, but not until the interwar years, the medical treatment-oriented viewpoint triumphed over the custodial one and was embodied in the Mental Treatment Act of 1930. This Act recognized that people could be treated voluntarily and not only as detained patients; it also provided for the asylums to be renamed 'hospitals'.

Moreover, even though for many years the Lunacy Commissioners and their successors on the Board of Control had pressed for improved medical and nursing input and had urged hospitals to forge links between psychological and general medicine, nothing much happened to foster closer working relationships between general and mental hospitals until the Second World War, when the advent of the new treatments provided a new sense of self-esteem for the psychiatric profession. The discovery of effective drugs finally elevated psychiatry to a professional plane alongside general medicine. Psychiatrists were proper doctors at last.

The scope for psychiatrists to treat acutely ill people as out-patients increased markedly at this time, and they began on a nationwide basis to press for more accessible local clinics where patients and their families would not be deterred from treatment by the stigma associated with the old asylums and the often long journeys to get there. Before long psychiatrists were demanding beds in general hospitals for the specific purpose of treating short-term patients with a good prognosis, such as those with depression or severe neurotic states. Guy's Hospital in London, which had a long tradition of employing physicians in 'psychological medicine', was the first London teaching hospital to establish an inpatient psychiatric clinic, the York Clinic, built with charitable funds in 1940.

Conditions in some mental hospitals in the 1940s and 1950s were appalling, often worse than when the hospitals had been opened a century earlier. Dr A. A. Baker, later the first Director of the Hospital Advisory Service established in 1969, reminisced recently in the *Bulletin of the Royal College of Psychiatrists* about his years as Deputy Superintendent of Banstead Hospital in Surrey in the early 1950s.

Conditions were very bad there. It had been grossly overcrowded during the war when patients from other hospitals had been put in to clear their beds for casualties. I was the only consultant on the female side which had 1,500 beds – seven wards of over 100 apiece, almost all of them locked. There were several wards which only took disturbed patients rejected by other wards; this was a very bad system. One of these had 100 or more patients ... there was no occupational therapy and patients just sat or stood around the outer edge of the ward in a state of apathy or tense frustration. The smell of paraldehyde [a heavy sedative] filled the air and some patients were persistently drunk and disorderly on it. They were in strong clothes

– garments which in theory they couldn't tear. ... On the female side alone there were 50 or more patients who were secluded the whole day, some having been so for many months or even years at a stretch. Time did not permit going round and assessing everyone.

There were wards at Banstead which were freer and more homely than these, and there were many better hospitals than Banstead, but these conditions were not unusual. Such hopelessly dismal environments inevitably drove doctors to seek an alternative way of working.

The wish of psychiatrists to move their patients out of the old asylums was thus motivated in part by concern for their patients but also by reasons of professional pride in raising the status of psychiatry. Doctors wanted their patients to be accepted as ordinary medical patients and to be treated in decent surroundings with all the facilities of the general hospital available to them. They also recognized that discharged patients were more easily followed up closer to home. And as it became more socially acceptable to admit to mental distress, a growing proportion of general psychiatric work was directed at less severe outpatient and acute cases and a smaller proportion of time was devoted to the care and rehabilitation of the chronically sick. Inevitably, treatable and less severe disorders started to occupy the attention of many psychiatrists, and the long-term patients were the losers.

The strong professional drive to move a substantial part of psychiatrists' work out of the asylums undoubtedly contributed to the run-down of the institutions. But this major shift in focus of the profession over the post-war years also had a catastrophic effect on the development of comprehensive care in the community, for reasons which will be explored in the next chapter.

Not all psychiatrists, however, chose to flee the asylums or focus only on 'treatable' conditions to the detriment of the long-term chronically sick. There was a small group of psychiatrists who were committed to policies which would benefit all mental patients including the long-term residents of the hospitals. Men such as Duncan MacMillan at Mapperley in Nottingham, T. P. Rees at Warlingham Park, Croydon, Donal Early at Glenside in Bristol and

R. K. Freudenberg at Netherne, Surrey all stressed the importance of open doors and the rehabilitation of the chronically disabled through meaningful social, domestic and occupational roles. They pioneered the development of day centres, sheltered work and small residential homes or 'halfway' houses. Most of the themes of community care were well aired in the late 1930s and 1940s, and solid progress was made by determined entrepreneurial managers. They were, however, hindered by the lack of the appropriate local authority housing and social welfare structures, and few of them envisaged a time when there would be no large hospitals as a last resort 'back-up'. A common theme throughout the 1940s and 1950s was the negative therapeutic impact of the institution itself on mentally disordered people. The regime, physical environment and isolation away from home and family were felt to militate against recovery. Furthermore, the institution was blamed for producing some of the abnormal behaviours found in long-term patients.

The total institution and antipsychiatry

Not surprisingly, the suspicion started to grow among doctors, sociologists and former patients that the mental hospitals were acting against successful rehabilitation and might themselves be causing some of the apathy, withdrawal and loss of personal care skills which were common in long-stay patients. Evidence accumulated that the ward environment could adversely influence the severity of symptoms and social adjustment of patients, although we now know that many of the residual problems of motivation of will and a feeling of discomforting distress in the company of others, which linger on following recurrent bouts of severe mental disorder, are an integral part of the process of the illness and not a result of environment.

Criticism of the institution grew much louder when two American sociologists, Belknap (1956) and Goffman (1958) published papers on their observations of daily life in large state mental hospitals. Goffman's book *Asylums*, published in 1961, was a searing critique of what he called 'the total institution', in which he included all those environments for living such as monasteries, boarding schools, residential homes for old people, prisons and orphanages, in which the inmates' entire daily experience is confined within the walls of the institution. He observed that the inmates were at the bottom of a highly structured hierarchy of staff. Doctors, who were at the top, had almost no contact with the inmates, senior nurses very little, and almost the sole day-to-day patient-contact was with domestics and untrained assistants. Inmates, it was argued, were robbed of their individualism and subjected to a dehumanizing, regimented daily regime designed to produce acquiescent conformity. Goffman's angry polemic targeted psychiatrists and nurses as the main villians of the piece but, curiously, perhaps because of the sheer accuracy and obviousness of his observations and also because he provided convenient arguments at a time when psychiatrists were lobbying to escape from the asylums, his work was accepted without offence. The subsequent antipsychiatry movement which arose in the 1960s was not, however, so readily welcomed by professionals in mainstream psychiatry.

Looking back now, thirty years on from the wave of excited intellectual interest stirred up by the two separate schools of antipsychiatry, the sum total of the achievements of the antipsychiatry movement are disappointingly small. Thomas Szasz, an American psychologist, published *The Myth of Mental Illness* in 1961. In it he wrote: 'I submit that the traditional definition of psychiatry, which is still in vogue, places it alongside alchemy and astrology and commits it to the category of pseudoscience.' If Szasz had stuck to that theme a great many people would have agreed with him. American psychiatry for middle- and upper-income patients was then dominated by psychoanalytically oriented psychotherapy. But Szasz went much further:

Strictly speaking disease or illness can affect only the body; hence there can be no mental illness. ... Psychiatric diagnoses are stigmatizing labels, phrased to resemble diagnoses and applied to persons whose behaviour annoys or offends them. ... If there is no mental illness there can be no hospitalization, treatment or cure for it. ... The introduction of psychiatric considerations into the administration of criminal law – for example the insanity pleas – corrupts the law and victimizes the subject on whose behalf they are employed. . . . Personal conduct is always rule-following, strategic and meaningful. . . . There is no medical, moral or legal justification for involuntary psychiatric interventions such as diagnosis, hospitalization or treatment. They are crimes against humanity.

Szasz perceived psychiatrists as agents of society's drive to control deviant and abnormal behaviour and believed that it was a dangerously short step from this to totalitarian abuse. Later revelations of psychiatric abuse in the USSR show how right Szasz was in this last respect.

Szasz's views had little impact on the theory and practice of mainstream psychiatry in Britain although professionals were appalled by his apparent denial of the value of attempting to relieve suffering and by his rejection of the cherished belief that mentally incompetent individuals had a right to treatment. British psychiatrists regarded Szasz as an office-bound psychoanalyst whose experience was limited to wealthy American neurotics and who had little experience or understanding of severe psychotic mental disorder, conditions which constituted the bulk of British psychiatric practice.

In Britain, Dr R. D. Laing had a rather greater impact. Like Szasz, he trained as a psychoanalyst. He was also convinced that mental disorder, including the severest psychotic breakdowns, was psychological in origin. His first influential book, *The Divided Self*, sought to demonstrate that abnormal belief and behaviour were the rational and understandable outcome of psychological influences brought to bear by other family members, undermining the individual's autonomy. The nuclear family, he argued, was often an oppressive social unit which, convenient as it was for ensuring society's cohesion, was a maladaptive environment for some people. Madness was a normal understandable response to 'mad' circumstances.

Laing and his followers established a number of treatment centres. These were houses which adopted a philosophy of acceptance of bizarre behaviour; they believed that a *laissez-faire* ethos and a style of communal living would see people through their madness. To many people, however, this was merely a 1960s' 'flower-power' version of the 'moral treatment'.

Laing's later writing became increasingly obscure and irrelevant to mainstream mental health services, but the antipsychiatry movement had struck a chord. While doctors and politicians were generally outraged by the views of the antipsychiatrists, many people who felt themselves to have been the victims of aggressive modern psychiatric practice, and were thus profoundly resentful of forcible treatment and involuntary detention in hospitals, found it an immediately attractive philosophy and used it to mobilize civil liberties activists to fight their cause, central to which was an attack on psychiatry as a profession and on the compulsory treatment of patients. The antipsychiatry movement was rambling, unfocused and frequently less than coherent and it is unclear what part it played in encouraging the closure of the mental hospitals, though it clearly provided a general groundswell of anger and concern. Throughout the 1960s and 1970s patients and their families were increasingly reluctant to accept psychiatrists' judgments unquestioningly, and a patients' rights movement grew up which culminated in the new Mental Health Act of 1983. In effect, the healthy public scepticism about the efficacy of psychiatric treatment which emerged in the 1960s and 1970s allowed other professionals concerned with mental illness, especially psychologists, nurses and occupational therapists, to emerge out of obscurity and play a more productive role in shaping the services. It also mobilized the voluntary sector movement to form an active and effective political lobby which later played an important role in promoting patients' civil rights.

The government adopts the policy of community care and asylum closure

The optimism of the 1950s, brought on mainly by the availability of new drugs and of new treatments such as ECT, culminated in the Mental Health Act of 1959 and the government's commitment to eventual closure of the large hospitals. The Act reinforced the voluntary treatment system, originally introduced in 1930 but to little effect, and for the first time enabled the vast majority of patients to be admitted without legal compulsion. At the same time, procedures and safeguards for compulsory detention and treatment

were tightened, so much so that Britain started to gain an international reputation for its forward-looking developments. The
Millbank Memorial Fund, for example, sent a party of American
psychiatrists to survey the scene. Dr Robert Hunt reported back:

Those of us who have had a good 'take' from the British 'vaccine' under-
went a revolutionary upheaval and emerged with a whole new set of
concepts about our patients, about our professional roles and we see almost
every detail of our work from a radically different point of view.

Visitors were particularly impressed by the spirit of partnership
which was growing between local government and the Health
Service.

The community care movement found a powerful political champion in Enoch Powell, the Minister of Health from 1960 to 1963,
aided by an exceptionally able civil servant, Enid Russell-Smith,
and by the Chief Medical Officer, Sir George Godber. At this time
government statistics showed a clear downward trend in the
number of occupied beds from 1954 to 1959, and Tooth and
Brooke, two medical officers in the ministry, estimated that if the
trend continued at the same rate, only half the beds would be
required by 1975. Although they have since been much criticized
for using the simple technique of projecting forward bed needs on
the basis of only five years' experience, in fact their estimates proved
to be extraordinarily accurate. It is also worth noting that the
authors of this influential report foresaw the need for asylum care
for a younger, chronically sick group who could not be discharged
early. What they did not foresee was the phenomenal growth in the
numbers of old people and the impact these would have on future
services. As a consequence, they were wrong in their predictions
about the date when the old mental hospitals could close.

It was not, however, the statistics alone which influenced Enoch
Powell in seeking to close down the long-stay mental hospitals and
substitute instead a system of community care. Looking back thirty
years later, he recalled visiting the large hospitals and seeing for
himself their 'horrifying overcrowding'. He witnessed dreadful conditions in some institutions and he was much influenced by the
quality and determination of some medical superintendents who

sought to create a new world of care outside the hospital. He also noted the dramatic improvements that intensive training programmes could produce in mentally handicapped people. He recalls:

The need of the acute hospitals was, as always, voracious but I was so struck by the need to support the mental health services I even shifted a few million up a line or two in one Region's plan just before it was published, so bad were their services for these people, something I had never done before or since.

In a powerful speech to the National Association of Mental Health, Powell spoke of 'the defences we have to storm' and of 'setting the torch to the funeral pyre'.

Powell's plan was

nothing less than the elimination of by far the greater part of this country's mental hospitals as they stand today. This is a colossal undertaking, not so much in the physical provision which it involves as in the sheer inertia of mind and matter which it requires to be overcome. There they stand, isolated, majestic, imperious, brooded over by the gigantic water tower and chimney combined, rising unmistakably and daunting out of the countryside – the asylums which our forefathers built with such solidity.

The 1962 Hospital Plan launched the official closure programme and Powell had every reason to be optimistic. In 1963 the first comprehensive survey of local government, health and social service plans, *Health and Welfare Plans*, indicated a thriving, buoyant and committed local government eager to rise to the challenge. The era of community care had begun and community care has remained official government policy since 1962.

4 The Disaster Years, 1962–1990

In the early years of the official policy of community care two linked themes were emphasized in policy documents. The dominant theme was a plan for short-term treatment of mental illness, just like any other illness, in district general hospital units, outpatient clinics and day hospitals provided by the NHS. The second theme, much less forcefully presented, was a plan whereby local government would provide a network of hostel and home accommodation, social work support, day care and sheltered work for chronically disabled people, in order to provide a real alternative to the back wards of the mental hospital. The first theme grew into a major symphonic work, the second was scarcely audible until the 1980s.

By 1974 there were 60,000 fewer residents in large mental hospitals than there had been in 1954, but very few services at all existed in the community. There were some day hospitals run by the Health Service, a few local authority hostels, an increasing but still small number of group homes and a handful of voluntary 'halfway houses', but little else. Many hospital beds were closed after their occupants had grown old and died, but many others were closed after their occupants were discharged into the community – in most cases these people simply 'disappeared' from the official statistics since no one followed up their progress or knew anything about their fate.

The early leavers were the most socially competent and best able to look after themselves and usually had few residual symptoms of mental disturbance. Some had recovered completely from mental disorder many years earlier, while others left because their families were prepared to provide support. The early exodus was largely driven by enthusiastic psychiatrists, many of whom, it ought to be said, did follow up patients for a year or two either as outpatients or through visits by a growing band of community psychiatric nurses. But there were no proper systems for keeping track of patients over an extended number of years and most psychiatrists were too busy with new patients to worry about those long gone.

Dr A. A. Baker's recollections of Banstead Hospital, published in The Psychiatric Bulletin of the Royal College of Psychiatrists (July 1990), make the process appear easy enough, albeit with some early reluctance on the part of the patients themselves.

There was a ward of over 100 patients who were active and ambulant; all had useful jobs about the hospital, in the laundry, the bakehouse and similar places. I went to this ward and had an open meeting and explained to them that I was willing to help contact relatives or friends, to find accommodation, to find work, to make sure they were financially viable, and offer follow up in the outside world. I asked for volunteers, and had none. So a week later, I did the same again, but suggested that if they were reluctant to talk to me, would they talk to the ward sister? There were still none. After a third such visit, the ward as a whole did a 'round robin' which they sent to the Minister of Health protesting that I was trying to discharge them! They certainly weren't oppressed or imprisoned. This particular block was needed for development, so over a year or so all the patients on that ward were transferred to others. Without any further effort on my part, many of them left the hospital; they seemed to find relatives that they didn't know existed before, and found jobs.

We do not learn what the relatives felt about this unexpected return from the asylum. We do know, however, that many of the arrangements made when patients first left hospital did not last longer than a few years. Circumstances change, relatives die, relationships do not work out as expected. Some who were discharged mentally well had further breakdowns. Many left their original discharge addresses and drifted into the large towns to live in lodging-houses and cheap hotels, seeking isolation and anonymity, persistently plagued by delusional ideas and troublesome hallucinatory voices. Some ended up in prison. No doubt there were many successes too but similarly we know almost nothing about them.

By 1974 it was becoming obvious that the expected development of community facilities had not occurred. James Collier, the civil servant responsible for mental health at that time, recalls observing that services for mentally handicapped people seem to have fared rather better since the government had set specific numerical targets for day care and residential places in a White Paper in 1971; it seems that visible government focus on this group had encouraged service developments. It seemed likely therefore that a similar White Paper for mentally ill people would achieve the same results and James Collier was able to persuade the Minister, Keith Joseph, to launch an initiative in this area. However, the economic situation had worsened markedly since 1971 and unemployment was rising. The White Paper, entitled *Better Services for the Mentally Ill* and published in 1975, admitted in tones of pessimistic realism that services were unlikely to be in good shape for the next quarter of a century.

Fifteen years further on and reaching the end of the century, we can see that this pessimism was justified. In many parts of the country the picture now is shocking. There are overburdened families in varying states of desperation doing their best to cope with a disturbed relative, and deranged destitute people sleeping rough on the streets of every town. Acutely disturbed patients are discharged from general hospital psychiatric wards into bed and breakfast hotels after only a few days in order to make room for more severely disturbed emergencies, and, paradoxically, up to a third of short-term psychiatric hospital beds are permanently occupied by homeless people who receive no help with rehabilitation and have no prospect of a sheltered home.

Yet there are still some 60,000 people left behind in the deteriorating wards of large mental hospitals, shuffled and reshuffled endlessly from ward to ward every few months or years as the process of 'rationalization' forces the amalgamation of the smaller uneconomic remnants of old ward communities. As the populations of hospitals become too small for them to be run economically, we are also beginning to see plans to shift residual residents across from their old home into a neighbouring aslyum. 'Transinstitutionalization' is the 25-letter word used as a euphemism for the cheapest possible warehousing of those who are left.

The picture is not, however, unmitigatedly bleak, for there are pockets of excellent services here and there. Indeed, given the difficulties under which staff work, it is quite remarkable what an innovative assortment of projects has emerged in recent years, though the overall picture is fragmented, uncoordinated, haphazard and extraordinarily variable from place to place. Where in Britain the patient lives is probably the most significant factor in determining the quality of the care he or she receives and there are areas of the country which are service deserts.

Specific targets were set in the 1975 White Paper for both the pace of bed closures in large hospitals and the growth of critical elements of a community service, notably residential places and day centre places to be provided by the local authority, and day hospital places provided by the NHS. Surprisingly, government statistics on the number of beds and day places currently available have been difficult to come by since 1986, partly because of the unnotified temporary closures of beds and ward 'rationalizations' mentioned above, whereby long-stay patients are shifted from ward to ward to save the overhead costs of running a half-empty ward. Since 1984 ward closures across the NHS have generated financial savings which have been used to fund the cost of staff wage awards, which year after year central government has declined to fund. Such 'temporary closures' slip by almost unnoticed in public planning documents yet they nearly always seem to become permanent.

Between 1974 and 1984 the number of hospital places for the long-term mentally ill reduced by a further 25,000 to around 80,000, bringing the total loss of beds since the peak in 1954 to 69,000. Community residential and day care facilities increased between 1974 and 1984 by only a fraction of the need. Only 3,500 local authority 'private or voluntary' residential care places were available and day care places fell short of the White Paper target by a staggering 48,000. Since 1984 there has been a further bed reduction to just over 60,000 in 1989, and a minimal increase in day places.

Bed losses do not, however, simply signal an exodus of long-stay patients out of the asylum and further deaths of old patients. The losses also affect the treatment of new patients. In most hospitals there is now no longer sufficient provision of accommodation in which a period of slow rehabilitation and recovery over a two- or three-year period can take place away from the 'hurly-burly' of a rapidly changing acute psychiatric ward. As a result admissions to acute wards are often terminated abruptly. A recent study in London of discharged short-term psychiatric patients found that patients felt they were offered no choice about their long-term care and were not involved in decisions made on their behalf, and that the arrangements for rehousing and day care were often inadequate and unacceptable to the patients themselves. Nor did they receive any practical help with getting welfare benefits or dealing with the social security system and they often had little understanding of the purpose of their medication. While most preferred living out of hospital to remaining inside it, many were living in emergency temporary hostels for homeless people or in bed and breakfast hotels paid for by the local authority. The majority were dissatisfied with their housing and half felt they needed more help and support to cope with their mental illness as well as with the problems of finding or maintaining a home and a job. It is clear that community care is failing many thousands of highly vulnerable people.

Since the early 1960s the mental health services have been the victim of political indifference, catastrophic reorganizations of the NHS itself, and of local authorities, inappropriate funding arrangements and, saddest of all, the persistent failure of the psychiatric profession to take an interest in the rehabilitation and continuing care of long-term disabled people. And during this same period another rapidly growing group has emerged with pressing health care demands, which has led to further problems for politicians, the social services and the medical profession – the growing population of very old people.

Political disinterest

Mental health services rarely find their way on to any political party's agenda. The sufferers, often from poor families, form an invisible minority with little political clout, and our society, dominated as it is by the clamour of the consumer voice, has other priorities for its health and welfare services. Consequently, mental health is traditionally given to the most junior minister in the Department of Health, one who is often cutting his or her ministerial teeth in an unpopular area while hoping for swift promotion to more prestigious office. Within the Department of Health itself mental health has also been viewed consistently as a fringe area, in spite of the fact that one pound in every ten of NHS expenditure goes (albeit reluctantly) in this area, and a staggering two-thirds of all social security supplementary benefit for board and lodging is now directed at adults with mental disorders or elderly people with dementia. In the late 1970s and 1980s particularly Enoch Powell's earlier vision of 'building cathedrals – services to the glory of society, with no demonstrable economic benefit' sounds woefully at odds with the realities of community care for the mentally ill.

Reorganizations

A retired public health physician and former Medical Officer of Health recently remarked, 'My whole career in the '60s, '70s and '80s was dominated by reorganizations. I can only remember two years when my service wasn't just recovering from one or preparing for the next.' By any standards, the organizations primarily responsible for providing health and social care in Britain are astonishingly complex. The government, of course, has overall responsibility, but below this comes the NHS, local government social services departments and other local government departments. Mental health services straddle the whole gamut, and people needing, or receiving, care often need to cross at different times from one service to another. It is frequently at the boundaries between services that failed 'baton changes' occur, and various reorganizations have taken place over the years, mainly for financial reasons, but also, it is claimed, in order to make these organizations more responsive to the needs of consumers. Unfortunately, the target consumer for all such reorganizations (where the consumer was seriously considered at all) was the short-stay patient with an acute illness (for example, a gastric ulcer or a broken leg), not the long-term mentally ill patient, and services for this group have suffered badly from the periodic reorganizations, particularly those in 1971 and 1974 which created a gulf between NHS and local authority services which has never been healed. In these structural changes, mental health services were catastrophically split down the middle simply because no one was thinking much about how the changes would impact on mental health services.

At the same time the reorganization of social services, recommended by the Seebohm Report, led to specialist mental health workers being swallowed up in larger 'generic' departments. Social services also became increasingly preoccupied with child welfare as this was perceived as a more glamorous area, and also because of widely publicized child abuse cases. The result was that the psychiatric social worker virtually disappeared. On the NHS side, psychiatry became increasingly integrated with general medicine as just one more specialty, and a rather 'down market', unprestigious specialty at that.

The result was that services for the seriously mentally ill became quickly submerged under tier upon tier of administration designed, paradoxically, to provide integrated hospital and community service for all health care services in a local district, but inevitably dominated at the top by the preoccupations of the more glamorous acute specialties. Since 1974 there has been no identifiable corporate group of individuals within a locality who can be identified as 'The Mental Health Service' – no one is responsible, no one carries the can. It is always someone else's responsibility.

Further NHS reorganization took place in the 1980s and yet another fundamental change of structure is outlined in the NHS and Community Care Act of 1990. This latest reorganization of the NHS, covered in the first part of the Act, was triggered by rising and apparently uncontrollable overspending in the acute hospital service, a wish to curb the power of hospital consultants, and by increasing public concern about the poor standards of care being offered by the hospital service. It is too early to say whether the planned changes in the hospital service will have a positive or negative effect on mental health, but there are fears of even further fragmentation and separation of services. The Community Care part of the Act, which has quite separate aims from the NHS reforms, is intended to bring about significant changes in mental health services and is considered in detail in Chapter 6.

Loss of local government power

The development of community-based mental health services depends crucially on the willingness and ability of local government authorities to spend money on providing appropriate housing; and on rehabilitation facilities such as day care and social care support in its widest sense, including the leisure and education facilities which other citizens enjoy. Since the early 1960s, the balance of power has dramatically shifted away from local government in favour of central government, and relations between central and local government have been steadily eroded by a series of measures designed to keep the lid tightly closed on local authority expenditure of any kind. The response has been predictable: left-wing local authorities have indulged in angry profligacy and right wing-dominated authorities have, in some instances, almost totally failed to spend anything at all on social welfare services for disadvantaged minority groups. Those in the middle have sometimes done what they could, but all in the interest of a 'minimalist' cash-limited environment. It is not surprising therefore that as hospital closures have proceeded in the NHS, local authorities have not responded as originally expected to patients' needs by developing the range of alternative services set out in the 1962 plan. Indeed, as early as 1975 the White Paper repeatedly referred to 'economic stringencies' and indicated that the government expected no improvement in local authorities' commitment to mental health 'until economic circumstances permit'. The government came quickly to expect nothing and most local governments did nothing.

Financial disincentives to developing community care

The rapid development of asylums in the nineteenth century was encouraged by the wish of local parishes to shift financial responsibility for long-term care on to county council asylums. In the late twentieth century a curious and complex set of financial arrangements provided incentives for both health and local authorities to shift responsibility for care on to another central government ministry, the Department of Social Security. Social security benefit is a welfare entitlement paid direct to an individual in need. The availability of social security benefit to assist with board and lodging payments in residential homes or bed and breakfast accommodation had the effect of shifting huge numbers of mentally disordered people out of hospitals and into private sector residential care. This was because health and local authorities faced with strict budgetary constraints quickly came to realize that, if they discharged patients into the community, the funding responsibility would pass elsewhere. Some observers have regarded this shift as a Machiavellian Tory government plot to stimulate the growth of private sector care and reduce the role of public authorities. But looking at the history of the funding changes, there is no evidence that central government had any notion whatever of the likely impact of the social security benefit arrangements in producing the 'transinstitutionalization' of mentally ill people from hospital to private 'care'. Indeed, in the late 1970s and 1980s the easy availability of social security benefit funding seems largely to have been fostered by government as a considered, though still none the less somewhat panicked, response to the urgent need for increased residential care provision for elderly people. Little thought appears to have been given to the effect the changes were having on mental health care.

Enormous sums of money are spent on mental health services in Britain though they come from various government purses. Ultimately, however, virtually all the money comes from the public in the form of direct central or local government taxation, although charitable sources and patients' families also figure. In 1990, approximately £2 billion was spent by the NHS directly on mental health services, a figure which represented some 10 per cent of total Health Service expenditure. In addition social services departments spend round about £50 million annually on residential and day care services for people with mental problems. Add to this a further £100 million spent on supplementary benefit for board and lodging payments and the considerable amount expended by prisons, courts and the police. Add to this, too, the growing amounts of money,

£500 million to £600 million in 1990, spent on supporting elderly people with senile dementia outside mental illness hospitals in residential and nursing homes. This figure represents almost two-thirds of all expenditure on residential care for elderly people, two-thirds being the proportion of people in residential care with mental disorder. Overall, the current direct care costs to the public purse of disabling mental disorder is approximately £3,000 million a year.

In the 1960s and 1970s, it was assumed that as hospital beds closed, money would be transferred from the NHS to local authorities in order to provide alternative facilities. To promote this transfer of resources (for it was recognized that the NHS would not cheerfully relinquish its funding) an ear-marked fund, called Joint Finance, was established in 1976. This was carved out of the NHS national budget but was to be specially allocated to mutually agreed schemes provided by local authorities or voluntary organizations. Joint Finance was therefore the carrot to promote better joint working of the divided public sector. It proved to be only a modest success, and though it made a small contribution to developing some innovative demonstration projects, it represented only 1 per cent of NHS total expenditure, and this had to cover services for elderly people, people with physical disabilities, children and adults with mental handicap as well as mental health services. Joint Finance grant was a specific sum allocated to a project for a number of years which then gradually tapered off; thereafter the intention was that the local authority would pick up the bill. As the budgets of local authorities grew tighter, they naturally became reluctant to commit themselves to additional expenditure for seriously dependent people in years ahead when their income could not be predicted. In the later years of the scheme the money was frequently spent on temporary support to voluntary organizations and on schemes which had a minimal impact on the overall shape of services.

The fact that Joint Finance existed may have discouraged health authorities from transferring money directly from their own budgets to local authorities, but there were also other disincentives. Government funding arrangements penalized heavily those local authorities who invested in community care services. How this came about is that, in order to restrain overall public expenditure, the government reduced the allocation of central grant if an authority spent more by raising local rates, or more recently, the community charge (or local tax). 'Rate capping', or 'poll tax capping', that is, preventing local government from raising local taxes, remains the ultimate weapon of central government to restrain big-spending local authorities. Under such circumstances it is not surprising that local authorities did not want to commit themselves to taking up Joint Finance or even to accepting a transfer of funds direct from the NHS, as the former would give them a long-term commitment which might prove embarrassing at a later date and the latter would merely be counterbalanced by a reduction in the central grant and, even worse, by financial penalties for increasing their spending. Thus for every extra million pounds an authority spent on community care services, a burden of up to £2 million could fall on rate payers because of loss of central grant and 'capping', unless other services were reduced to compensate for the cost of the community care developments.

Added to this is the natural tendency, mentioned earlier, of all bureaucracies to hang on to their funding, a tendency from which the NHS is not exempt. Indeed, it has successfully retained mental health funds by using these to cover the rapidly growing costs of in-patient hospital beds for the mentally ill, and there has been minimal transfer of resources to local authorities.

During a period when thousands of beds closed and when mental health's share of the NHS cake remained steady, the proportion of funds spent on in-patient beds remained much the same. Over this period, however, the cost of an in-patient bed for a mentally ill person doubled. In part this was due to much needed increased staffing levels on acute psychiatric wards, with nurses, occupational therapists, psychologists and doctors, plus improvements in the community psychiatric nursing services, and in part it is due, less admirably, to a direct shift of resources out of long-stay care beds and into new acute psychiatric units developed in general hospitals. But the key reason for the dramatic increase in in-patient costs is that as patients have died or left hospital, there have been only marginal savings on the overall costs of running a hospital. To save significantly on staffing costs, for example, a whole ward of twenty to thirty people needs to close at once and a piecemeal reduction in patient numbers has no great effect. To save substantially on such overhead costs as water, light and heating, a whole ward block of fifty to 100 beds needs to close. To save the enormous infrastructure costs of an entire decrepit Victorian institution (for example, building maintenance, gardeners and grounds, administrators, telephone operators, catering department, pharmacy, etc.), the whole hospital has to close. When half a dozen or a dozen patients move out of hospital into a home of their own and their beds are closed, there are minimal savings in the hospital which can be passed on for care in the community.

Thus in order to develop services outside the hospital, bridging finance is required for many years until all the funds can be finally released on the closure of the hospital. Such funds are not, of course, just the cost of running the hospital. The capital costs of building, converting or leasing property for residential and day care need to be found many years before the hospital is closed, so while in theory the costs of community provision should easily be covered by the money raised from the sale of large hospital sites, some of which are situated in prime residential or commercial development areas, the income cannot be realized while the hospital is still partially occupied. Thus large capital sums are required 'up front' to provide alternative accommodation for discharged patients.

In the 1980s, Regional Health Authorities introduced capital and 'ongoing revenue' bridging funds in a small way, usually targeting one, or perhaps two, institutions in their Regions. But the funds were simply inadequate to cover the huge need. The inexorable decline in the number of beds continued and patients continued to move into places which cost the NHS and local authority nothing. Ever since the run-down of the asylums began, patients who were thought fit for discharge but who had no family or friends to return to, have tended to drift to cheap hotels and hostels in inner city areas. These cater for single homeless people seeking basic shelter, food and anonymity for a small sum of money which falls well within welfare benefit limits. Others, of course, did not settle in to even such basic accommodation and became vagrants, dossers, derelicts.

But as well as the inner city hotels and hostels, a new trade grew up in the 1970s. It began at English seaside resorts where landladies running cheap private hotels and bed and breakfast accommodation were facing hard times as a result of English summers and increasingly popular cheap package holidays which swept British holiday-makers off to Spain and other sunny destinations. Ex-psychiatric patients were attractive alternative customers – they were year-round residents, funded generously enough by social security benefits, and were generally quiet, socially reserved and often inept at complaining even when the circumstances they were living in were unsatisfactory. Besides, many had little choice as there was no way back to the hospitals for them. They were welcomed by proprietors who generally had no experience what-soever of the needs of their residents and little understanding of mental disorder. In the 1970s in any seaside town on the south coast you would find dozens of dispirited, isolated people; all were unemployed and spent most of the day walking along the beaches and around the town or sitting in cheap cafés and public libraries as they were usually forbidden to stay in their lodgings during the day. Some of these establishments were good and their proprietors were kindly and concerned. Many, however, were characterized by multiple-occupancy rooms with beds squashed into every corner, poor washing and bathing facilities and a total lack of any social amenities. They were new versions of the private madhouses of the eighteenth century. Many consultant psychiatrists working in mental hospitals discharged their patients to these 'homes' quite unaware of the reality of the conditions to which they were consigning their patients.

Most of these private homes are now registered with the local authority and are regularly inspected. Conditions have improved, but the residents remain an additional unsought burden of responsibility on local social services authorities and often, too, on the district psychiatric services.

By the late 1970s there was no one left in long-stay wards in mental hospitals who could easily be discharged without follow-up.

Those remaining were either too physically sick or old, too emotionally or behaviourally disturbed to be discharged to unsupervised homes, or too dependent on other people for help with the daily tasks of life – washing, bathing, feeding and so on. The options for such patients were few; either they had to go to the increasing number of private nursing homes and residential homes springing up for elderly people, or alternative provision had to be made using NHS money. Large numbers of physically disabled and elderly people who were considered sufficiently well-behaved and free of excessive mental symptoms were moved into ordinary private residential nursing homes, but the most seriously disturbed had to be left behind.

A further reorganization of the NHS took place in 1983 and created mental health or 'priority care' units of management in which NHS elements of the care were all planned and managed under one responsible unit general manager. The government encouraged the development of 'priority care services' – broadly all those services in which continuing care in the community is essential – and on a wave of optimism considerable capital investment was made in such services in the mid-1980s. Unfortunately this was too little too late. By then most of the damage had been done – twenty years of thoughtless discharge of vulnerable patients could not be undone, and the new plans focused almost exclusively on services to help those patients who had been left behind in the institution cope once discharged into the community. No new money was made available for the ever-increasing numbers of new patients with long-term needs who were constantly recycling through the new district general hospital acute psychiatric units. Such new patients had generally entered the system in the last twenty to twenty-five years and had never been part of a long-stay community; there were also many chronically ill people who had never had any contact with services and who were receiving no help at all.

Patients who moved to private sector board and lodging accommodation or to residential homes were rarely followed up by the consultant or his team beyond the first few weeks, in part because the distances between the hospital and the area where large, cheap properties suitable for conversion to private institutions were plentiful was likely to preclude much visiting. The NHS effectively shuffled off high-cost in-patients to a low-cost system remote from the statutory services.

In spite of all these problems, some high-quality and innovative projects were developed in these thirty years, generally by committed voluntary organizations working with housing associations or by local authorities prepared to provide property for conversion. The 'group' homes movement, in which four to six ex-patients live together in an ordinary house, sharing household tasks but supported by professional staff from a voluntary organization and the statutory services, was a fashionable and often successful solution for less disabled people. Psychiatrists with a real interest in long-term care and considerable determination could, if they formed the right links with external agencies, build an impressive network of community houses. Usually these rare and precious 'rehabilitation' enthusiasts were trying to run a district psychiatric service for acute short-term patients at the same time. As combining the two roles successfully is a tricky and difficult business, most psychiatrists decided that they had neither the inclination nor the skills to try, and concentrated instead on their acute work.

Perverse funding systems have thus acted as a serious disincentive to collaboration between agencies, and large sums of money remain 'locked in' to partly occupied old hospitals while local authorities are discouraged by current arrangements from spending appropriately. The NHS and Community Care Act of 1990 proposes some streamlining of funding arrangements so that social security benefit for residential care is channelled through local authorities following an assessment of an individual's needs. This should have the effect of improving the targeting of these funds but it will also impose a cash-limit 'ceiling' on the government's expenditure in this area. These changes will not now take effect until 1993. From April 1991 there is also a specific mental health grant for social services to use on provision of community services. The funding arrangements for this are similar to Joint Finance and it is thought unlikely that it will have any significant impact. The

Treasury has also given a cautious nod to some private developers to advance money before the final sale of hospital sites so as to provide bridging finance for community-based replacement services; however, the complex rules suggest that the Treasury is more ambivalent and suspicious about these unconventional finance arrangements than might at first appear.

The rising tide of an ageing population

One key reason for the slower than expected run-down of large hospitals is that as patients who have been ill for twenty or thirty years have left the hospital, empty places have filled up with elderly people with 'senile dementia'. In the 1980s almost all patients admitted explicitly for long-term care with no expectation of discharge, have been old people over the age of 75 years. By the late 1980s more than a third of all psychiatric hospital admissions were elderly people and this proportion will continue to rise until well into the twenty-first century.

It has been estimated that two out of every three elderly people who have ever lived on this earth are alive today. At the beginning of the twentieth century there were 300,000 people over the age of 75 years in Britain. By the end of the twentieth century there will be something over 4 million, and a total of 10 million men and women over retirement age. The population of old people has grown much faster than the population of young people, so we now have a society in which there is a rising percentage of old people and a falling percentage of young and middle-aged. Elderly people now comprise 16 per cent of the population, whereas in 1900 the figure was only 4 per cent. So there are not only many more old people around than ever before, but they largely depend for their pensions and other health and social welfare support needed in old age on a proportionately smaller young and middle-aged working population.

Elderly people are also living longer. More than at any other time in history, a person has a good chance of surviving into their eighties, nineties and beyond – there are now at least 3,000 centenarians in Britain. These changes in the age structure of the population have come about as a result of improvements in sanitation, nutrition and general living conditions towards the end of the nineteenth century and into the twentieth. Improved living standards caused a dramatic fall in the numbers of babies who died at birth or in early childhood. The children of large Victorian and Edwardian families began to survive the hazards of childhood and the scourges of TB and other infectious epidemics which afflicted young adults in earlier generations and lived to a ripe old age.

A further change then occurred. As people's living standards improved and parents could be more confident that their children would survive into adulthood, they planned fewer babies. The numbers of births began to fall at the end of the last century and levelled out at a much lower number. So a fall in the birth rate, an increased life expectancy and improved survival into very old age has given rise to an ageing population not just in Britain (though here, at least, we are world leaders) but in every developed country of the world.

Women survive longer than men as a general rule so that in the over-75 age group there are now twice as many women as men. And it is not just the wonders of modern medicine which are causing people to live longer. While many individuals have benefited from specific treatments and now lead fuller, less handicapped and more active lives as a result of medicine and surgery, this does not account for the ageing of our population, which mainly reflects a triumph over poverty brought about by the increasing wealth of a nation with a successful industrial, agricultural and service infrastructure.

It is also important not to exaggerate the extent of disease and disability in old age. In general, people between the age of 60 and 75 years keep remarkably healthy and active. The problems of old age emerge most commonly in people over 75 years and especially in those over 85 years. Even then, it is a minority of these 'very old' people who have serious disabilities or long-term illness. Thus the majority of elderly people remain mentally well until the end of their days. Four out of five people over the age of 85 years have no problems with their memories and can concentrate with as much rigour and attentiveness as they ever could. Senility (or senile dementia as it is more properly called) is not the inevitable consequence of ageing and, in fact, affects only a small proportion: perhaps five in 100 people of retirement age have some form of dementia or serious confusion as a result of physical illness. But while the proportion may be small it is the sheer *number* of elderly people with mental disorder which raises a very serious and rising problem for the sufferers, their families, their neighbours and for the health and social services provided by the state.

Mental disorder is now the primary reason for entering institutional care in old age. There are now nearly a million elderly people in Britain with mental disorder of some kind, including dementia, severe confusion, mental handicap or depression. Most of them remain at home, cared for by members of their family (often an elderly spouse), but something like a quarter of a million confused old people now live permanently in residential care, either in homes or in hospitals. Most elderly people with mental disorder do not come into contact with specialist psychiatric services, and even when they need 24-hour supervision they are far more likely to be cared for by local authorities in ordinary old people's homes, in private residential homes or in geriatric beds provided by the general medical services of the health service. But those who do come the way of the psychiatric services, usually because of the seriously upsetting emotional and behavioural problems which are sometimes a consequence of dementia, often become long-stay patients in old mental hospitals, ending their days in totally inappropriate, anonymous, run-down, understaffed wards designed to rob them of their last shreds of individuality. Dementia sufferers who come to a mental hospital for the first time in old age now form approximately half the long-stay population of old mental hospitals.

The ageing population has had a dramatic impact on mental health services. In order to satisfy the rising clamour for improved community mental health services to assist GPs and social services staff in caring for elderly people with mental disorder at home, and in order to provide care for the most severely affected in hospitals, considerable resources have been carved out of the overall mental health budget in the last fifteen years and directed towards the elderly. Almost all District Health Authorities have appointed new specialists in 'psychogeriatrics', that is, the psychiatry of old age, and have acquired specialist teams of nurses, occupational therapists and psychologists. The money had to be found from somewhere and in most authorities it was diverted from resources which originally provided long-stay care in mental hospitals for younger adults with chronic mental disorder, especially resources originally provided for people with schizophrenia and other lifelong disorders. Society finds it relatively easy to ignore strange, deranged, isolated younger people living rough or out of sight in bed and breakfast seaside hotels, but it is more difficult to ignore a frail confused old person wandering at night, or to let an old neighbour die from self-neglect and starvation. Old people with dementia get into the 'caring' system by hook or by crook. If all else fails, an emergency hospital admission brings shelter and care; it may perhaps not be of the right kind, but it is a solution of sorts.

The profound and continuing effect on health and social services of the escalating numbers of very old people is of fundamental significance. Over the next forty years, unless the investment in services significantly exceeds the 2 per cent annual increase that is required merely to meet the need for services for the increasing numbers of disabled old people, there cannot be (in the absence of a miracle) any improvement in services for those other groups of people who have long-term disabilities. Between 1983 and 1988, the government identified four 'priority care' groups – people with physical disabilities, mental illness and mental handicap, and elderly people. Many Health Service authorities made no conscious effort at all to shift resources into these groups, but whether managers realized it or not, money did move. Nationwide, services for elderly people soaked up most of the identified 'priority' resources. The money was not spent on improving services but simply on providing the same level of service to keep pace with the demographic changes. Mental health services gained nothing overall although services for elderly people with dementia did begin to improve.

Elderly people with mental disorder have very special needs and I cannot ever recall meeting a sufferer or a relative who felt that a mental hospital could provide the right kind of environment for the continuing care of someone with dementia. The rising tide of dementia sufferers deserves something a great deal better.

The influence of psychiatrists

From the 1940s to the early 1960s, it was psychiatrists who were the pioneers in developing and improving services. But as psychiatry became increasingly a medical specialty, it focused more and more on specific medical and psychological treatments of individuals with short-term, potentially reversible conditions, and it largely lost interest in patients who did not recover, particularly those in the dismal 'back wards' of mental hospitals and those supported at home by families who had long given up hope of a cure. Psychiatrists began to regard patients' social and cultural background as merely an interesting backdrop against which the drama of acute illness was enacted. Government planning documents might push the idea of a 'comprehensive' community service for all sufferers, and most doctors paid lip-service to the concept, but the more prestigious the consultant post finally attained at the end of training, the better the chance a doctor had of avoiding the responsibility of caring for the long-term sick.

I began postgraduate training in psychiatry in 1972, with the advice of my medical school professor firmly fixed in my mind: 'Stay away from mental hospitals, they'll give you bad habits.' I followed this advice assiduously for five years until I reached the point in my training when I could no longer avoid working in a mental hospital. I still managed to complete my training, however, without ever having worked with a senior colleague interested in the rehabilitation and care of long-term sufferers. I had no idea whatever of the practicalities and problems of establishing community-based services. Nor was there anything in the syllabus for the examinations of the newly formed Royal College of Psychiatrists to encourage study in this area; psychiatric training was about medical diagnosis and the treatment of individuals. A 'good' postgraduate training covered a three-year period comprising six monthly attachments to consultant 'firms'. These would be engaged in various types of acute psychiatric work, to which the trainee served an apprenticeship, learning to use the therapeutic approaches espoused by individual consultants, some of whom might use drugs and physical treatments, some psychoanalytically oriented psychotherapy, some group therapy and so on. Experience of other kinds of work was available, with children and families, for example, or services for drug or alcohol abusers, but most of a trainee's time was spent in general adult acute work. This was followed by a further four-year period of 'higher' advanced training, moving jobs each year, at least one year of which was spent in a teaching hospital unit. Again, almost all the emphasis throughout the four years was on short-term treatment.

The syllabus of the Royal College of Psychiatrists has scarcely changed in twenty years: 'social and community psychiatry' is still regarded as a 'branch' of psychiatry rather than the rootstock on which all services should be developed.

It is easy to understand why British psychiatry, and, indeed, psychiatric practice around the world, became so dominated by the particular needs of short-term patients. For a start, doctors who became consultants were trained as I was and simply did not see much of the long-stay patients. In the 1960s and 1970s junior doctors in mental hospitals were recruited mainly from among the thousands of overseas doctors from the Indian sub-continent and the Middle East who came to Britain with bright hopes to train as surgeons or physicians but discovered that general hospital work was hard to find and ended up as extra pairs of hands in jobs unattractive to British graduates. I recall that in 1972 the training course organized for the West Midlands regional rotation scheme was regularly attended by thirty junior doctors. There were only three British-trained graduates on the course, all of us employed in the Birmingham teaching hospitals; the rest were Asian and Middle Eastern. This sad exploitation of overseas doctors ended only when anxiety about protecting the future career prospects of British graduates influenced the government to restrict immigration. The happier legacy of this period is the contribution now being made to services in Britain by those overseas doctors who found they enjoyed psychiatry and had the persistence to struggle up the ladder to consultant status.

There are persuasive arguments in favour of basing most short-term treatment in district general hospitals. Advocates of general hospital units point out the many advantages over the old mental hospital and also their superiority in some ways to small, localized centres specifically for people with mental health problems. The general hospital is usually quite conveniently situated, with good public transport, it is open twenty-four hours a day and is familiar and unthreatening to the local population. It is possible to walk in and out without being identified as 'a mental patient'. Furthermore, many patients find it reassuring and comforting to be 'ill' rather than 'mad', 'having a breakdown' or 'emotionally disturbed'. Ill people are accorded the privileges of rest from work without guilt, a non-judgmental attitude of sympathy from friends and relatives, and are given the hope of treatment and recovery which can have a very beneficial effect on mentally disordered people searching for an explanation of their puzzling experiences. General hospital units are also usually well staffed, in new bright surroundings and with far more money invested in them than in the old mental hospitals. The physical environment and staffing levels are close to other on-site facilities for other 'physical' specialties, which ensures that the mental health services do not become too much of a 'cinderella service' compared with other specialties. The presence of psychiatry on site also encourages better liaison with other services and advice is also available for patients of other doctors and for people coming into the casualty department in a state of mental distress.

The presence of a psychiatric unit in a general hospital or teaching hospital encourages junior doctors to train in psychiatry and provides new trainees with an experience which is not dissimilar to other specialties. Recruitment of junior doctors to psychiatric training has therefore improved immeasurably as a result of medically oriented training and the emphasis on general hospital work. Furthermore, the investigative facilities of a general hospital, such as a good x-ray department, are increasingly important with the rise in the proportion of elderly people needing treatment, due to the close links which exist in old age between physical illness and disability and mental disorder.

Such reasons are sound and important, but there has been a

heavy price to pay for these advantages. General hospital- and teaching hospital-based psychiatrists, concentrating like all other medical specialists on acutely ill short-term patients, have their offices and secretaries many miles away from the old mental hospitals. Whereas, prior to the move to general hospital units, long-stay patients were on the site where the consultant worked and were thus a constant reminder of the need for better care and rehabilitation facilities outside the hospital, now such patients might only be visited once a week or fortnight, or even less. Many newly appointed psychiatrists, especially those working in the new, prestigious academic teaching hospital units which were established in the late 1960s and 1970s, had few contacts with mental hospitals and did not provide any care at all for long-stay patients. Professors of psychiatry and teaching hospital consultants who provided a role model for junior doctors in training usually chose not to provide a service to residents of a specific geographical 'catchment area', but instead took patient referrals selectively from GPs and other psychiatrists, concentrating on patients with the specific psychiatric disorder which was the focus of their personal research programme.

It did not take long for junior doctors to realize that life as a psychiatrist in a teaching hospital or general hospital without any 'catchment area' responsibility was professionally stimulating, allowed time for medical research, and was more likely to lead to academic preferment or, for those so inclined, private practice. It was also much, much easier and less stressful work than taking on the diverse, complex problems of catchment area work, which involved dealing with urgent and unpredictable crises in the community, with sometimes dangerous and difficult people and with long-stay patients in run down, old, inadequate wards, all at the same time as attempting to find time to plan a better future for patients.

In London a two-tier system of care had been in place since the Maudsley Hospital was established. Under this system the Maudsley operated as the hub of a wheel whose spokes led out to a ring of London County Council mental hospitals. The Maudsley had a concentration of nationally, even internationally renowned consultants and a cadre of ambitious young psychiatrists. It prided itself on

being a centre of academic clinical excellence,
hospitals were staffed by asylum doctors of low statu
to provide care for huge numbers of patients from
London. In the 1960s and 1970s, as general hosp
more numerous, a similar, nationwide two-tier system developed
whereby the most seriously disturbed patients – who were difficult
to manage in ordinary hospital units or who needed security – and
old long-stay patients were catered for in mental hospitals, while the
daily activity of the local acute psychiatric service focused on the
general hospital. Psychiatrists who took on catchment area responsibilities perceived their work largely as focusing on acutely ill
patients rather than on the long-term sick. As psychiatrists moved
out of the mental hospitals, most of the other professionals (such as
occupational therapists, psychologists and so on) moved with them,
leaving behind an old guard of demoralized and disaffected nursing
staff to cope as best they could, knowing that as further beds closed,
their jobs would go too.

It may appear that I have been hard on psychiatrists, and it is true
that the majority of general hospital psychiatrists worked with a very
demanding, acutely ill population of short-term patients who could
not be ignored. They felt they had little time to do anything else.
The ethos of the profession was concerned with excellence of
diagnosis and treatment and during these years there was an
improvement in the standards of medical practice offered to
seriously disturbed short-term patients.

Psychiatrists have often been deeply resentful of the taunts of
social work colleagues, local pressure groups and voluntary organizations about their adoption of the 'medical model'. The truth is
that although all psychiatrists acknowledge the profound influence
of family, culture, class and race in the onset of disorders, and the
importance of providing the right kind of environment on discharge, they have failed to grasp the key role which they as professionals could play in developing new-style services in the
community. They have somehow felt that they were therapists, not
Mr (or Ms) Fixits, and that developing new services was simply not
a doctor's job. While it is true that doctors are not well trained in the
principles or practice of rehabilitation, and that other professionals

ch as psychologists, occupational therapists and senior nurses are often better fitted for this work, because of the power and influence of consultant psychiatrists other professions simply could not take over this task without the ungrudging support of their psychiatrist colleagues.

Gradually, though, a small number of other professional workers did begin to focus their skills on the needs of the long-term patient. Some psychologists, in particular, have shown the way forward and now the 'big names' in rehabilitation are all psychologists, not psychiatrists. Developments would, however, have moved much faster had there been greater enthusiasm and backing from psychiatrists.

Psychiatrists, therefore, have opted out of service development, and the most potent vision of the future has been created by others, notably by voluntary organizations such as MIND (National Association for Mental Health) and managers and planners in health and social services. At the moment, however, psychiatrists still exercise enormous influence because of their medical professional background and because they belong to the only health profession which holds a licence to prescribe extremely powerful drugs. When and if other professions acquire this power, as they are now beginning to do in some other countries, psychiatrists had better be sure they know what their role is or they may find themselves expensive dinosaurs.

It is by no means too late for a change in orientation to take place. There are encouraging signs that as a result of pressures from NHS managers, academic psychiatrists in teaching hospitals are realizing that they must demonstrate their usefulness to the NHS or lose their expensive facilities. Furthermore, psychiatrists in general and teaching hospitals are realizing that the increasing numbers of chronically sick people who now occupy their acute psychiatry wards for months or even years are doing so because they lack appropriate supported housing. The realization of their plight and of the 'grid-locking' which results in the acute services is finally driving home the need for a more comprehensive service for both short-term and long-term patients in the community.

Even though psychiatrists have not on the whole played the role originally expected of them in the closure of the hospitals and the development of community alternatives, a handful of committed rehabilitation specialists have accomplished very significant changes in their own districts. There is a number of large hospitals where individual consultants have ensured that every discharge was carefully planned to a network of supported houses and homes linked permanently to a support team. They have provided, where possible, for rapid readmission for those who felt unhappy or unsettled in their new homes and ensured that a slow, unpressured approach helped uncertain people to a feeling of mastery over their own potential. I witnessed such a service in operation at Goodmayes Hospital, Essex in the 1970s (see Chapter 10). Leaving hospital could and should have been as positive an experience for patients nationwide.

In summary, we can trace the failure of community care for mentally disordered people to political neglect, detrimental NHS and local authority organizational changes, loss of local government power, financial disincentives to effective delivery of care, the increasing need for resources by an ageing population and, last, the failure by psychiatrists to participate in the development of services for people who need long-term care.

What is required to foster good community care is clear:

- Political commitment and government leadership
- Organizational changes within the health service and local authorities which facilitate transfer of resources from hospitals to community services and permit an effective operational structure for practical delivery of care
- Radical restructuring of the way existing financial resources are used to support community care
- Recognition of the impact of demographic changes and of the consequences for funding other services
- A radical change in the training of psychiatrists towards a community-oriented model of practice which focuses on the treatment and care of the most seriously disturbed mentally disordered people who need continuing support.

5 The Nature of Mental Disorder and Problems in Treatment and Care

Mental disorder presents very special problems for those planning services, problems which are inherent in the disabilities created by mental disorder and in the response of relatives and the wider community to this form of distress. It is not, perhaps, altogether surprising that these serious and profound problems, particularly when allied with major demographic changes, should have given rise to the political, economic and professional difficulties outlined in the previous chapter.

The term 'mental disorder' is preferable to 'mental illness' because while there are many people who suffer from quite clear biologically determined abnormalities of the brain which give rise to mental disorders and which deserve to be called 'illness' as much as any bodily disease, there are also many forms of mental distress which do not fit so happily into the concept of illness. 'Symptoms' often represent normal emotional human responses to adversity but are either experienced in an exaggerated form or seem to have emerged out of time with the events which triggered them. Sometimes they do not seem to be related to external circumstances at all. Another good reason for using the term 'mental illness' sparingly is that while many sufferers and relatives find it reassuring and helpful to explain puzzling and distressing conditions in terms of illness, there are numerous sufferers who experience what is happening to them as an integral part of their being, their personality.

The all-embracing concept of mental disorder as 'illness' can also lead to a mechanistic medical approach to diagnosis and treatment which focuses on *symptoms*. These often respond best to drugs and physical treatments, but often are the least troublesome problem the sufferer has to cope with. Emphasizing the medical problem and ignoring the social difficulties which may result from it are a result of trying to treat mental disorder as if it were no different from a broken leg. But mental disorder, unlike a broken leg, can affect the emotions, senses, reasoning powers and the ability of a person to form normal social relationships. It can lead to strange behaviour and profound changes in personality which make daily life difficult and work impossible.

Most people with mental disorder suffer from mild or short-lived conditions that do not interfere permanently with their ability to lead a normal life, although work and home life may be very difficult to cope with for a while. But those relatively few people with serious and long-standing mental disorder, especially those who have a relapsing, recurrent condition, often need a great deal of help from other people to lead a semblance of 'normal' life. It is this aspect, the dependence on others for help in managing the daily business of life, not clinical problems, which characterizes all those groups of people who have been identified in official government policy documents as in need of 'community care'.

This book is not concerned with people with a mental handicap, (or, as they are increasingly referred to, people with learning difficulties). Every ten years or so campaigners with the best of intentions seek to remove the stigma of being born with an abnormally poor intellect as a result of a failure of brain development by changing the way we refer to the individuals concerned. What used to be called mental subnormality, 'backwardness' or mental retardation has now been relabelled again, and perhaps this strategy does stimulate new thinking and provide new perspectives and attitudes to individuals' problems. People with learning difficulties have also emerged from the shadow of the asylums and in many ways have fared rather better in terms of the provision of community care services than people with mental disorder. They benefited from clear government guidance in 1971 which channelled more resources into this field, and a vigorous and effective campaigning voluntary sector lobby of parents of handicapped children has emerged. There was also a fortunate lack of interest on the part of most of the medical profession which allowed other professional groups such as psychologists, educational experts, rehabilitation therapists and private and voluntary organizations to apply their skills, creating a diverse range of appropriate and innovative services. Nevertheless, families caring for a mentally handicapped child or adult still complain about the same 'community care' problems as are described in this book and many of the solutions outlined in later chapters apply equally to the care of this group.

This book is therefore concerned with people with mental disorder acquired in later childhood or adult life. However, abnormal states of mind cannot all be lumped together. The value of an accurate psychiatric diagnosis is that it gives some guidance to the likely course and outcome of the disorder and it allows professionals to choose the best approach to treatment and care. Diagnosis is usually relatively easy in psychiatric practice since it is based solely on recognizing a characteristic constellation of symptoms; and the way a disorder starts – for example suddenly or over weeks or years – and progresses over the lifetime of the individual, are also important in understanding the person's needs now and in the future. There are few blood tests, x-rays or physical investigations which help in diagnosis, although some rare disorders due to physical abnormality can be ruled out by investigations and, in the case of elderly people in particular, as we have seen, the relationship between mental disorder and physical illness is a close one. Even the newer ways of scanning the brain, such as nuclear magnetic resonance imaging and positron emission tomography, are not yet proving helpful in identifying specific disorders.

Getting the diagnosis right is a helpful start, but it is never enough to provide comprehensive guidance as to a plan of care for an individual. Medical diagnosis must be accompanied by an assessment of the life circumstances of the individual in terms of personal relationships, family life, culture, race, educational attainments, housing, employment, social environment, physical health and previous life history.

Mental disorder in the general population

At some point in their lives, most people will experience a period of mental distress lasting some weeks or months. Many of us are familiar, for example, with the distress of grief following the death of a close relative. Other seriously upsetting events and circumstances also cause similar feelings, but while death happens at a point in time and within a year or two most people will have recovered from the worst symptoms of grief, many people have to cope year after year and for the foreseeable future with similar profound distress but with no hope of a solution. Up to a third of people consulting their general practitioners have significant distressing feelings which are sufficiently persistent to interfere with their concentration at work and create problems at home. At any one time between twelve and fifteen adults in every 100 will be going through a period of what doctors refer to as 'depression' or 'anxiety', but which may not be identified in that way by the sufferer. Often the main complaints are physical – of being tensed up, tired, suffering from headaches, backache, 'eye-strain', difficulty in sleeping or palpitations and pain in the chest. Worrying, tearfulness, sadness and hopelessness are more often present when the person can identify the event which triggered off the feelings. Fortunately, most people who suffer in this way recover their good spirits within a few months, but in some people the problems can be extremely distressing and go on for many years. Women are more likely than men to suffer from symptoms of this kind and to consult their doctors about it; men in distress seem more likely to vent their feelings of tension in anger, heavy drinking and difficult behaviour, but they too are liable to get depressed and anxious when life goes awry.

These 'milder' forms of psychiatric problem are almost always coped with by individuals with the help of relatives and friends and their GP; there is seldom recourse to a specialist service. However, while doctors may refer to these problems as 'minor psychiatric morbidity', they do not feel 'minor' to the sufferers whose whole lives may be blighted by disabling and distressing symptoms which preoccupy them to the extent of ruining their family relationships.

When people refer unkindly to others as 'just neurotic' they usually mean someone who apparently worries unduly and is easily upset about matters of small consequence. Some individuals are born with more worrying, introspective personalities, but we all get 'neurotic' and develop upsetting symptoms if life's circumstances get bad enough.

GPs also not infrequently see patients whose mental and physical problems are caused by persistent drinking of too much alcohol or by excessive use of drugs or where the main problem is one of being born with an unusual personality which causes a lifelong inability to form close, rewarding personal relationships.

Mental disorder creates a great deal of distress and is a common cause of being off work 'sick'. A great deal of minor distress is not officially recorded in sickness notes and all figures are serious underestimates. However, in 1987 162,000 people in England and Wales were recorded as receiving invalidity benefit as a result of mental disorder which kept them away from work for more than six months at a time, and a further 64,000 men and women were recorded as away from work for periods of anything from a few days to many months as a direct result of mental disorder. Sickness certificates for short spells of illness rarely record mental distress as the cause and probably hundreds of thousands of short absences attributed to 'flu', a 'virus', 'headaches' and so on are, in reality, caused by emotional upsets.

Depression and related disorders

The commonest more serious psychiatric disorder is severe depression. Three or four out of every 100 adults suffer from depression severe enough to warrant specific treatment with medication; one or two in every 100 will be sufficiently disturbed that they will require specialist psychiatric treatment. These people may be admitted to hospital if the condition interferes seriously with their ability to care for themselves, if they stop eating and drinking, or if suicide is being considered sufficiently seriously that they are in danger of harming themselves.

Depression often starts with the milder symptoms described

THE NATURE OF MENTAL DISORDER 91

earlier but can become a very severe relapsing condition which requires months or years of treatment to prevent suicide or death by self-neglect. On the whole, the more severe depressions tend to come in middle age or later life though they can happen at any age. Severe depression affects every aspect of a person's thinking, feeling, conversation, behaviour and physical health. Feelings of depression are extremely unpleasant: sufferers feel generally ill, fatigued and keyed up and are tense and anxious for no apparent reason. Waves of panicky fear sweep over them, often accompanied by a feeling of impending catastrophe. They feel irritable and cannot bear noise, but on the other hand a feeling of fearfulness makes them cling anxiously to other people and seek constant reassurance and company. Such feelings are often worse during the early morning and gradually improve during the day.

Depressed people feel as though they are looking at the world from the bottom of a dark pit. The future seems hopelessly gloomy and they feel they will never recover. Thoughts of death and suicide intrude. They feel inferior to other people and generally worthless and either blame themselves needlessly or blame others, acting in a suspicious, hostile, unfriendly way. Depressed people may sometimes begin to develop wrong ideas – delusions – for example, that their home is falling apart, that heating and domestic appliances have broken, that they have sunk into poverty or that they have brought catastrophe to their dearest relatives by their own misdeeds. Depressed people sometimes, too, begin to believe they have a serious physical illness, perhaps cancer or AIDS.

It is not surprising that people with a severe depression often attribute their problems to illness because depression affects the way the body works physically. Thinking, speech and movement all slow down and sometimes sufferers slow up so much that they sit motionless, hardly speaking. Appetite is lost and sleep becomes lighter and shorter.

Before specific medical treatments were available severe depressions used to last anything from a few months to several years – three years were thought to be usual. The sufferer would remain in hospital cared for by staff who would often have to feed, dress, wash and do everything for the patient. Their mental distress was almost unbearable to watch, trapped in distressing delusional ideas from which only time would release them. But most patients did recover fully in time and were discharged.

Specific antidepressant drugs have helped to treat severe depressions by releasing sufferers from most of the worst symptoms until nature takes its course. These drugs are not, however, miracle cures for everyone with depression, as the manufacturers are inclined to claim, but rather they tone down the more distressing symptoms, and provide the sufferer with an expectation of recovery.

There are some families where the liability to develop depression is inherited. While recurrent episodes of depression are rare, when they do keep returning 'out of the blue' every few years or even every few months, a person's whole life may become dominated by what must be genuinely thought of as 'illness'. This sort of depressive illness is sometimes accompanied by episodes of extreme overactivity, garrulous, pressured speech, grandiose ideas of superefficiency or genius and a cheerful, ebullient but irritable mood. These periods of 'hypomania' are often extremely enjoyable for the individuals concerned, particularly in the milder phases, but can be devastating for their families as they tend to spend money in a profligate fashion and incur massive debts. Swings of hypomania and depression are referred to as 'manic-depressive disorder'; this condition affects perhaps one person in 200 at some time in their lives but only a tiny proportion are ill so frequently that they are readmitted to hospital every few months. The drug Lithium has helped many sufferers to stay on a 'straight and narrow' normal mood; it does not, however, help everyone and is a toxic drug which needs careful supervision.

People who suffer from the severer forms of depression or manic-depressive disorder figure very prominently in the development of satisfactory community care plans. About a quarter of all patients who have been in hospital for many years and who still live in long-stay mental hospital wards were at one time diagnosed as having an 'affective' disorder, that is, depression or manic depressive disorder of a severe or relapsing kind, and some still experience episodes which are not easily treated.

Most people who have depression are treated by their GPs, a

minority are referred to psychiatrists and a small proportion of these are admitted to hospital for treatment; a few become long-term patients. Although there are elderly people in whom recovery still takes some years and who need daily supervision if they are not to starve to death or commit suicide, the majority of people admitted for treatment are discharged home from hospital within six to ten weeks, and then a long slow process of recovery to 'normal' takes place over a year or two.

In between times of depression sufferers are usually completely well, functioning normally and in control of their own lives. They would be surprised to be told they needed 'community care', but when episodes return every few months life becomes more chaotic as it becomes impossible to hold down a job or care for children. Close relationships deteriorate under the strain and, inevitably, chronic disorder often brings with it the dissolution of family ties. In such circumstances some form of community care may be essential.

Schizophrenia

There are approximately 300,000 people in Britain who have at some stage in their lives been diagnosed as suffering from schizophrenia or a closely related condition. Half or more of these individuals have a disorder which has a profound impact on the course of their lives. Indeed, if schizophrenia did not exist, the asylums would never have been built.

A quarter of all hospital beds in Britain of all types including medical and surgical beds are occupied by people with this one diagnosis. Two-thirds of all patients who have lived in mental hospitals for twenty years or more have been diagnosed as having schizophrenia, and of the current total population of the old mental hospitals (some 60,000 in all) 20,000 people have schizophrenia, a disease which can exact a terrible toll over a period of years. Their disabilities are further compounded by physical ageing, the effects of a poor hospital diet, by heavy smoking, the adverse long-term side-effects of potent drugs and by the consequences of an impoverished institutional environment. Nearly half of the rapidly accumulating 'new', 'long-stay' patients in general hospital psychiatric units who have been in hospital for more than a year and who require intensive help and support also suffer from schizophrenia.

The relatively small numbers of people – 20,000 or so – inside the long-stay mental hospitals, compared with the quarter of a million who are in general hospitals or, more commonly, outside hospital altogether, are worth emphasizing here. For the most part such sufferers live in ordinary houses and flats with their own families or on their own. A lucky few live in special supported or sheltered accommodation and an unknown number live rough, on the streets, in hostels for single homeless people, cheap lodgings and private hotels. When concerned campaigners talk of halting the closure of the mental hospitals, it is perhaps as well to remember that fewer than one in ten people with chronic schizophrenia are in mental hospitals. Keeping mental hospitals open for the sake of schizophrenia sufferers is like closing the stable door thirty years after the horse has bolted.

The figures also highlight why it is so misleading to focus 'community care' only on those who are planning to leave hospital and settle in the community. Even if we had sufficient funds to provide good care for the closure of all the remaining mental hospitals tomorrow, we would still not have tackled 90 per cent of the need.

Schizophrenia is a disorder of the brain. It affects roughly the same proportion of people in all societies and countries which have been studied. Seventeen million people worldwide are estimated to be sufferers. The condition is remarkably similar all over the world, which is curious, considering how very different are the cultures in which we live. The particular tragedy of schizophrenia is that it usually begins in early adult life between the late teens and mid-twenties after a normal, often even a highly promising, childhood and adolescence. It sometimes, however, begins out of the blue in mid-life or in old age, but the later it starts the less likely it is to have the devastating impact on the person's whole life that the early-onset forms of the disorder have.

The cause of the illness is unknown. We do know, however, that inheritance plays an important part and that whereas only one in

100 of the general population develop the illness, one in ten of children who have one parent with the disorder will develop the illness in later life. If one identical twin develops the disorder the other twin has a 30–40 per cent chance of developing it too.

While these odds demonstrate that the genetic influence is strong, it is obvious that there are other factors at work, possibly influences in early childhood. But while an enormous amount of research has been done on the influence of parents and family life, nothing conclusive has emerged. We do, however, know that in later life symptoms similar to those in schizophrenia can develop after a head injury, a stroke, brain tumour, long-standing epilepsy or as a side-effect of some drugs, all of which points to a simple organic cerebral brain disease being the most likely explanation. The problem is that while it is usually a great relief for the family and friends of a sufferer to learn that this strange and frightening condition is an illness, there are thousands of sufferers who do not feel 'ill' in any way, resent being regarded as 'sick', and will not be helped at all by this explanation. Since their needs are the key issue we are addressing in this book, the experience of the disorder from the point of view of sufferers and their families must be considered.

At first the sufferer may simply become more withdrawn, quiet and self-preoccupied, spending a lot of time alone in his or her room and perhaps not performing as well at school or college or at work. Thinking becomes muddled and thoughts cannot be kept in order; conversation may become jumbled, vague or may never get to the point. Odd ideas crop up and come to occupy many hours of apparent inactivity. The most incomprehensible problem to others is that sufferers start to hear 'voices' or even sometimes to 'see things'. 'Voices' are 'heard' as real, 'out loud' voices; indeed, they are as real to the sufferer as someone talking in the same room and may often be experienced as rude, abusive or unpleasant. Not surprisingly, the victim tries to understand why and how these odd occurrences are happening and often produces bizarre explanations as to who the voices are and why other people are trying to interfere with his or her thinking and daily life. Complex delusional plots full of 'mad' ideas can be created; for example, that the sufferer is being persecuted by the IRA, or controlled by the Russians through the telephone wires. As the individual becomes more and more pre-occupied with his or her inner life, so contact with the real world of home and family may seem to lessen. Sufferers may seem to become less able to be close to others and may become awkward and gauche in company and unable to respond in social situations. Relatives describe the feeling of a 'glass wall' developing between them and the sufferer which makes it difficult to sustain a loving relationship.

Schizophrenia is frightening for the sufferer, who often feels suddenly plunged into an isolated nightmarish world of terrifying experiences. He or she may react with terror, panic, aggression or despair, and may also become destructive and threatening to relatives or suicidally depressed. In order to exert some control over an uncontrollable world, he or she may develop irritating repetitive habits or refuse to wash, change or have his or her belongings touched.

Acute, 'florid' attacks of schizophrenia with full-blown delusions and hallucinations may only happen once in a persons's life but more commonly they recur, perhaps in a few weeks or years. Once the 'liability' to attacks has started, sufferers remain highly vulnerable to the effect of distressing circumstances such as stressful family and interpersonal relationships or upsetting events such as bereavement, redundancy or moving house. Over the years the condition seems to sap an individual's energy and motivation to do things. Relatives often complain that 'He can but won't.' In reality the person is quite unable to raise the energy to do things at the normal speed or maintain interest for any length of time, and this inevitably means that holding down a job or looking after a household becomes very difficult. On the other hand, the more peculiar, distressing symptoms like delusions and hallucinations seem to become less distressing and intrusive as the person matures. In this respect the condition tends to improve and, given the right medical treatment in the early years and skilled support, sufferers can live satisfactory and fulfilling lives although they seldom reach the potential promised by their childhood intellectual level and early personality. Two-thirds of sufferers experience some effects of schizophrenia for the remainder of their lives after a first attack.

The role of drugs in schizophrenia

Drugs play an important part in helping people with schizophrenia. Modern 'antipsychotic' medication was first introduced in the 1950s and chlorpromazine (Largactil) is still widely used today and is very effective, though many different related medications also now play a part. All such drugs act by blocking dopamine receptors in the brain. Dopamine is a chemical which transmits messages from one brain cell to another and is one of the many 'neurotransmitters' in the human brain. It is not known why blocking the release of this substance improves the symptoms of schizophrenia, although such drugs work best on overt symptoms such as hallucinatory voices, delusional ideas, confusing thoughts and strange behaviours. They also have a calming effect on someone who is overactive or in a state of over-excitement, but they are less effective on the more disabling long-term symptoms such as withdrawal, loss of motivation and inactivity. Some patients also complain that the 'dampening' effect of the drugs (for example, lethargy, tiredness, etc.) are worse than the symptoms.

While many drugs are taken in tablet form with the effects lasting over a few hours or days, some are now available in long-acting injectable forms which last a month or so. These 'depot' preparations – Modecate and Depixol are the commonest – are prescribed to improve the chances of a person avoiding a relapse following recovery from an acute episode. Without continuing medication, three-quarters of patients relapse within a few months, while with medication less than half relapse – clearly, while drugs help they are by no means an infallible protection. Other factors such as a stressful home environment or major untoward changes in social circumstances are also important in triggering further episodes.

There is a minority of patients who do not respond at all well to medication and who may be seriously disabled by continuing 'psychotic' symptoms for several years. It is this group who contribute to the younger adults labelled 'new long-stay' patients who, after a first illness, need close supervision over a number of years.

There is also one very major problem with drugs. Although the immediate unpleasant side-effects – tremor, stiffness, drowsiness and so forth – can all be reduced if the dose is adjusted and carefully monitored over time, every individual suffers from the significant, unpleasant long-term effects of such medication, the main one of which is 'tardive dyskinesia' (TD). TD is a movement disorder involving abnormal involuntary writhings of the mouth, tongue, facial muscles and, later, the limbs. These side-effects may start to occur many years after the individual first began taking antipsychotic medication and tend therefore to occur in older people who may have been taking medication for twenty or thirty years. TD is often untreatable, is distressing and disabling and indicates permanent damage to the brain.

The dilemma for both doctors and patients is that while half of sufferers will either not need or will not benefit from long-term medication, the other half benefit in a major way, living fuller, happier lives free of illness as a result of drugs. Often, however, we do not know which half will benefit from drugs. Drugs also mainly treat *symptoms*, and probably do not influence the course of the underlying disorder. As the penalties of long-term treatment can be grim, there is an urgent need to know which groups of individuals can most benefit, so that not everyone is subjected to long-term injections which they might not need.

Dementia in old age

Dementia is simply the medical term for what used generally to be called senility. 'Senile', however, merely means 'old', and since the majority of old people never have any serious mental problems at all, it is inaccurate to lump together two quite separate concepts. 'Dementia' is not normal ageing, but a process which affects only perhaps five in every 100 retired people. However, it gets commoner as age advances so that people in their mid-eighties have a one in five chance of developing dementia. It is the sheer numbers of such old people in the population which have determined the enormous and rising importance of dementia as a cause of mental disorder in the population as a whole. But in addition to dementia, old people also suffer from mental disorders such as depression, just like the rest of the population. Over a million old people in Britain have a serious chronic mental disorder, some three-quarters of them arising from dementia.

Dementia denotes a group of progressive diseases of the brain that slowly affect all the functions of the mind and lead to a deterioration in a person's ability to concentrate, remember and reason. Dementia affects every area of human thinking, feeling and behaviour. It starts insidiously and it can be months or years before the penny drops for relatives that something is seriously amiss. It often starts with simple forgetfulness, an apathetic loss of interest in life in general or a loss of concern or warmth for relatives. The way a person is affected and how this develops depends on the progress of the illness in the brain and also on how each individual's personality reacts to and copes with increasing mental impairment. The major symptoms are progressive forgetfulness, particularly for events in the recent past few hours or days, failure to grasp what is happening around one, leading to misinterpretations of events, confusion about daily events, and repetitive questioning. Many patients gradually lose their former personalities and some become permanently perplexed and anxious, constantly seeking reassurance; others become changeable and irritable; some sadly become suspicious, accusatory and act in a verbally aggressive or punitive way towards former friends. Speech problems are very common in dementia; language slowly becomes more difficult and speech may be confined to a few simple words. Dementia can also lead to wandering out of the house in a puzzled state, self-neglect and a failure to perform normal household chores; the social niceties of ordinary behaviour are abandoned. Gradually sufferers become unable to care for themselves and grow dependent on others for dressing, feeding, bathing and using the toilet. Physical health may be good in the early stages but at a later stage balance and mobility are affected and the individual may become chair-bound or liable to falls.

The illness lasts anything from two to ten years or more and in general the earlier it begins in life – and it can, rarely, begin in the fifties and sixties – the more rapidly progressive is the illness both in terms of its severity and the length of time before death. There is no cure. Dementia is a slow terminal illness which gradually robs sufferers of their mind until they become very different from their former selves. Sufferers do not, however, become 'vegetables'; they remain people with feelings, worries, anxieties and human needs.

There are two main types of dementia. About half of all people with dementia have Alzheimer's disease, a condition in which a characteristic biochemical change in the cerebral cortex results in abnormalities in transmission of messages across neurones. The cause of Alzheimer's disease is unknown. The other common cause of dementia is 'multi-infarct' dementia, in which many small 'strokes' of the blood vessels cause small areas of the brain to die. It is common in people with a history of high blood pressure, in those who have suffered a major stroke affecting their limbs and in people with other circulatory problems such as coronary artery disease. Multi-infarct dementia is notoriously difficult to distinguish from Alzheimer's disease but it tends to progress more erratically with sudden changes as further small strokes occur.

In addition, there are other rare causes of dementia which account for less than 10 per cent of all cases, though most elderly people with dementia will have one of the two main types or even a mixture of the two.

The key problem presented by dementia is that sufferers lose their ability to control their own lives and become entirely dependent on other people for all their daily needs. Sufferers often feel perfectly fit and well and regard themselves as capable of carrying on their lives as before, something which adds to the difficulties of those trying to care for them. More than with any other mental disorder, sufferers need steadily increasing practical help from other people as the disease progresses and it is for this reason that so many eventually enter a residential home, a nursing home or a long-stay hospital ward.

Other mental disorders

About three-quarters of those people who live in hospitals or homes as a result of severe mental disorder fall into one of the categories described above – severe depressive illness, manic-depressive disorder, one of the schizophrenias or a closely related illness, or a dementia. The remaining quarter of all such patients have a very broad range of problems. There are, for example, younger people brain-damaged after head injury from a traffic accident; people who have developed brain damage after years of heavy alcohol abuse; and a few people who have personalities so different from others that they are unable to sustain an independent life because of profound lack of motivation or forethought. These last people often have a lack of ability to plan or shape their own lives or feel too anxious and isolated if they live alone outside of a very supportive home life or institution. Usually these individuals have entered hospital at a crisis point in their lives many years earlier and somehow got 'stuck'. There are also still a few individuals who puzzle new staff; they wonder why these individuals have become long-stay patients. Attempts to discharge them have repeatedly failed because they have had insufficient support and they are usually referred to as having a 'personality disorder', a catch-all phrase with little specific meaning.

The difficulties of providing satisfactory care in the community for people with mental disorder

Relapse and recurrence

People with a mental disorder do not stay in the same condition for months or years on end. In this respect they are like sufferers from physical illnesses such as rheumatoid arthritis, where episodes of illness flare up out of the blue every few months or years. Even elderly people with dementia, who tend to deteriorate over the course of years, may have times of worse confusion or may suddenly lose a skill, such as using the gas fire, which has been crucial for maintaining them in their own home with little supervision or practical help. People with schizophrenia or severe depression characteristically relapse from time to time and florid symptoms of illness may appear out of the blue. Relatives often learn to detect warning signs such as withdrawal or preoccupation with curious, wrong ideas that have lain dormant since the last episode, and very often there is an obvious stressful trigger which precipitates an acute attack, such as physical illness, loss of a job or the death of a close relative. It is during a florid period of illness, when the sufferer is in a state of serious distress, locked in a private unbearable isolated world, that the risk of violence or suicide is greatest. Contrary to popular belief, most people with schizophrenia are not violent towards others. They are much more inclined to be passive, shy and retiring. But the few who are driven to violent acts as a result of delusional ideas are often in the throes of a relapsing illness. Violence is often directed at people with whom they feel a close but ambivalent relationship – for example, a mother, spouse or child – and suicide is also distressingly common. Indeed, it is estimated that one in ten people with a diagnosis of schizophrenia will eventually kill themselves, and people with severe recurrent depressions are also at high risk of harming themselves.

Getting the right professional help to the sufferer at an early stage during the course of a relapse is crucial. Time and again relatives complain that the services do not take sufficient notice of an escalating deterioration in someone's condition until they have actually threatened to harm themselves or others. A mother of a 30-year-old man with schizophrenia said:

He'd gone off his food and begun to talk about his face changing shape again. He got very worked up about a supervisor at work he doesn't like. He kept saying he was changing the shape of his nose. I got the GP and he said there was nothing to worry about but that he would come back next week – he didn't seem to realize I can sense when Michael's 'going off'. Three days later, after spending forty-eight hours staring in a mirror, Michael carved the end off his nose with a kitchen knife.

More active medical intervention could have saved Michael from painful reconstructive surgery and future embarrassed shame brought on by his former delusional ideas.

David, a man in his late forties living with his elderly mother, became increasingly tortured by voices of people he believed were trying to harm him. He suspected that his mother, on whom he had always depended for a home and much support, might be in league with the voices and trying to poison him. He felt friendless, alone and deeply depressed. He talked of doing away with himself. His mother was keenly aware of his ruminations and concerned for his safety. At times she was also frightened of what he might do to her.

Over the course of a few days the GP saw him and arranged a home visit from a psychiatrist a couple of days later. The psychiatrist agreed to admit him once a bed was available but did not think the need was urgent. Two days later David cut his throat in a suicide attempt which was not fatal. His wound was sutured in the casualty department of the local hospital. He had to wait many hours without supervision in casualty for an ambulance to transfer him to a psychiatric unit and he suddenly disappeared from the hospital alone in a distraught state. No one followed him and his family never saw him alive again. The remains of his body were found three months later in a burnt-out room of a derelict hotel ten miles away. The coroner's verdict was 'open' but suicide was the likely truth.

These two cases illustrate that professionals need to be vigilant, alert, responsive to both sufferers and relatives, available twenty-four hours a day and willing to intervene when the condition is changing rather than wait for a crisis. Conventional hospital out-patient services are rarely organized in a way which provides easy access and a swift response. It is also a great deal easier for professionals to respond appropriately when they know the patient personally or where good records of the sufferer's previous problems are available in confidence to the individual professional suddenly faced with having to respond to a developing crisis. Services therefore need to be developed in such a way that the right, up-dated information is collected and made readily available to those responsible for making rapid decisions.

'There's nothing wrong with me': rights and risk

One of the most difficult dilemmas which mental disorder presents for both families and services is that many sufferers do not regard their problems as requiring any intervention or help from medical or social services. Rather, they seek what they regard as more rational solutions to their perceived problems. Miss Thompson, for example, was a 64-year-old single woman living in a terraced house in Muswell Hill, North London. She believed that the Roman Catholic Church, on the instructions of the Pope, was organizing a repeat performance of the gunpowder plot to blow up the Houses of

Parliament. For most of the twenty or so years that her beliefs had been present she had kept them to herself, well aware that other people regarded them as foolish. But from time to time the ideas became so frighteningly real to her that she tried desperately to persuade the local police, Citizens Advice Bureau, post office and her Member of Parliament of the imminent risk. Dismissed as a harmless, eccentric spinster and frustrated by the police in her attempts to reach the Prime Minister in Number 10, Miss Thompson was finally admitted to a psychiatric unit against her will, under the Mental Health Act, after creating a noisy disturbance in the public gallery of the House of Commons. She remained adamantly defiant and refused treatment while in hospital, believing that the hospital staff were conspiring to prevent her from doing her public duty. She also became increasingly distressed by persecutory voices and ceased to eat or drink, believing that her food was 'contaminated'. She was finally given drug treatment under the provisions of the Mental Health Act and over the course of three weeks the ideas gradually receded and she returned to being a calm, quiet, rather self-contained but competent person. After discharge from hospital she accepted monthly injections of a drug prescribed to prevent further relapses but refused it after six months. She remained fairly well for three years when another 'flare-up' occurred, almost identical to the first.

Elderly people with dementia similarly also rarely recognize their own failings. They feel fit, well, just like their old selves. They may recognize they have memory problems but do not perceive the impact these have on their ability to care for themselves or their homes. Repeated offers of help may well be refused.

Over the past twenty years in particular there has been an active debate about how far it is justified to impose unwanted treatment on individuals who do not consent to it. Our notion of a citizen's right to freedom and choice can mean, in the case of someone with schizophrenia or dementia, the freedom to live in squalor, to die of starvation and self-neglect or to be driven to suicide by living in an internal mental hell. But it can also mean allowing someone the right to live in the community, free of restraint, unburdened by unpleasant drugs and a good deal happier than they would be if

incarcerated in a mental hospital. Freedom for the individual therefore implies being allowed to take risks, make choices and determine one's own future. Some risk-taking on the part of carers and
the community at large may also be required.

On the other side of the argument, severe mental disorder can
deprive an individual of the capacity to make reasoned, informed
judgments about his own health and safety. We expect doctors and
other professionals to treat unconscious patients without consent, as
long as they act in the best interests of the patients. Society surely
owes a similar 'duty of care' to people who are suffering from
mental conditions which interfere with their ability to make rational
decisions about their own care.

The Mental Health Act of 1983 attempted to provide a framework for making decisions in individual cases about whether compulsory admission to hospital was justified. It also laid down
conditions under which a legally detained patient's consent to
treatment can be dispensed with. The Act allows for compulsory
admission and treatment of individuals in the interest of their own
health or safety, or with a view to the protection of other persons. In
fact, the statute is fairly broad and some civil liberties campaigners
have complained that it is too lax and allows doctors and nurses a
dangerous freedom of action to impose unpleasant treatments.
Psychiatrists, however, responded to the new Act with deep resentment at what they regarded as the imposition of unwarranted
controls on their traditional clinical freedoms. Many took fright and
simply stopped recommending compulsory admission for people
whose health was clearly deteriorating but who were not yet sufficiently deranged to endanger life and limb.

The Act is now probably under-used or used too late because of
a wide misunderstanding as to its aims and intentions. Encouraged
by certain psychiatrists, the media seized on the Mental Health Act
as a root cause of the neglect of seriously disturbed schizophrenia
sufferers and, in a series of moving articles in *The Times* in 1987
about the plight of schizophrenia sufferers in the community,
campaigning journalist Marjorie Wallace repeated the myth that it
was the Act itself, not doctors' lack of understanding of the Act,
which prevented doctors from treating their patients adequately.

It is true that the 1983 Act is not perfect. In some areas it is rather woolly, in others too prescriptive. One problem is that it was formulated during a time when most treatment and care was provided in hospital. It did not take account of the development of community services, the growing practice of treating people at home and the aim of maintaining people with long-term mental disorders in the community. Its focus is on those few patients who are detained in hospital for compulsory treatment. But, nowadays, the most pressing need is for a legal framework for caring for people in the community, particularly those who are mentally incapable of making decisions about their own care, such as sufferers with dementia. However, the focus of professional concern has been those who actively refuse treatment, rather than those who are unable to express an opinion. Pressure has been growing for a compulsory 'community treatment order' which would allow psychiatrists to treat people with relapsing disorders, such as schizophrenia, on a continuing basis without admitting them to hospital. This would require major new legislation and, to safeguard people from abuse, such an order would need to be hedged around with major restrictions and constraints so that the usefulness of such an order is questionable. Nevertheless, there is a tiny minority of people with very serious relapsing illnesses who are currently detained in hospital for longer periods than they need to be because of the difficulties of maintaining treatment outside the hospital after discharge. Some minor amendments to the present Act might assist such patients, without putting other people being treated in the community at risk of too much restriction on their freedom.

The law is not to blame for the neglect of people with long-term disorders in the community and no change of statute will magically solve the problem. The Code of Practice for the Mental Health Act, published by the government in 1989, should give confidence to psychiatrists, nurses and social workers to intervene at an appropriate, early stage when it is clear that someone is beginning to relapse and needs treatment quickly.

In fact, only 13 per cent of psychiatric hospital admissions are of people detained under the Mental Health Act and no statute can resolve all the tensions which arise in individual cases. People with mental disorder are never like unconscious patients or babies; even those with profound disturbances have a will of their own and feelings and attitudes which should be respected. Although relatives often find it distressing and painful to see a disturbed relative living alone, unprotected and vulnerable, for the individual that may seem preferable to living in an institution or even in a family or small group.

Fundamental philosophical differences lie at the heart of the many disputes and disagreements which have surfaced periodically between the two major voluntary organizations campaigning on behalf of schizophrenia sufferers, MIND (National Association for Mental Health) and the National Schizophrenia Fellowship (NSF). MIND is committed to the cause of self-determination, liberty and freedom of choice for patients, and the NSF places its emphasis on the right of any suffering individual to receive care and treatment, even when help is refused as a result of impaired judgment. The NSF position therefore emphasizes society's duty to care for those who cannot make rational judgments about their own care and has led to serious disagreements with MIND over such issues as the future of mental health services and the closure of the old mental hospitals.

Traditionally, doctors have tended to espouse the rather paternalistic view, favouring the Duty of Care side of the argument. It is, frankly, nearly impossible to witness the disintegration of a fellow human being into a state of deluded despair and not feel that, if you were in his shoes, you would want someone to take control, care for you, treat you and try to restore you to sanity, even if there was only a small chance of the treatment working. For parents, watching an adult child's disintegration with schizophrenia is often a more difficult tragedy to come to terms with than the death of a child in a traffic accident, and it is parents and professionals who form the backbone of National Schizophrenia Fellowship. The concerns of MIND, on the other hand, arise from their observations that enforced psychiatric treatment can be cruelly repressive and excessively controlling, can fail to take account of an individual's wishes and is frequently not very effective. Without doubt, cavalier attitudes still dominate much formal psychiatric treatment and some hospital regimes are still unbelievably restrictive and rule-bound.

There is no correct solution to this dilemma and the decisions taken for each individual need to be worked out in discussion with the person, his or her family and the various professionals so that decisions are reached after full consultation and with all views being listened to and acknowledged as relevant. In general, the more accessible and friendly the local services are, the less problem there is in persuading mentally disordered people to accept help willingly.

The long-term effects on personality of severe mental disorder

Providing care of the right kind to mentally disordered people over many years is made more difficult by the disabling impact of severe disorder on personality. As years go by, some people with schizophrenia become increasingly withdrawn, suspicious and isolated. They often shun the company of others and prefer to live on their own, not in family groups or with other people where frequent contact has to be maintained, as in sharing mealtimes or a sitting room. It is these individuals who feel most uncomfortable in an ordinary family environment and who most appreciate the relative anonymity of a working men's hostel or temporary hotel where no one pries or tries to form friendships. When community care services are being established it is important to take account of an individual's wish for privacy and allow those who wish to spend time alone to do so. Communal living is far more stressful in an ordinary house with four or six people living in it than on a thirty-bedded psychiatric ward in a spacious old mental hospital. For some people, living in small groups is simply not an adequate substitute for a home of one's own.

Prejudice and public fear

The public's perception of mental disorder is of the raving lunatic or homicidal maniac. The term 'psycho' is usually used in the tabloid press to mean a violent murderer. In fact, the vast majority of murderers have no history of mental disorder – they are as 'sane' as you or me – and the vast majority of mentally disordered people pose no threat whatever to anyone, except perhaps themselves. Violence is a rare occurrence even in acute schizophrenia and is by no means as common as the public perceive it to be. The media, of course, particularly tabloid newspapers like the *Sun*, enjoy a good story, and accounts of mayhem and murder are made juicier by the extra titillation of the fear engendered by the spectre of madness. The vast majority of patients are in practice more likely to be victims than offenders.

But the general public does not just have a general, unfocused fear of mental disorder. People feel awkward and uncomfortable in the presence of anyone who looks or acts differently from the social norm. They do not want to mix with people who are overtly disabled in any way – the fear and prejudice that prevent wheelchair-bound thalidomide victims being given equal job opportunities is the same fear that generates campaigns to stop discharged mental hospital patients living in a house in a local neighbourhood. 'Not in my back yard' has become the derogatory term with which professionals dismiss the ignorant rejection of plans to settle mentally disordered people outside hospital and 'NIMBYs' are held responsible for disrupting many plans for community care.

The most famous recent example is the legal action brought by the Cheltenham and Gloucester Building Society against Bath Health Authority who had bought an 'executive home' on a new residential estate to provide sheltered accommodation for six discharged adult patients. These people were continuing to receive treatment and support from the health authority staff and their new home was intended as a model of good community care. The Building Society developers feared the residents would 'lower the tone' of the neighbourhood, become a nuisance to neighbours and reduce the resale value of all the estate houses. They invoked a clause in a covenant which stipulated that the houses should be used only for ordinary residential family accommodation. The legal question, of course, turned on the definition of what is ordinary family accommodation and the case achieved notoriety when the Health Authority lost in the High Court. Several other organizations then invoked similar covenants to prevent discharged patients being settled nearby.

There is clearly therefore a need for a major programme of public education as to the realities of mental disorder. Fear and hostility can be countered by familiarity and knowledge. Organizations planning community care projects must also be sympathetic to the concerns of local people and must invest time and energy in introducing local people and neighbours to the proposed scheme and to the individual residents. Local councillors and community and church leaders often hold the key to persuading the local population, and a sympathetic approach to the people's real fears usually produces good, supportive neighbours, particularly if the neighbours know to whom they can turn for instant help should they need it.

Prejudice and fear of the unknown, and distaste for the abnormal and unusual, cannot, however, be overcome easily; we all carry deep-seated fears of being embarrassed or made to look foolish and we all feel guilt and shame about not doing enough. It would be altogether easier for us if mentally disordered people were put away out of sight in some comfortable institution far from the rest of us. But such notions are quite impracticable and, in any case, take no account of the wishes of mentally disordered people themselves. Therefore, for community care to work – for it must work – society must start to accept the presence of 'funny-looking', oddly behaved people living and being cared for amongst us. Acceptance will follow understanding and familiarity, but the process will take time.

6 Providing a Comprehensive Service

Having examined the characteristics of mental disorder and the various structural and organizational problems which must be overcome, we are now in a position to look at some of the proposed solutions. First, however, it is important to understand how services are perceived by users who, in the main, suffer from the disorganization, lack of coordination and disparate funding of services in different geographical areas of the country. Listen to the views of two women, both in their early fifties, with adult children, who live in the London Borough of Southwark. Let us call them Mrs Smith and Mrs Jones.

Mrs Smith is a widow living in a small council flat in Bermondsey. She works as a primary school teacher's reading helper in a local school. She has two sons, both married with families, who live at some distance, and an older sister living in Brighton who cares for a disabled husband. Mrs Smith's 82-year-old mother lives with her and has severe senile dementia. She is totally dependent on her daughter for help with bathing, washing, dressing and feeding. She is still agile but is unable to control her bladder and has anaemia and a recurring chest problem. Her memory is extremely poor and she cannot sustain a normal conversation. She frequently gets up at night, thinking it is daytime, and wanders round the flat. Several times she has wandered out into the street while Mrs Smith was asleep, although now the front door is kept double-locked at night to prevent this from happening. Mrs Smith comes home from school four times during the day to make sure her mother is all right and she is also usually up three or four times in the night to attend to her mother. She has a break one night a month when her sister comes from Brighton to stay overnight; on these occasions Mrs Smith sleeps soundly on the sofa in the living room. Mrs Smith described the problems as follows:

I get a lot of help and I'm very grateful but somehow it doesn't seem to add up to a great deal. I feel exhausted all the time from the sheer hard physical work and never getting a proper break. Not having a good night's sleep is the main thing and not knowing how long it'll go on for. Every week she gets worse and yet it could go on for years. I feel I'm cracking up, always on the verge of tears, but I can't let her down. She was such a marvellous mother, slogged all her life for us and she just dreaded going into one of those homes. I'll keep on as long as I can. I've got a list of phone numbers, it seems like fifty, of different people who have been involved – the doctor, the home help, district nurse, chiropodist, social worker, hospital doctor, Age Concern, the Red Cross, the old people's home where she went for a break and dozens more, I hardly know who they are. I'm always short of money, she needs such a lot of extra things, you wouldn't believe the money I've spent on bedding, laundry, special chairs, clothing. We both need a break but I can't afford a holiday and you wouldn't believe the hassle of organizing for her to go into a home for a fortnight. This year they said she was too 'far gone' and she'd have to go into hospital if I wanted a holiday; getting a definite date for that was impossible so I couldn't book anything. The home help does a bit of cleaning but frankly that's the least of my worries. The district nurse comes to give her the monthly vitamin injections for her anaemia – takes about ten seconds and she's gone. The community psychiatric nurse comes occasionally – I never know when – and she sympathizes; nice girl but she doesn't actually do anything useful. And as for social workers – it's never the same one twice. They say there's too many children with problems round here to worry much about the old – well, they'd damn well have to worry if *I* wasn't here doing all the work wouldn't they?

Now let us listen to Mrs Jones. She is exactly the same age as Mrs Smith and came to Britain from Jamaica in 1957 as a 20-year-old with her father (a skilled motor mechanic who came to work on the London buses), her mother and her three brothers. Her parents have done well; her father became one of the first Afro-Caribbean councillors in inner London. Mrs Jones married a welder from Antigua and had four children. They bought a tumbledown Victorian terraced house near the Elephant and Castle, cheap because it had an old man as a sitting tenant on the top floor. Their one major problem started when their 19-year-old son was diagnosed as having schizophrenia. That was five years ago.

He's unrecognizable as the boy we once knew. He spends most of the day in his room writing letters – crazy, mad letters no one understands. He lets waste bits of paper pile up in his room – he won't let me touch them. He doesn't talk to us about his problems – he scarcely talks at all. But he's so rude, he seems to think his troubles are all our fault. He thinks we're in league with the police to get rid of him and now my husband won't have anything to do with him, he leaves it all to me. He's got a fear of water – don't know why – and just won't bath or wash. He smells dreadful. His room's a dustbin with *lists* of objects pinned all over the walls – no, I don't know what it means. Every now and again he gets so worked up he hits me or his sister. When he's really crazy and violent or says he'll kill himself, he goes into hospital – for about a month, usually. That happens once a year or so. But that's no relief. Some of the nurses are black but the doctors are white. They don't really understand us. I reckon they use more of the heavy drugs on blacks than whites. Getting him to hospital is something I dread – you wouldn't believe the struggle to get people to understand how bad it is – it's usually building up for weeks but until he's practically killed himself or someone else, no one wants to know. And when he comes out of hospital, it's like they've forgotten he exists – just a couple of visits from a nurse. They want him to have injections every month – I don't know if they help or not – but he says they slow him up and make his legs ache and he can't think straight. He may be right – he seems like a zombie when he's on them, but then about a month after he stops having the regular injections he gets happier for a while, then gradually all the funny ideas begin again.

Sometimes he just wanders off for days on end – we get frantic, not knowing where he is. He's got no money, and his Giro seems wrong every week. No one helps him with it. He says he wants to work but how is he ever going to find work when normal fit boys can't get work round here? There's nowhere for him to go for a bit of company – he won't go to the day hospital because he thinks they'll make him take drugs. It's heartbreaking to see him wasting his life away. I wish there was someone I could talk to about the problems – someone who'd keep an eye on him and watch for him getting bad and get the doctor to do something, sooner; someone who'd help him with money, a job, get him out of the room for a bit, give us a break too.

Both Mrs Smith and Mrs Jones complain of feeling unsupported and isolated, and stagger from crisis to crisis without knowing who to turn to. Their dependent relatives have very different kinds of problem and they themselves need different kinds of help. Mrs Smith needs someone to help her with the practical side of caring, to arrange respite breaks, coordinate the nursing input and ensure that the hospital and local authority services work together *with* her. Mrs Jones needs a closer and better relationship with the psychiatric services; she needs to get them to listen to *her* needs and she also needs someone to provide practical help with money problems for her son, someone who can discuss work opportunities, recognize his need for friendship and help him think about his future.

The practical problems Mrs Smith and Mrs Jones are both experiencing are a result of operational difficulties in the way the services are organized and delivered in the community.

Lack of money to make choices

Most sufferers and their families simply have insufficient money under their own control to make choices about how they wish to be helped. Money empowers people to choose for themselves what kind of accommodation they need, how much assistance with household chores they require, and how much help they need from neighbours or private agencies. Money doesn't solve everything but it gives a sense of control over some of the options. Certain welfare benefits such as attendance allowances and invalid care allowances make a small contribution to the care of some individuals but the sums are very small, particularly when compared with the costs of providing residential or hospital care. Inadequate personal income and lack of assistance in this area are a major problem for many mentally disordered people and their relatives.

Local variability of commitment and funds

There are extraordinary disparities between one area of the country and another in the commitment of funds to mental health services from local authorities and health authorities. For example, in 1986, inner-city north-east Newcastle-upon-Tyne spent £7.43 per head of population per annum on mental health services, while Redbridge, a prosperous outer London suburb, spent just £0.49 per head per annum. NHS spending varies as widely. In 1986 Mersey Region Health Authority spent proportionately over double what Oxfordshire Region spent. To make matters worse, there is no evidence that lack of spending by social services is compensated for by increased NHS spending, or vice versa; indeed, the financial allocation seems just as likely to be low from both authorities, as it has been, for example, in the London Borough of Lambeth, or very good in both authorities, as traditionally has been the case in Newcastle. Nor has the growth of private sector nursing homes and specialist hotels been evenly spread across the country; indeed, these tend to be concentrated in those areas where cheap large houses were available for conversion, or in traditional holiday areas. Prosperous rural and coastal areas are often over-provided with this sort of accommodation, while inner-city areas, where far more people with serious mental disorder live, are desperately short of such places.

Confused responsibilities

Once a person leaves hospital, no one is 'in charge' of that person out there. Whereas a patient living inside a hospital has one named doctor – the consultant – in charge of his or her treatment and one named person – the ward sister – responsible for the nursing care he or she receives, outside the walls of the hospital no one person is responsible for assessing the individual's needs for a range of services and for then making sure that the required services are delivered. A younger person, for example, may need help with housing, assistance in finding a way through the complex welfare benefit system, help with using the local rehabilitation facilities at a day centre or day hospital, help in planning a return to work, and so on. What is needed is one named individual who is responsible for assessing that person's total needs, deciding who should do what, coordinating the efforts of the various health professionals and for ensuring that, from the 'consumer's' point of view, the various services are integrated and one hand knows what the other hand is doing. Importantly, the appointment of one named individual also ensures that there is someone to turn to when help is required.

Insufficient staff with the right training

When a hospital patient is unable to perform the activities of daily life for him- or herself, staff are on hand to help; such staff are called 'nurses', though in reality ward staff do little that requires a skilled qualified nursing background. What the staff provide is understanding and tolerance of difficult behaviour; they also assist with the practical caring tasks of washing, dressing and feeding, and they encourage, supervise and train patients to carry out these tasks for themselves. They ensure, for example, that meals are eaten at the right time, that appointments are kept, that a daily routine is adhered to and that patients do not neglect themselves or put themselves in danger. In the community, however, people called 'nurses' are not available to do these practical things. They are people who visit, oversee, inspect, give medication and observe, but they are involved with patients only intermittently and are not present twenty-four hours in a day. None the less, in very many cases 'hands-on' care is still required and there has been a distinct failure to understand the needs of discharged patients for continuing support of this kind. A yawning gap exists in the supposed overlap of services between the home help and the nurse, which needs to be filled by a small army of 'hands-on' carers. However, the creation of such a workforce of carers requires a heavy investment in training and recruitment as well as substantial on-going budgets. Yet such carers do not need to be highly skilled, though they require careful selection, close supervision and extensive in-service continuing training. While many local authorities are now organizing care of this sort for disabled elderly people living at home, the similar needs of people with chronic mental disorder have by no means been as widely recognized.

The sideline role of general practitioners

Family doctors treat and care for over 95 per cent of all mental disorder. They refer on to specialists only a tiny proportion of people with mental disorder, usually those with severely upsetting or difficult problems such as new psychotic illnesses, very severe depression or disabling anxiety disorders. Generally, however, family doctors receive very little training in the management of severe chronic mental disorder in spite of the fact that they may be frequently called on to give advice and may often have to decide when to recommend a period of hospital treatment.

GPs also complain, quite rightly, that hospital staff making, for example, discharge plans for a group of patients to a new home or hostel sometimes neglect to discuss the plans with the primary care team – normally the local general practice together with its team of doctors, nurses and other specialists – yet expect the GPs to pick up the pieces when something goes wrong. The reason for this may well be that the hospital consultant is reluctant to let go medical responsibility for former patients and thrust them on to a local GP, but he is not normally easily available when off duty or working in a clinic many miles away. Thus responsibility for the discharged patient often ends up with the GP, whether this outcome is planned or not, and few GPs have been prepared by vocational training for a more involved role in community care services. GPs and their primary care team of nurses and other staff must be involved more fully in the central task of planning and delivering services.

The problems of community care are not just financial

Government money, channelled via local government and the NHS, or through income support benefits into the pockets of sufferers and their families, is essential for effective community care services, but it is not enough on its own. More and more money from public taxation has been put in to such services one way or another, yet the services still do not work in a foolproof way, for a number of practical reasons. Future services must be structured and organized so as to avoid the pitfalls: an organizational structure is required to facilitate the smooth cooperation of all the individual parts of a service and ensure that there are no wasteful overlaps and no gaps.

Much analysis of what is wrong with current systems has been undertaken. In the last few years many policy analysts, professional organizations, charitable bodies and government-funded bodies have made recommendations on how the NHS and local authority structures should be changed in order to develop community care more effectively. One of the organizations concerned is the King's Fund, founded by the beneficence of King Edward VII to assist hospitals in London, though its role today is to develop policy on improving the organization and management of health services throughout Britain. In 1987 it published a report on its observations of specific community care projects which were felt by local people to be successful. Four key elements common to all the successful services were identified.

1. *Clear values and principles about what the services were trying to achieve.* All the individual professionals, managers and planners, together with the local people the service was designed to serve, shared a common vision as to what they were aiming for, often based around the concept of providing a more 'normal' home life for patients who had previously lived in an institution.

As we have already seen, it is more difficult to agree a common vision for the development of mental health services than for other services because of the differing philosophies with which people approach individuals' rights to refuse treatment and to take personal risks. Often dramatically opposed views are held by consultant psychiatrists, for example, on one side and the local MIND group on the other, on what comprises a good mental health service. When this happens, however, opposing parties are usually willing to work towards a common view if they are brought together for joint discussions by a neutral 'arbitrator' or facilitator, for example, a senior respected manager or an elected member of the local public or voluntary services. With goodwill, even people with apparently 'extreme' views may find, sometimes to their surprise, that there is much common ground.

2. *The views of the recipients of the services were considered.* Mental health services are traditionally planned without any reference whatever to the views of those on the receiving end. 'Consumers' or 'users' have traditionally been regarded as having no realistic, lucid, practical views to offer, and many professionals feel that the very nature of mental illness precludes users of services from making a sensible contribution. While this may be true, in part, for acutely disturbed patients, for those who are unable to express themselves clearly or for those with advanced senile dementia, it is not true of most people who depend daily on mental health services. Even when people are very severely disturbed they can express legitimate choices about whether they wish to be alone or in company, occupied or relaxing, about the food they like, about whether they would prefer silence or a music-filled room, and so forth. Most users, once recovered from an acute phase of illness, can make a contribution far beyond such simple choices, and can be involved in planning the shape of services, provided their opinions are sought and listened to. Such consultation, though a problematic and difficult area, is vital for proper service planning and is considered in greater detail in Chapter 8.

Relatives are also 'consumers' and they too must be involved in service planning; they know the problems at first hand in a way which professionals can never do. The King's Fund found that good projects involved families in the planning of services and built them in to the system in such a way that they felt their important role was appreciated. Relatives and sufferers should feel that they are in control or, at least, have a powerful voice in what happens to the individual.

Relatives, of course, do not always agree with the individual about what is best for him or her and they may not agree with professionals trying to help the person either. There will inevitably be disagreements and sometimes these may prove insoluble. But while this may be true for matters concerning individual patients, as family relationships often develop severe tensions and problems, it is rarely true of the relatives of groups of patients who, when involved in planning and running services, show collective good sense and experience in addressing practical problems. The role of relatives is also discussed in Chapter 8.

3. *The skills of doctors, nurses, social workers and other professionals were valued.* In some areas of Britain local voluntary organizations, or perhaps one of the arms of the public sector services, have become so disheartened by the lack of commitment and enthusiasm on the part of local psychiatrists and psychiatric nurses for developing a new style of service away from their traditional hospital base that they have decided to go ahead and develop a new service without any support from the consultants and hospital staff. On the whole, such services tend not to serve severely mentally disordered people but to concentrate instead on less seriously dependent people. Generally, links with other services are poor and the contribution that doctors and nurses can make to specific treatment is entirely lost.

Typically, exasperated health service managers in some areas have developed 'community-based teams' of nurses, psychologists and therapists working with people living at home, while the local consultant has remained firmly ensconced in his hospital office, near his admission ward and at some distance from the team. This separation creates inevitable tensions between the team and the consultant, which are inimical to good multidisciplinary work. Consultants are often fearful that these new styles of service will lead to the quality of care of acutely ill patients on the wards suffering; they believe that the focus of community work is away from those who are most in need or are concerned that if they work in the community they will lose the professional day-to-day support of consultant colleagues. All these issues can, however, be satisfactorily resolved with tact and consultation, and overall, it is usually better to be patient and to move slowly, gradually involving reluctant or sceptical professionals and attempting to meet their anxieties, than to go it alone. Professionals have training and experience which are valuable in planning services; ignoring them almost always leads to an inferior service.

4. *Recipients of good schemes had access to local community facilities available to the local population at large.* Local facilities such as libraries, swimming pools, tennis courts, further education classes, bingo, cinemas, pubs, working men's clubs, parks, concerts and

church services are, in theory, for the use of everyone, and if people with mental disorder live day in and day out inside the confines of a suburban house and never use such local facilities or participate in the life of the community, they might just as well remain behind the walls of an institution. Ordinary people spend their leisure time using such facilities as well as shopping, meeting friends in local cafés or pubs, visiting friends at home, and so on. People with mental disorder may well have difficulty in doing some of these things but often they would like to try, particularly if they are accompanied in the early exploratory stages, and are helped to achieve confidence in using facilities for their own enjoyment. Local authority education and leisure department can often be usefully involved in planning and developing services and in the education and training of staff. They are usually also very willing to create special opportunities for individuals to become accustomed to new experiences such as going swimming, to help them become familiar with an unknown and perhaps daunting routine before 'plunging in' with the general public.

In addition to the above elements, the King's Fund also identified several other factors which determined whether or not a community care scheme would be successful. They were:

1. *The presence of an entrepreneur.* Successful schemes always had someone who could be identified as the driving force, someone who pushed and who steered the project through to a satisfactory launch. This leader, the champion of change, was frequently a consultant responsible for the area service, or a general manager within the NHS or social services, or the director of a voluntary organization, but it could be anyone with sufficient enthusiasm, knowledge, commitment and determination to persuade others to collaborate and to get people who control resources to part with their cash. However, to ensure that projects do not collapse when the 'entrepreneur's' work is finished, the service system has to be established in such a way that it can continue if necessary without that person's contribution.

2. *A focus on action.* Community care plans are often bedevilled by too many people from too many organizations spending too much time in

endless meetings where no decisions get taken and where ideas and enthusiasm become diluted and, eventually, dissipated into thin air. The way in which community care projects get off the ground quickly is to have a small project team of three or four people with the task of steering it through from start to finish, working under the guidance of a strong chairman. This small group needs the authority to make decisions on behalf of organizations who hold the purse-strings and therefore must be made up of individuals who are trusted and respected within their own organizations. Such small project teams rarely spend much time meeting or writing reports – they just get on and do it.

3. *Intersectoral integration*. This grand term merely means that successful community care schemes are usually a joint initiative of two or more service sectors, that is, a local authority and a voluntary organization, a local authority and the NHS, the NHS and a housing association, and so on. There is, for example, a sheltered home in the south of England for ten adult patients recently discharged from a psychiatric hospital, where the large house is privately owned by the manager/proprietor and the staff are employed by a local voluntary organization but trained and supported by the health service. The consultant psychiatrist and a team of community nurses from the health service are actively involved in supporting and visiting the scheme, and the home is registered and inspected by the local authority who also provide a social worker to provide links with other local services. Every resident has one member of staff who acts as a personal 'key worker', responsible for making sure that the care plans drawn up by the professional staff and the individual residents are implemented.

4. *Local neighbourhood focus*. Each geographical area served by different teams of people from different organizations needs to be small enough for all the individuals to get to know each other, so that good personal working relationships are fostered and liaison between services is optimized. Services organized across large District Health Authorities covering 200–300,000 people cannot possibly provide a local, friendly, easily accessible service. Sufferers and families need to be able to walk to the main services in their

neighbourhood or to catch a bus into a local centre no more than a mile or two away. Services should be provided near enough so that people do not to have to venture further than their local shops or post office. Thus the office base for a local service should cater for a local population of 10–20,000 people, although in inner-city areas the number can be larger because of the greater density of population. In some rural areas the population served may need to be even smaller if villages are far apart.

In practice, the majority of services can be provided locally, but there are none the less certain disadvantages in carving a district up into 'patches' or 'localities'. Rigid demarcation lines can leave users with no choice at all about who they wish to be treated by, and getting along with and trusting the professionals who are responsible for providing help is a crucial factor in whether a service user will stay in touch with the services and persevere with treatment. So a small neighbourhood system often works best if service users know that they can, if they wish, choose to be treated in a neighbouring locality by another consultant. In addition, more specialist services such as those for mentally abnormal offenders, where there are usually only one or two expert practitioners in a large district, often have to be organized on a larger scale than is ideal for patients, simply because there is no other practical way of making the service available to everyone who needs it.

5. *Multidisciplinary collaboration.* Good community care services work best where skilled professionals work comfortably hand-in-hand with unskilled staff, families, neighbours and voluntary organizations. Service teams should comprise people from different professional backgrounds, although it is still not uncommon to come across teams called 'community mental health teams' which consist entirely of nurses from the health service or of social workers from the local authority. Multiprofessional teams bring a range of educational backgrounds, training and expertise to bear on the management of individual cases, which ensures that care is not dominated by one single professional approach.

The same principles apply in planning and delivering a new service. A range of disciplines and organizations ensures that all relevant points of view are considered, although this does not mean that every Tom, Dick and Harry has to sit on the planning committee; rather, their insights and experience are gained through their active participation in informal discussions at the planning stage, and through consultation at all stages in the development process.

The organization of community care

The structure and organization of public services do not, at present, foster service developments which match the King's Fund recommendations, and the need for an overhaul in the way services are organized has been recognized for some years. In late December 1986 the Audit Commission for local authorities in England and Wales published an influential report which severely criticized the existing public sector framework for community care services. The Audit Commission conducts 'value for money' studies across the whole of the statutory public sector responsible for community care, and its report, *Making A Reality of Community Care*, was revolutionary in its recommendations and hotly debated by professional staff in the NHS and local authorities. The Commission's brief was not only to address the problems of mentally disordered people but also to make recommendations on community care for elderly people and everyone with long-term physical or mental disabilities. It decided that only fundamental, structural changes to the organization and management of services would bring about the environment necessary for locally integrated community care to flourish. It proposed three such major structural changes.

First, it recommended that local authorities should be made responsible for all long-term care of mentally handicapped and physically handicapped people, except for the rare few in need of permanent 24-hour medical supervision, who would remain the responsibility of the NHS.

The second recommendation was that a single budget should be established for the care of elderly people in the community, with contributions from the NHS and from local authorities. The amount paid would be determined according to a centrally agreed formula, and the budget would be controlled by a manager who would purchase services from whichever public or private agency gave the best value for money. The manager of the budget would be supervised by a joint board of representatives from local statutory services and from health and social services.

Third, the Audit Commission recommended that for mentally *ill* people the NHS should continue as the main authority responsible for care, but the possibility should remain for developing a central budget similar to that proposed for elderly people; alternatively, the NHS should have the ability to purchase local authority services on a contractual basis.

These proposals for major structural changes had considerable appeal. The notion of a lead agency with overall responsibility for developing services or for buying in the necessary services from local statutory, private or voluntary agencies would make clear where responsibility should lie. It thus gave a framework for developing a system of accountability and for monitoring and reviewing the service provided to individual clients. These proposals for 'top–down' changes, which effectively sought to redraw the service boundaries, would probably achieve little, however, unless the real operational problems of delivering the service to individual clients were also tackled. Fortunately, the practical operational problems were addressed in the next important report to be published.

The Griffiths Report

As a direct result of Audit Commission criticisms and other recently published reports, the government announced that Sir Roy Griffiths had been invited 'to undertake a review of the way in which public funds are used to support community care and to advise on the options for action which would improve the use of these funds as a contribution to more effective community care'. The announcement was carefully worded to stress the financial aspects of the study but it none the less generated a good deal of hopeful excitement as well as sceptical anxiety.

Sir Roy was a popular choice; he was managing director of Sainsbury's, the retail grocery chain, and was known to be a pragmatic and sensible man accustomed to issues relating to the provision of complex services. His previous government report, in 1983, on the restructuring of senior management in the NHS, had brought about very significant improvements to the administration of hospitals and community services and, since 1983, he had been immersed part-time in health care issues in his role as Deputy Chairman of the National Health Service Board. When he embarked on his enquiry he was clearly favoured by the government, but his report of his findings, *Community Care: Agenda for Action*, published in early 1988, created government consternation. While it was widely acclaimed by public sector authorities, voluntary organizations and professionals – though inevitably with some interagency squabbling and professional quibbling – its proposed 'agenda for action' was perceived as even more far-reaching and revolutionary than the Audit Commission report, although in fact many of Griffiths' recommendations were themselves derived from the Audit Commission's findings, translated into practical proposals.

It is important to understand Griffiths' proposals because some of them formed the basis of new government legislation in 1990, although other fundamental recommendations were, unfortunately, rejected – something which may well cause difficulties in the future, as we shall see later. The Griffiths Report recommended the following:

1. There should be government action to promulgate a definition of community care values and a set of objectives to guide developments. A new Minister of State should be appointed in the Department of Health with responsibility for ensuring that national policy objectives are consistent with resources available to public authorities charged with meeting those objectives.

Griffiths regarded central government leadership in establishing policy objectives as crucial. His proposals would have prevented the political indifference and the civil service's lack of interest, noted earlier, which have blighted the development of mental health services.

2. Local authority social services should be responsible for identifying all people with community care needs in their area, for

assessing such needs, for arranging for individuals to receive social, domestic and personal care, and for ensuring that other authorities such as housing and health services are alerted to their needs.

3. The individual and his or her particular situation and needs should be assessed by a care manager, a local authority member of staff who would develop and manage an individual package of services assembled from the various local options. This care manager would be the person 'in charge' in the community, working closely with the client's family so as, for example, to arrange appropriate day care, liaise with the housing department on an application for a flat, keep in contact with the community psychiatric nurse about the client's mental state and need for medication, and so on.

4. In order to channel most effectively the social security funds then available to individuals to enter residential care, the benefit would no longer be paid direct to the individual. Instead, local authorities would be the 'gatekeeper' and would be able to choose to use such funds to provide care in the client's own home, if that was a more satisfactory arrangement than residential care for the individual concerned.

5. Griffiths strongly recommended that funds for community care should be separately identified in the public expenditure planning process and allocated to local authorities in a 'ring-fenced' budget so that community care monies would not 'leak' out into education, housing or leisure services on the decision of locally elected members.

6. Local authorities should become the planners, organizers and purchasers of care services, but not direct providers. Griffiths believed that a greater diversity of service options would develop if the independent sector, voluntary organizations and private companies were encouraged to compete for contracts for domiciliary and residential care services: indeed, there is evidence from initiatives in services for people with mental handicap that having a multiplicity of different service providers stimulates creative innovations in services in a way which monolithic public sector services seem slow to do. Griffiths' plans thus once again brought local

government firmly to centre stage as the proper place for initiatives for the local population.

7. Health authorities were encourage to restrict their services to health care only; that is, to the diagnosis, treatment and rehabilitation undertaken by doctors and other professionals employed in the NHS. The NHS was advised not to provide housing and social care but to hand over responsibilities for these community care developments to local authorities.

8. GPs were to have an important role in alerting social services to the social care needs of their patients. Griffiths also recommended that GPs should satisfy themselves that social services had considered the needs of individuals, a clear attempt by Griffiths to involve GPs more in the provision of services.

9. Finally, Griffiths was concerned to ensure that the quality of services was regularly inspected and suggested that local authority registration and inspection units should be strengthened and supported by a national inspectorate.

Griffiths' solutions were radical but, potentially, highly effective. His emphasis on government leadership, the creation of an identified and 'ring-fenced' budget, the clear attribution of responsibility to local authorities and the appointment of nominated 'care managers' are fundamental to the delivery of a coordinated service. The principles were sound but none the less there was great fear amongst mental health service professionals about the Report's practical implementation.

The clear advantages of Griffiths were as follows. First, responsibilities for care for the chronically handicapped in a community were to be given to those elected by the local population; thus the electorate would, in theory, have greater control over the way local services are provided. Second, the NHS would focus more on acute hospital care; thus chronically sick patients, who lack media appeal and who have never been able to compete successfully for resources within the NHS, would have a substantial part of their budgets protected within the proposed community care grant. Third, effective operational planning of services for individuals would be fostered by the appointment of care managers who would have more flexibility to be innovative and would also work within a clear system of accountability to senior managers.

There were other advantages, too, in that the proposed arrangements would give a clear focus for informal carers and relatives; such carers would no longer have to find their way through a maze of local services. There was also the possibility of a more flexible use of facilities in the statutory, voluntary and private sectors, and, finally, the powerful influence of doctors over the lives of the chronically disabled would inevitably wane, a process of 'de-medicalization' which is largely to be welcomed as medical and nursing skills are only a small part of the required professional skills. The new arrangements might, therefore, provide a better balance of skills and better opportunities for employing unskilled local people.

Many psychiatrists, unsurprisingly, did not like Sir Roy's proposals. They were concerned about their own roles but they also felt there was no historical evidence of local authority commitment to mental health services and they therefore feared losing hard-won resources to these authorities.

A further drawback was that at that time most local authorities had neither the trained staff nor the organizational structure to manage a community care programme effectively. Recruitment of trained staff was a continuing problem for local authorities and training of non-professional grades of staff was almost non-existent. Another difficulty for local authorities was that they had not developed a culture of objective evaluation; few used good research methods to evaluate the costs and benefits of innovative schemes. As dependent individuals are not vociferous consumers, ordinary market forces cannot operate in the same way as might be possible for the acute sector.

The most worrying feature of the proposals, however, was whether local authorities had either the ability or the will to implement the recommendations for mental health services. Although most local authorities take as their priority the provision of services to their electorate, an appreciable minority have elected members whose priorities are concerned largely with the advancement of an ideology, a situation to which the streets of some London boroughs, for example, provide mute witness. Some councils refused under any circumstances whatever to purchase private services and would rather deny a disadvantaged person access to care than buy it privately. Others had so mismanaged their own social work departments that they no longer had sufficient staff to fulfil their minimum statutory responsibilities to children at risk of abuse or to operate the Mental Health Act. The prospect of handing over total responsibility for the care of the most vulnerable people in society to such local authorities was felt by some to be profoundly disquieting. There were also councils of an altogether different political complexion who knew full well that most of their electorate would not make an issue if they skimped the care of minority, socially disadvantaged groups.

It was therefore felt that any new arrangements should ensure that no council could ignore its responsibilities, although no effective legal mechanism existed for central government to impose Griffiths' 'ring-fence' budget on local authorities.

In spite of these anxieties, the Griffiths Report contains the most impressive proposals on the effective delivery of community care services. Its proposals are workable and provide a framework for services which can be applied at all levels from the government at the top right down to the professional worker in direct contact with the recipient of services.

Caring for People, 1990: the government's plan

The Griffiths Report was published in early 1988 but the government then fell silent. The proposal to delegate responsibilities to local authorities was anathema to the Thatcher government in particular as it profoundly mistrusted local government and had progressively weakened its influence. The only advantage of the proposals from the government's point of view was that they offered the possibility of appearing to reduce central government expenditure, a cause dear to the Tory heart. Some sceptics also felt that community care was in such a mess that it would be quite convenient for the government to transfer future blame for failure on to local councils.

The government's prolonged sixteen-month silence over the Griffiths Report naturally led to much speculation, rumour and gossip. Policy discussions at ministerial level appeared to focus mainly on the hoary old issues of which agency should take lead responsibility, but finally, in 1989, the government took a decision which was considered unthinkable only a year earlier, that is, that local authority social services departments should be given lead responsibility for community care and for all services including mental health, but with some additional controls added in the latter case, the single most controversial of Griffiths' proposals.

Under the new arrangements the role of the local authority will be to assess needs in their locality, set local priorities and service objectives, and arrange the required care by designing, organizing and purchasing it. In order for this to be effectively implemented, social security benefits and existing community care monies are to be channelled through local authority social services and these funds will also be available to support individuals at home. If the new arrangements are adequately funded and properly implemented, they will comprise the first major government initiative to foster care at home rather than in institutions. The new arrangements also address the government's concern over the escalating social security bill for residential care, in 1989 running at £1 billion per year.

There were, however, enormous and seriously worrying gaps in the government's *Caring for People* White Paper, its response to Griffiths. Griffiths, for example, wanted decisive central government action to ensure that clear objectives and priorities were set, but no such central direction was contained in *Caring for People* and no mechanisms were devised by which the government could ensure that local planning and implementation were consistent with national priorities; indeed, no such priorities were set. Also, without the appointment of a minister with specific responsibilities, there seems little likelihood of the essential interdepartmental links developing between the Ministries of Health, Social Security, Housing, Employment and Education.

The government also failed to take up the recommendation to 'ring-fence' community care budget allocations, except in the case of mental health services where they did agree to a specific grant which would only be spent on community care service plans developed jointly by the health and social services. Other monies will not be separately identified from the general rate support grant from the Department of the Environment, a decision which will make it very difficult to identify exactly what is being spent on services by individual authorities.

In spite of these problems, the proposals do have the potential for righting the current gross geographical imbalance of services, though only if the resources made available to and by local authorities genuinely match the local costs of domiciliary and residential care. The allocation of resources to authorities must be linked not only to social need in terms of the levels of disability locally and the age and social class patterns of handicap and mental disorder, but also to the local costs of delivering that care. Geographical accident must not be allowed to disadvantage individuals in their ability to gain access to good local care.

It seems, too, that certain specific proposals in *Caring for People* relating to the care of mentally disordered people are something of an afterthought; certainly they read that way. It is generally felt that in the past local authorities have dragged their feet in taking on their responsibilities to care for mentally disordered people, and the Minister of Health, Roger Freeman, outlined further plans for this group to Parliament the day after Secretary of State Kenneth Clarke's speech on community care; these were, clearly, some last-minute additions to the government's package of proposals. The responsibility for the assessment and organization of care would, it was proposed, be with local authorities, as for other care groups, but health authorities would have an influence over social care spending plans. Furthermore, health authorities could no longer discharge patients without an individual care plan being approved and agreed with the local authority. This last-minute addition went some way to satisfying the psychiatric lobby who had pressed for continuing health authority control.

Overall, the most welcome part of the White Paper was the clear commitment to continue with the policy of closure of the large institutions, though in a more controlled fashion. Even though reactionary voices were raised in opposition to this, both in Parliament and by some campaigners, (particularly the National Schizophrenia Fellowship, who wished to reverse the policy on the basis of the misguided notion that this would remove the problem of homeless, drifting, mentally disordered people), the disasters of the past thirty years of unplanned discharge cannot be reversed by bolting the stable door now. In the main, however, most people welcomed the proposals, among the most heartening of which was one to allow developers to invest private capital in hospital closure programmes in order to enable the right kinds of alternative accommodation to be developed.

The White Paper, *Caring for People*, was a partial response to Griffiths and it can be fleshed out into a workable comprehensive policy; it became law in June 1990 with the passing of the NHS and Community Care Act. In fact, the proposals for community care received very little media attention throughout the bill's passage through the Houses of Parliament because other parts of the bill, those which proposed a new organizational structure for the general hospital and community services, represented the most fundamental change to the NHS since its inception in 1948 and therefore deflected attention away from the community care proposals. Health authorities, doctors, nurses, professional organizations, trade unions, administrators and managers were seriously at odds over whether the proposed reforms to the hospital service were beneficial or disastrous, and the all-consuming nature of the massive organizational 'shake-up' preoccupied the NHS and the media almost to the exclusion of anything else. Community care proposals were perceived by many NHS staff as essentially to do with social care, something which could best be left to the local authorities.

In between the publication of the White Paper and the passing of the new Act, the government decided that in view of the work required on the hospital services, it could not expect its community care proposals to be ready by the proposed launch date of April 1991, so in early 1990 it announced a two-year delay in implementation until 1993. Once again, community care was to take a back seat while the hospital services received the main attention.

There are a few District Health Authorities who are already

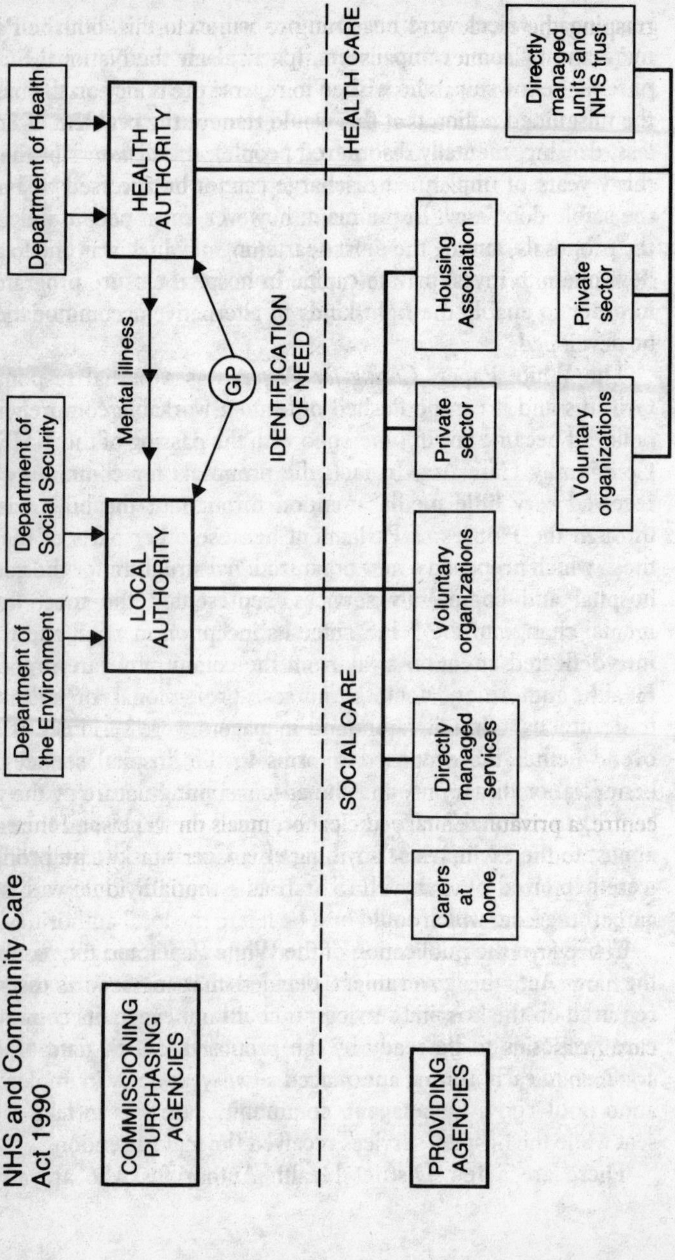

Figure 4 NHS Organization Structure
NHS and Community Care
Act 1990

grasping the nettle and beginning to work closely with their local authority colleagues to ensure the implementation of the community care proposals, but close joint working is very patchy across the country. Enthusiasm largely fizzled out when the delay in implementation was announced, and the *ad hoc*, laissez-faire government approach of letting authorities decide for themselves how fast and how enthusiastically to move on the proposals is exacerbated by a lack of ministerial drive and an absence of central government leadership in the mental health field.

Care management

Care management practice, which has been mentioned earlier, is so fundamental to good community care and such a key part of Griffiths' and the government's proposals that a further word about it is necessary here. Care management, or case management as it is sometimes called, is a concept which developed in the United States in the mid-1970s and is growing rapidly in popularity in Britain. In this system one individual worker, employed by an agency responsible for community care services, is appointed to assess the needs of an individual client, plan a comprehensive set of services for the individual, coordinate the various services and follow up the individual's progress over time. The services themselves may be provided by a number of different agencies, for example, a voluntary respite 'sitting in' service, a local authority day centre, a privately employed cleaner, meals on wheels, a community nurse, and so forth, but it is the care manager's task to pull all these together into a scheme which best suits the individual, his family and other close supporters.

There are many advantages to having a care manager, 'someone in charge out there', and this has long been recognized as essential, although in the past this recognition has not been focused on as closely as under the current care management system. Such a system has the following advantages:

1. Services are built round an individual's needs in a flexible way, rather than people being forced to comply with existing service

patterns, whether or not they find them convenient or useful.

2. Care managers can use financial resources efficiently, especially when they are planning services for a group of people with widely differing needs and have a flexible budget to use at their discretion.

3. The individual service user and his family have one named contact, one phone number to call for information, help and support.

4. There is one person responsible for ensuring that the individual does not 'slip through the net' or drift away from the service, a factor which is particularly important in mental health services.

5. Care managers can become advocates and supporters for their clients.

Care managers can come from a wide range of professional backgrounds though social work professionals are probably best trained for the role. Others, however, such as senior nurses, therapists or even people without specific health care qualifications can be trained to do the job. What is critical is that care managers should be able to command authority with the various service agencies and with others such as consultant psychiatrists, probation officers, senior housing managers and so on, as one of their key tasks is to cajole, encourage and, at times, bully services out of government and private agencies.

Care management is at an early stage of development in Britain but, if the experience in the United States is anything to go on, we can be optimistic that the system will promote for the recipient a better coordination of services and a better quality of community care.

Developing a seamless service

The new community care plans do not, however, directly link together the NHS and local authorities in order to improve coordination of services. Figure 4 above shows how few direct links exist between the two authorities. The plans exhort those responsible to bridge the gulf but do not themselves bridge it. Griffiths had in fact suggested that rather than try to create new bridging structures by organizational change, it would be better for both statutory authorities to have clearly defined responsibilities and roles which did not overlap. He suggested, as I describe earlier, that the NHS should confine itself to health care, and local authorities should be responsible for social care. Thus most long-term care for people who require a lot of daily support would be the responsibility of the local authority rather than, as formerly, of the NHS. The idea, under the new plan, is that, over a number of years, the local authority will contract with a wide range of voluntary and private agencies to provide a spectrum of different services which it pays for. It will purchase the total range of care needed by local people with mental disorder and, meanwhile, the NHS will restrict itself to providing a psychiatric service for these individuals in whichever setting is most appropriate.

These proposals are, however, made much more complex by the existence of old long-stay wards in hospitals whose main function, quite clearly, is social care, yet which for many years are going to be run by the Health Service. Griffiths realized that this situation could not be changed overnight, so under the new regulations the NHS will still be allowed to carry on providing long-term care if it wishes.

A further problem is that no one is quite sure exactly what defines *health* care and *social* care, since an individual's progress in responding to treatment is often measured by an improvement in the performance of social care tasks and everyday activities. This being so, specific rehabilitation programmes for people with mental disorder frequently use a therapeutic approach which practises and rehearses ordinary activities so as to help people regain confidence in managing the business of life. It is therefore perfectly possible for social care to be provided in an ordinary household with rehabilitation and personal development as its main purpose; in other words, the therapy itself is of a social care nature. Under such circumstances, it is not at all clear which statutory agency should take the leading role in developing such therapeutic houses and homes, something perhaps which explains why the government has now proposed a specific grant for mental health services in the community which can only be spent by the *joint* agreement of local health and social services.

The specific grant, introduced in April 1991, should encourage authorities to plan together so that a broad spectrum of services is developed and there are no gaps for individual patients to fall down. One commonly heard complaint from relatives is that 'I was told she was too disturbed for the council day centre as they couldn't stop her from wandering out', yet 'The doctor at the day hospital said they only took short-term cases, people who could get better and move on.' Too 'bad' for the council and too 'good' for the NHS is a recurrent problem, and, therefore, a *range* of services is needed to care for all possible problems, however unusual, complex, worrying or burdensome an individual's difficulties may appear.

In some parts of Britain health services and local authorities are beginning to work together to develop an overall plan for services in their area. Fortunately, the NHS reforms and the community care changes share some unifying principles which should encourage the two statutory authorities to work together more closely.

1. The role of the responsible local statutory authority is to develop an overall strategy for the shape of services for the local population in a defined geographical area. The authority must develop a plan for the design and development of a service, set priorities and determine the most appropriate set of services for its residents, within the constraints of its resources. The authority will be purchasers and enablers of care, but not necessarily a provider of care.

2. The management of services will be via contracts. Authorities will develop specifications for services and then reach contractual agreements with provider agencies such as voluntary or private organizations. Public authorities have, however, minimal expertise in this area, though they have 'cut their teeth' by developing 'specifications for contracts' for non-care services such as cleaning and catering. Developing an effective contractual style of management is a challenge which has, in the main, still to be faced across the public sector.

3. A 'mixed economy of care', with care being provided on similar terms by public and independent sectors, is not particularly new to local authorities, although the contracting of care from multiple organizations has not been a key policy in the past, more an *ad hoc* response to specific local problems. Getting the right balance of 'in house' provision and 'contracted out' services will vary from one locality to another and will reflect local authorities' employment policies as well as the availability of effective local voluntary organizations. It will also reflect the propensity or otherwise of the private sector to invest in the provision of care services. Clearly, both statutory authorities will need to develop new attitudes and approaches to the 'other world' of the independent sector.

4. Local authorities will need good information on the costs, quality and volume of services needed and provided. While the NHS has been developing its computerized data-bases and information systems for general hospitals with astonishing rapidity, community care services lag far behind. Both authorities will need to invest substantially in information systems over the next decade if they are to maximize the amount of care they can squeeze out of their constrained budgets.

5. Last, but possibly most important, both public sector services are moving towards more 'explicit' accountability for the use of their resources. While the NHS has become increasingly concerned with ensuring that there is a hierarchy of individuals with responsibility for achieving certain objectives, and an increasing commitment by individual doctors, nurses and therapists to agreed aims, local authority staff have also come under increasing pressure from elected council members and, behind them, the voting electorate, to demonstrate that their service departments have effective management structures and are truly accountable.

These common features should therefore enable health and local authorities to develop a common philosophy about the style of delivery of mental health services. They also highlight the relative inexperience of both authorities in certain key areas, although benefits of cooperation between authorities, such as in the development and sharing of computer information systems for work in the community, are obvious.

When professionals who work in mental health services talk of an 'integrated, comprehensive, seamless service' they mean a service where acute hospital beds, hostels, group homes, community teams and services for people in their own homes, are all managed as one service with one team of people who have total responsibility. In practice this is rarely achieved by health services and local authorities and almost never includes private and voluntary sectors. Nevertheless, most professionals aspire to a flexible, easily accessible service where 'users' can move rapidly between home, day care and hospital when the need arises. One of the major anxieties about the new NHS and Community Care Act is the further fragmentation of services, with health services even more isolated and hospital-bound, yet still consuming massive resources. One radical but simple solution to this problem is joint buying consortia.

Buying consortia

Under this system the two statutory authorities would create a new organization where NHS resources for mental health services and the local authority social services resources for domiciliary, residential and day care services would be pooled. This new organization, or consortium, could have powers delegated to it to design and buy services across an area coterminous with the local authority boundary. Indeed, the local authority *must* be the key agency around which services are designed if we are to make the best use not only of social services but also of housing, education and leisure facilities.

Apart from the clear advantages of having a joint strategic plan for mental health services, a joint buying consortium would have much enhanced buying power and could lead, too, to considerable economies in developing information systems and a pooling of skills in service development and the maintenance of standards of care. Figure 4 shows diagrammatically how the new community care proposals by the government are currently planned. Figure 5 shows how a Joint Purchasing Consortium would work.

There are, of course, drawbacks to this proposal. Indeed, the

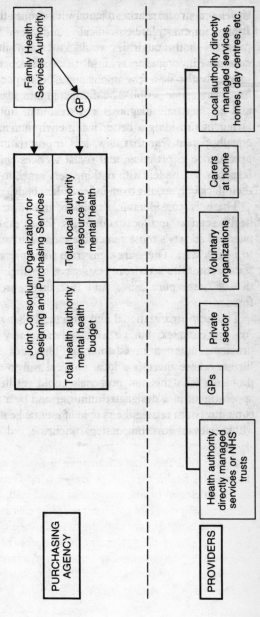

Figure 5 The Seamless Service
A Buying Consortium for Mental Health Services

issues and structures are so massively complex that this is inevitable. It may, for example, be politically 'undeliverable' in many areas at present – both authorities would lose some sovereignty over their current funds and may find this unacceptable. There would inevitably also be a fear among some NHS professionals that their hard-won services would be dissipated into a 'support only' service and that accurate diagnosis and treatment would be sacrificed in favour of providing a better living environment. There will be an equally potent fear that new, less appropriate priorities may take precedence in planning, and social services council members may fear they will be left with nothing very much to do if they delegate their decision-making to an independent body.

There is considerable suspicion and mistrust between many health services and local authorities, but a real commitment to the needs of society's most vulnerable members could drive both sides to a fresh start. There are signs from some parts of the country that some authorities are already exploring, albeit gingerly, the possibilities of 'joint purchasing' and that this represents a good way forward.

The new organizational and structural changes proposed in the Act are complex, but go a considerable way to addressing the problems outlined in Chapter 4. They can also be developed further where there is a local political will to do so. Any serious problems with the new proposals could yet be addressed by the appointment of a designated minister and by a strong government commitment to raising the profile of mental health service planning within relevant government departments.

7 From Principles to Practice I

For the first time in many years there is hope that by means of the NHS and Community Care Act of 1990, imperfect and incomplete though it may be, the fundamental organizational and financial changes needed to foster good community care have been made. But the general public does not have a clear understanding of what community care services are trying to achieve, partly because people with mental disorder are the focus of philosophical and ethical disagreements about their care, disagreements which create confusion in the minds of a public unfamiliar with the issues. The story of the growth of community care and the closure of the asylums has been dominated by unseemly public disputes between different professional and voluntary organizations, all of them committed to developing mental health services but with very different ideas about the routes to be followed. Thus one organization will expound in the media about the urgent need to 'slow down the hospital closures', while another will follow hot on their heels, saying, 'Close the hospitals as rapidly as possible.' Clearly what is lacking is a single, explicit, cohesive vision of the future which inspires collaboration between professionals, voluntary groups and the sufferers themselves, and which could also drive political action.

The Victorian asylum movement was successful largely because of a unanimity of views on the subject by most men of influence. Perhaps if we look beyond superficial disagreements we may find that today's men and women of influence share fundamental beliefs and that these beliefs can inspire a common approach to community care.

This chapter outlines what society should seek to achieve for people with mental disorder.

Principles of community care

The purpose of community care services should be to help individuals achieve and sustain a fulfilling and rewarding life when this has become difficult as a result of mental disability.

The philosophy that underpins this statement of purpose is the belief that every individual human being in our society has rights of citizenship and the potentiality to participate as a citizen, irrespective of gender, ethnic origin, cultural background or physical or mental ability. Thus every recipient of community care has rights and entitlements, and also responsibilities, and the aim of community care services should be to enhance the ability of an individual to live independently in as 'normal' a way as possible. There is, of course, much argument about what is 'normal', but in general it should mean that every adult person lives in a home of his or her own or with chosen friends or family members, that he or she has daily purposeful occupation, whether in paid employment or not, and that the person has social contacts and interpersonal relationships which are emotionally satisfying.

The goal of social independence, of helping people to 'look after themselves', is a very important one, but many individuals with long-term mental disorder may also need specific medical and psychological treatment to lessen the burden of symptoms; from time to time they may also need extra supervision, care and shelter. Community care support, therefore, may well be a starting-point in a process designed to provide an individual with, ultimately, true independence and a generally fuller life.

But although it is easy to write fine-sounding words about the vision which should inspire community care services, it is much more difficult to put them into practice. It would also be a lot easier to implement a new service from scratch, without the legacy of old hospitals and the current hotchpotch of uncoordinated services. However, we have inherited such a legacy and we need, too, to work with existing services. We have, therefore, two quite separate tasks.

The first is to design and construct local services for the majority of mentally disordered people who live in their own homes and who may use mental health services for only a few weeks every few years. The second is to resettle individuals with long-term mental disorder, who have been left behind in the old hospitals, back into their home localities, and support them with a network of services.

In order to translate an overall vision into practice, some general principles must be followed for both these groups:

Consultation and participation

Recipients of services, whether they are referred to as users, clients or patients, are entitled to be consulted about their treatment and care and to participate as fully as possible in decisions about their lives. The law provides that no medical treatment or other care should be given without the valid consent of the individual, except in the case of those detained in hospital under the Mental Health Act of 1983 and in certain other exceptional circumstances.

Self-determination and autonomy

Services should aim to promote individuals' capacity for self-determination and autonomy and to enhance their ability to make realistic choices for themselves. In order for this to be achieved, users need *information* on future possibilities and options.

A normal environment

Services should be provided wherever possible in ordinary houses and homes rather than in institutions. A home of one's own is a fundamental requirement but should be provided in the way best suited to an individual's needs.

Minimum segregation

Individuals should be restricted and segregated from the general community as little as possible. As far as their disabilities allow they should have the opportunity to participate in normal community activities. Promoting a policy of minimal segregation does not, however, preclude the provision of protection from abuse and harm.

Protection and asylum

All human beings have the right to be protected from physical and mental harm, abuse and exploitation. Services should be able to provide temporary or permanent 'asylum' in the sense of a haven or retreat when someone requires shelter and protection from the pressures of the external world.

Small scale

It is generally better to provide services on a small rather than a large scale. For example, the numbers of people living together, or the numbers of people attending a day centre or place of work, should be as small as is consistent with the successful functioning of the facility.

Local

Services which are organized locally are usually more accessible and friendly than remote, distant ones.

Environmental solutions are better than special services

Wherever possible it is better to provide a person with the living conditions and equipment to do things for him- or herself, rather than providing special services. For example, it may be better to provide a schizophrenia sufferer with personal transportation to enable him or her to reach a day centre rather than laying on transportation.

Alleviation of distress

Services should have as a primary goal the alleviation of distress, by providing a programme of treatment, care and support based on the unique needs of an individual. Distress does not just arise from the symptoms of mental disorder but also from the consequences of the disorder as they affect the social and occupational life of the individual. Services should also aim to enhance the individual's own ability to cope with distress.

The concept of normalization

The principles outlined above all use the notion of 'normality' or 'ordinariness' and it is worth considering further what this means for people with mental disorder.

The American word 'normalization' is now used increasingly in official planning documents to describe the concept, as far as possible, of providing services in ways which maintain mentally disordered people in, or return them to, 'as normal a life as possible'. The problem is that just like the 'moral treatments' of the nineteenth century, normalization has come to mean different things to different people, and professionals who have espoused the concept of 'normalization' often proselytize their views with a religious fervour which, though often motivating to fellow staff, can be alienating to those who are unfamiliar with the concept. Wolf Wolfensberger, an American professor of education and rehabilitation working with mentally handicapped people, was a particularly powerful influence on the 'normalization' movement, especially in the 1970s and early 1980s. His basic idea is that 'normalizing' services are those in which the ultimate goal of the service is the creation, support and defence of valued social roles for people who are at risk of social devaluation. This definition received, and still receives, much support, although, in the context of helping those with mental disorder, it has been agreed that Wolfensberger's concept fails to take account of the realities of many mental disorders.

For example, I visited a 'community rehabilitation house', a converted Victorian house in the suburbs of a northern city, where ten adults lived and the concept of normalization was applied. All ten residents had been long-term patients in a large psychiatric hospital, were severely disabled and had been discharged only after a lengthy period of active rehabilitation. All had their own bed-sitting rooms and used shared, though generously provided, bathroom facilities, as well as communal dining and sitting rooms. Physically their new environment was a major improvement on where they had previously lived, a dormitory-style long-stay ward.

The house was staffed round the clock since many of the

residents needed practical help with everyday tasks and several still displayed 'odd' or difficult behaviour. Even so, some residents had started to venture out to local pubs and shops and were slowly becoming part of the community.

One resident was, however, noticeably unshaven and smelly and there was evidence, too, of urinary incontinence. He would never have been allowed to remain looking like that in the regimented environment of a long-stay ward, but the staff of the house were striving to apply their understanding of the principles of normalization. One explained, 'It's his choice to be that way. He has the right not to change or wash, a right not to conform to social conventions.' Another member of staff wasn't so sure: 'He won't wash because he believes the water is poisoned and poison gets through his skin. Medication doesn't seem to make any difference. But I think we should at least make him look and smell normal – no one else will sit near him or talk to him because he's like that.' The two members of staff were still debating the issue of whether he should be bathed and shaved, whether he liked it or not, when I left. In this instance, a well-meaning effort to give an individual the right to choose how he led his life – arguably a choice which any 'normal' person enjoys – had led to that individual becoming increasingly isolated and rejected.

The worthy objective of 'normalization' should therefore lead to the implementation of care practices and procedural policies which are appropriate for those with mental disorders and it should not be applied in a rigid and obsessive fashion. Professionals and family members have to be very clear about an individual's own internal experiences and personal needs; clearly it is no good pretending, for the sake of normalization, that delusions, hallucinations and abnormal moods do not exist and that aberrant and unsocial behaviour is not a real and sometimes pervasive aspect of mental disorder. Above all, care plans must recognize the influence that such symptoms may have on the ability of a sufferer to live a 'normal' life.

Criteria for community services

The principles set out above focus on the treatment and rights of the individual but there are also principles which apply to systems of care. A workable set of such principles was described by the National Institute of Mental Health in the United States in 1980 and these are equally applicable in Britain today. A service system comprises a network of professionals and/or volunteers who accept responsibility for providing assistance to vulnerable people to meet their individual needs and develop their potential without their being unnecessarily isolated or excluded from the community. The ten criteria for an effective system are:

- There must be mechanism for *identifying persons in need* and for reaching out to those willing to participate; it may also at times be necessary to reach out to those who do not wish to participate but are at risk of harm to themselves or others.
- The system must offer service-users assistance in applying for and obtaining *financial entitlements* in the form of income support and disability allowances
- It must offer *24-hour crisis assistance* so that individuals are not left untreated or unsupported during an acute episode of illness, no matter what time of the day or night a crisis arises
- It must provide opportunities for *social rehabilitation*
- Services must be provided *indefinitely* and be available for an individual's lifetime if necessary
- Services must provide adequate *medical and psychiatric treatment* on a continuing basis
- Services must provide *back-up support for family friends and members of the local community* in order to minimize the burden of care which falls on other people's shoulders
- The system must engage voluntary groups, community organizations and other members of the *local community* to maximize involvement in normal community activities
- The system must operate so as to protect *patients' rights* and ensure their *civil liberties* are not denied them
- Finally, the system must provide for the coordination, integration and binding together of services so that they function as one

'*seamless service*', providing all the elements which one individual requires (this is the function of case management described in Chapter 6)

Having established service criteria, it is necessary to assess every individual who needs services along two dimensions: first, in terms of the *ordinary needs* of every citizen, and second, in terms of the special needs generated by mental disorder.

Ordinary needs include adequate income, shelter, food and clothing, plus protection from physical harm, a means of daily occupation and the opportunity for emotional, spiritual and social fulfilment.

The *special needs* of a mentally disordered person are for specific medical and psychological treatments and procedures. These special needs are dictated by the characteristics of the mental disorder and by its severity, duration and treatability. Special needs may include, for example, the need for medication, hospital inpatient care or outpatient review, regular monitoring of blood levels of specific drugs such as lithium, investigation of physical health problems, supervision of medication by community psychiatric nurses, perhaps a special diet, and so on.

Once the 'ordinary' needs of daily life have been successfully provided, mentally disordered people living in the community need regular skilled review of their mental state to ensure that medical, nursing and psychological expertise is used to best effect to minimize the impact of the disorder. In general, the fewer mental symptoms people experience and the less preoccupied they are with an internal abnormal world, the more able they are to live successfully in the community.

The remainder of the chapter considers ordinary needs in greater depth and services for special needs are discussed in Chapter 8.

Adequate personal income

Adequate personal financial resources are an essential component of community care and an essential prerequisite, too, of dignity and self-worth, but, surprisingly, the financial needs of people with mental disorder are often ignored or, at the other end of the scale, such people are at times even treated rather like children – they are provided with pocket money for 'treats' but all other financial decisions are taken out of their hands. In fact without sufficient regular income, individuals can make few choices about their lives.

In Britain today, financial support for long-term unemployed people is provided through a complex system of social security benefits, while other special arrangements exist for people with long-term disabilities. The system is, however, extremely difficult to negotiate and even the most competent citizen would find the task of tracking down his or her welfare benefit entitlements a daunting one. (Readers who doubt this should look at the bewildering array of welfare benefit leaflets in their local post office.) The old hospitals used to employ special patients' monies officers whose sole job was to ensure that patients' income and capital assets were administered for their benefit both while in hospital and on discharge. Very few general hospital units, however, have recognized how important this service was to individual patients and now it usually falls to a beleaguered social worker to take on the complex task of sorting out welfare benefits; social workers are not, however, experts in this field and it is a time-consuming task that few of them relish.

Indeed, a study in Hackney in 1990 of the work of mental health professionals working in a community team supporting people at home found that no less than a quarter of their working time was spent on working out welfare entitlements. One said, 'Being articulate and diplomatic and having saintlike patience and dogged persistence have become key attributes needed to prise out money that should be available as right.'

Any comprehensive community care system must ensure that all service users have ready access to skilled help from someone who is trained to assess their entitlements, to negotiate on their behalf with the Department of Social Security and other agencies, to assist with budgeting, offer financial advice and, where the individual desires it, hold benefit books and cheque books and arrange for regular bills to be paid and financial commitments to be planned.

Welfare rights and patients' monies' officers are, indeed, needed in every service and not just in community care, but at present there is doubt as to who should pay for them. The NHS used to fund such officers when patients lived in long-stay hospitals, but as people moved into the community their role was forgotten. As new services develop, health and social services should agree between them how they are going to allocate the responsibility for ensuring that every mentally disordered person has sufficient income to live on without the fear of poverty. Our welfare state provides every citizen with the entitlement to such income, but mentally disordered people find it particularly difficult, without assistance, to benefit from such entitlement.

Physical and environmental needs: housing and personal care

Shelter, food, clothing and protection from physical harm are the basic essentials of life, and personal care to maintain cleanliness and health, and domestic care to maintain a clean and safe living environment, are minimal necessities. At its most basic, 'shelter' is a place of protection from the weather and a safe place to sleep, but people also need a home of their own, an environment which provides security, familiarity and a haven from the external world.

People with mental disorder are no different from anyone else in wanting to live in good, decent housing, and local authority housing departments and housing associations are often willing to discriminate in favour of mentally disordered individuals in making properties available for rent, provided they can be assured that tenants will receive the right support and help from skilled professionals when they need it. Many local authorities have 'special housing needs' panels which consider individuals who have specific needs as a result of mental or physical disabilities. Tenants allocated homes in this way do of course pay rent and local taxes just like everyone else, although the sad reality at present is that many councils have such long waiting lists of homeless people and families living in substandard accommodation that people with mental disorders face great competition for housing. Indeed, there is a desperate shortage of accommodation to rent, especially in urban areas, and the housing stock that exists in these areas is often poorly maintained and badly managed. Perhaps the greatest challenge for mental health services in the 1990s is securing adequate housing for former patients in the community.

Some of the criticisms which are voiced by service planners and professionals when thinking about ordinary housing for long-term patients is that it is 'too expensive', or that 'They can't cope on their own,' or that 'They'll be affected by the same stresses and strains that put them in hospital in the first place.' But community services for mentally handicapped people have demonstrated that it is possible to provide for quite severely disturbed, multiply-handicapped people in specially adapted ordinary flats and houses, as long as there are sufficient well-trained staff to provide good-quality care round the clock, and provided the staff themselves are well supported by senior professionals with the right experience. Mental health services have unfortunately been generally reluctant to follow this good example and are still developing too many large group homes and hostels which create too many segregated communities of mentally disturbed people.

If community care is to function properly, suitable housing must be affordable on the low income support funds available for unemployed disabled people. Inevitably, therefore, the individual must usually rent accommodation rather than own a property. But perhaps more thought could be given to assisting such people to buy homes of their own. In Britain the majority of people aspire to owning their own home and those who do acquire a certain position in society. Indeed, they are keen to advertise the fact by stamping their personalities on their home, something which is evidenced by looking at homes in Britain which have passed from public to private ownership. If we take seriously the idea of valuing individuals as citizens, then instead of using bridging capital from the sale of hospital sites to purchase large houses and hostels outright, a means could perhaps be found of lending capital to individuals as an initial down-payment on a property or a share in a property. Such an initiative might also attract investment capital from building societies and other lenders and thus assist Regional Health Authorities with their cash-flows.

It is important not to be inflexible when looking at housing options, although sometimes it seems that dogma is of overriding importance to staff and, indeed, more important than finding solutions which suit individuals. While the basic aim of a service should be to provide people with ordinary homes of their own, there are many former long-term hospital patients who would not wish to live alone after many years of living in close proximity to other patients; such people may feel more comfortable living in a three- or four-person flat or house, or perhaps in a sheltered group of flatlets where communal dining rooms and recreational facilities echo the arrangements in ordinary sheltered accommodation for elderly people. Unfortunately there is very little hard research evidence as to the sort of residential provision which best suits people with differing levels or types of disability, and fashions change as new ideas evolve. Nevertheless, certain specific elements of good practice remain:

- Residents should have the same *security of tenure* as normal tenants, even if they spend weeks or months in hospital every now and again.
- Residents should have their *own rooms* and access to bathroom and WC facilities, preferably of their own, or shared with no more than one or two others; tenants sharing a house are *not* like a family of adults and children in an ordinary house where intimacy allows much more comfortable sharing of facilities
- Residents' rooms should be *private*, *lockable* and large enough to provide a comfortable sitting space, with *room for entertaining* guests and facilities for preparing hot drinks and snacks
- There should be sufficient staff both day and night to ensure that all residents have access at all times to *physical and emotional support*. How this requirement is implemented will obviously vary enormously with the level of disability of individual residents and it is normally more economical in staffing terms for there to be a fairly even level of disabilities among the residents of one unit. However, it is difficult to say if this is desirable from the residents' point of view, or whether they would prefer to live in a mixed group of people with differing levels of disability; when

asked, most patients express a preference for being with others who do not have behavioural problems. Such a preference is scarcely surprising but may be difficult to accommodate in specially designated homes and hostels.

- A home is a place for sleeping, retreating to in the evenings, storing one's personal possessions and for relaxing in private. It is not a place where one spends all day, every day, cut off from other people, and self-contained large units which provide all residents' daytime activities on site face the danger of becoming merely 'wards' in the community, new types of 'closed' institution. There must, therefore, be active commerce between the home and the outside world of shops, pubs, libraries, parks and neighbours.

- Finally, both staff and residents must be able to summon skilled medical and nursing help very quickly both day and night. This is particularly important in the case of people with serious behavioural problems or continuing florid symptoms of psychiatric disorder. However, the difficulties involved in providing a safe and reassuring environment for staff working with this group of people are one reason why so many professional staff still clamour to retain the old asylums; in such asylums staff know they can summon help at a few minutes' notice from a neighbouring ward and from resident medical staff. In order to provide the same sort of instant help and emotional support to staff as well as residents, it may be necessary to site a house supporting potentially disturbed people near to a hospital site with acute psychiatric admission wards, for although technology can link many homes to one central point, it cannot provide the reassurance of instant personal help in times of emergency.

Core and cluster

The concept of linking an administrative central service 'core' with a dispersed cluster of homes of people receiving long-term services was developed in the 1970s, and still retains its appeal. Under such a concept the 'core' is the central base for professional staff who are engaged in the rehabilitation and personal development of individuals living in the homes; it may also serve as a training base for staff, a research base for the evaluation and monitoring of the service and a place where the residential care staff meet to exchange ideas. It is often based at a Community Mental Health Centre (CMHC), although if it is, it is important that the supervisory and rehabilitation staff operate separately from the staff who provide the routine day-to-day mental health service, otherwise the needs of those in crisis may quickly push the needs of long-term sufferers into the background.

The 'cluster', under such an arrangement, is a dispersed group of residential facilities and ordinary dwellings scattered round the locality in which individuals receiving the service live. 'Core and cluster' is thus not a visible 'village' but, rather, an invisible administrative structure comprising a wide range of facilities of differing sizes and levels of staffing to suit a spectrum of disabilities.

Half-way houses

People sometimes find that their housing requirements change and seek after a period to move on to different kinds of residence, particularly into flats of their own. When this happens, the decision to move should be theirs alone and there should be no pressure to shuffle people round from house to house as their level of social achievement improves or deteriorates. The idea of 'half-way' houses, where discharged patients lived for a year or eighteen months and then moved to ordinary independent living, became fashionable in the 1960s. But it soon became apparent to the pioneering voluntary organizations that established them, such as the Richmond Fellowship, that patients who had been mentally unwell for years did not miraculously become capable of independent living in a short space of time; they often needed permanent help and support and coped particularly poorly with changes in their environment and lifestyle.

Family placement schemes and boarding out

The aim of these schemes is to place individuals, usually on a permanent basis, as lodgers with a landlady or family, where they can live as family, participating in home activities as much as possible. The idea behind such schemes is derived from children's fostering schemes and although they suit a small minority of less disabled former patients, the hosts normally need a great deal of regular help and support from professionals for the scheme to succeed and there must also be close monitoring and supervision of the quality of care provided. Nevertheless, these schemes play a small role and they are particularly useful for people who need a short break away from their own families and for carers in need of respite; they can also help someone moving towards a more independent life from a closely sheltered environment.

Occupation/participation: day care services and work

We all need to give form to our lives by pursuing a common goal with others for a purpose which has social value; in other words, we all need worthwhile occupation or, more prosaically, work. Work is usually thought of as paid employment outside the home, but purposeful work inside the home, providing domestic, physical and emotional comforts for others, can be equally rewarding. Daily purposeful occupation gives form to our lives, and if mentally disordered people are unable to participate in ordinary work inside or outside the home, consideration needs to be given as to how the absence of normal occupation can be compensated for.

Day care

The number of day hospitals run by health services and day centres provided by local authorities and voluntary organizations has grown slowly but steadily over the last forty years, although there remains a great deal of confusion about the purposes of day care, and professionals from different services have differing expectations and aims. NHS professionals normally perceive *day hospitals* as a possible alternative to hospital admission for people who are acutely ill and cannot be treated as outpatients or at home, as a place for recently discharged short-term in-patients to attend for a period while settling back into normal life, and as a place to treat, monitor and give social support to long-term patients who would otherwise live isolated lives. Day hospitals usually have generous staffing levels of doctors, nurses and therapists, an ambitious therapeutic programme, at least on paper, and an ethos geared to continuing rehabilitation. Many are sited in hospital grounds near the in-patient unit.

Day centres, in contrast, are described in Department of Health guidance notes as providing for 'clients' needs for shelter, occupation and social activity', although they also provide a break for caring relatives and a break for the individual away from home. Day centres are usually less well staffed, and therefore cheaper, than day hospitals, are run by staff with a wide variety of non-medical qualifications (for example, in social work, education, occupational therapy and industrial therapy), and usually depend heavily on unqualified helpers.

In spite of the differences in the declared aims of the two sorts of day care, and in their staffing, studies have found very little difference between them in terms of what the people who use them actually do. In most day units, whatever they are called, attenders normally spend a good deal of time chatting to other attenders or sitting about watching the world go by, doing nothing very much. Craft activities – weaving, pottery, printing, painting, woodwork, metalwork and so forth – may be offered for attenders but are only modestly popular, and increasingly units are focusing on developing the skills required for ordinary life, such as shopping and cooking, and on some forms of regular task-oriented activity which mimic the skills required for work, such as operating a computer keyboard. If doctors are employed in a unit the amount of time they spend with a patient may be as little as fifteen minutes twice a week for a short-term attender and an astonishingly low four or five minutes per week for a long-term attender.

In fact, the majority of attenders at day hospitals and day care centres are long-term service users. From the user's point of view, day care offers somewhere to go during the day, a new environment, a free or cheap meal, somewhere to meet other people, recreational activities and someone to talk to when things aren't going well. However, what they get from the service often falls far short of what they need. A study carried out in the mid-1980s in a South London day hospital and in local day centres examined the ordinary, every-day needs and specific treatment requirements of attenders. The researchers found that one-quarter really needed sheltered work of some kind rather than the informal craft and recreational activities which were on offer and that a further proportion would have benefited more from a social club of a less structured kind. Other studies have found that while managers and staff prize highly the 'therapeutic' discussion groups which flourish in many day care units, there is less evidence that users rate them as valuable and no evidence that people with long-term mental disorder gain benefit.

Current day care services have other problems, too. For example, attenders are usually expected to get there under their own steam; ordinary ambulance services have been reluctant to ferry day patients, and local ambulance service personnel are not trained to understand why an able-bodied young man lacks sufficient motivation as a result of schizophrenia to make his own way half a mile down the road to the day hospital. However, negotiating the public transport system may simply be too difficult for someone with mental disorder and 'dedicated transport' using specially trained personnel, though expensive, is often the only feasible solution.

Day care is clearly in need of a radical rethink and a wider choice of services is required than is now available. Perhaps what is needed is smaller, more easily accessible places that can be reached on foot and where closer attention is paid to the social needs of users and to identifying individuals' choices about their requirements for leisure, work and education. More use could also be made of educational techniques to improve interpersonal social skills and increase levels of educational attainment, particularly as many long-term attenders are handicapped not just by their mental disorder but also by poor schooling and impaired learning ability.

There is concern, however, that providing separate, specially labelled services which only mentally disordered people can use is not only extremely expensive but also encourages a discriminating attitude towards already stigmatized people. The creative use of existing clubs and leisure facilities could go much of the way to addressing this concern.

Work and employment

For many day care attenders, the service provides an alternative to going out to work. But it does not feel to them like real work and there is no financial reward and rarely any specific long-term achievable objectives which can be shared with others. The challenge of providing real work for long-term mentally disordered people has not been tackled successfully in Britain. Between 70 and 80 per cent of psychiatric admissions are unemployed and almost all patients now being discharged from long-stay wards have no work. The domination of mental health services by the NHS, which is traditionally concerned with specific medical treatment rather than other aspects of care, has meant that expertise in this field is very thinly spread across the country.

The importance of work and employment to those with mental disorder has, however, been recognized since Victorian times. John Connolly in his book *The Construction and Government of Lunatic Asylums* (1847) wrote:

Among the means of relieving patients from the monotony of an asylum and of preserving bodily health and at the same time of improving the conditions of the mind and prompting recovery, employment of some kind or other ranks highest.

The Lunacy Commissioners wholeheartedly agreed and severely castigated Boards of Guardians who did not provide daily occupation and incentive rewards for the majority of patients. They noted that asylums had a tendency to provide employment on farms and in workshops for the most competent and socially organized patients and there were some remarkably successful asylum farming ventures; for example, in the early twentieth century Cane Hill Hospital became famous for its herd of pedigree pigs. Such ventures, however, left out those who were most disturbed or withdrawn and hence who found it most difficult to work; these were left to idle their time away on the wards, and it was always a struggle to find sufficient financial investment in equipment and raw materials to establish and maintain occupational ventures.

In times of full employment, employers are more willing to take on disabled people of all kinds and there is a direct economic incentive to ensure that those who can work do. During the Second World War, for example, a number of government initiatives stimulated thinking about the resettlement of disabled people into open employment by channelling them through a period of 'industrial rehabilitation'. In the 1940s and 1950s Britain was still predominantly a manufacturing society, and preferred schemes tended to foster manual workshop skills. Pioneering NHS industrial units in large hospitals thus took on subcontracted work from local factories. By the 1960s enthusiasm for such industrial-type resettlement units was waning, and the rising unemployment of the late 1960s and 1970s made it increasingly difficult for people with chronic mental disorder to find work on the open job market. At the same time, the more able-bodied and work-fit patients had already been discharged from hospital, leaving behind a more seriously disabled group, who were unlikely ever to resume open employment, plus new short-term patients who needed assistance to return to their former work rather than the development of new skills. Moreover, Britain was increasingly shifting from a manufacturing economy to a service-based economy where quite different and, often, more sophisticated social skills are demanded of employees.

People with long-term mental disorder have many problems in holding down a job. These often relate not so much to poor manual skills or dexterity, although they may be slower than usual in completing tasks, as to problems in maintaining drive and interest, in adhering to a regular timetable and in forming the relationships with fellow workers which are necessary to effective completion of work tasks.

It is often difficult to predict which patients will be able to develop effective work skills, and some quite seriously disturbed people with persistently odd behaviour can work effectively while others with few overt symptoms of mental disorder may have great difficulties. The transition back to work is easier, however, if individuals have worked previously and have skills to fall back on. Many schizophrenia sufferers, however, find that they can no longer achieve previous levels of attainment after the onset of the disorder and need to adapt to less challenging work.

It is now recognized that many seriously disabled patients cannot be resettled into open employment but their need for real work can be met, none the less, by providing a special working environment where good job performance and long-term achievements are rewarded. It is difficult, however, to accept the concept of work which is non-profit-making or which may even cost the providing employer a substantial amount of on-going revenue funds, and until now there has been a great reluctance to fund such initiatives. The NHS has invested little in work schemes, although a few innovative services have established enterprises in such areas as gardening and horticulture, catering services and computer programming or word processing activities. Following the transfer of responsibility for social rehabilitation of discharged patients in 1993 from the NHS to local authorities, greater emphasis may be given to developing work schemes.

Sheltered work ventures provided specifically for identifiable groups of people with special needs always run the risk of seg-regating people with mental disorder from the rest of the com-munity; whenever possible, therefore, it is desirable to link such initiatives with 'for-profit' enterprises away from large old hospital grounds, however tempting it may be to use cheap old buildings and land on hospital sites. Local large employers could also be encour-aged to establish departments providing work experience for people with long-term disabilities, provided they received financial incen-tives in the form of capital grants and revenue support: employers should not be expected to provide charitable funds or investment, although they can provide an atmosphere of tolerance, access for sheltered workers to the benefits which other employees enjoy (such as sports and canteen facilities), and a willingness to consider these supported workers for more general employment if they make good progress. Specially recruited supervisory staff could be paid for by the local authority or by some other scheme initiator.

Voluntary organizations, notably local branches of MIND, and others specially created for the purpose, such as the Peter Bedford Trust, have developed a variety of sheltered work schemes. Some are service agencies providing painting and decorating, gardening and catering services to the local community; others have developed workshops which concentrate on one business activity – baking, furniture renovation and picture-framing are examples.

For people who have a realistic chance of developing their social skills sufficiently to re-enter open employment, other creative approaches have been used to place them in work. In the 1980s the government-funded Manpower Services Commission (MSC) sponsored a scheme whereby the employer paid a percentage of the salary and costs of a partially disabled person's employment in proportion to the individual's assessed percentage contribution to the job in terms of how it would be performed by an average non-disabled person; MSC paid the balance. Sheltered Placement Schemes of this kind have, however, been more successful with physically disabled and mentally handicapped people than with mentally disordered people as it is easier to assess the proportionate efficiency of people with physical disabilities and mental handicap. It is much more difficult to predict the performance of someone with mental disorder, and the process of assessment of an individual in a real situation requires time and skilled judgment.

New ideas do, however, appear from time to time. Once such has recently been copied from a well-known initiative in New York whereby the rehabilitation organization guarantees to the employer that an identified job will be done satisfactorily. The employer pays only one salary but two or even three workers will be identified who can perform the task, either working part-time or acting in concert on a full-time basis. If the workers fail to perform, the supervisor will guarantee to do the job himself or assist the workers to do it. Usually these 'cooperative' placements are temporary; successful placements lead, it is hoped, to full-time employment and the identified job is then made available for another placement.

Work schemes of this type are, none the less, especially difficult to fund, and neither the NHS nor social services have regarded them as their responsibility, a situation which must change if we want to provide a more fulfilling life for people with mental disorder. Some of the money that is currently channelled into day centres and day hospitals would probably be better spent in creating work schemes.

There remain, at the same time, two unsolved problems which have proved detrimental to the establishment of work schemes. The first is the 'poverty trap', well recognized in open employment, whereby those who acquire poorly paid employment lose part or all of their social security 'income support' benefits. Clearly, there need to be realistic incentives to reward effort and performance; payment in kind, by supplying goods and other services, is no substitute for cash. What is particularly required is for the government to review the rules on benefits paid to people who receive income under therapeutic work schemes. The second problem for such work schemes is the lack of trained staff with the necessary technical, commercial and entrepreneurial skills to set up and run a business for people with mental disorder. A new order of recruits is required, and a new set of skilled trainers should be established to develop careers in this rewarding area of work.

Emotional, spiritual and social needs: friendship, leisure and personal growth

Human beings have a need to feel valued, to possess self-esteem, to experience affection and warmth for others and to be liked and loved in return. The pursuit of happiness through developing rewarding emotional ties with other people is something most of us spend a good deal of our lives attempting. People with mental disorder have very special emotional needs and those with schizophrenia may find it virtually impossible to form close, mutually rewarding relationships; indeed, they often feel more comfortable with an accepting, tolerant but 'arm's length' relationship where emotional demands are few. But almost everyone needs friends and someone to confide in who is non-judgmental, sympathetic and understanding. Service planners have rarely acknowledged the need for emotional support, yet services need to be organized to foster the well-being of existing relationships and to help people develop new ones.

Human beings also seek meaning in their lives, a deeper spiritual understanding of their purpose which gives us our moral framework. While for many people religious faith provides a spiritual backdrop to their lives, for others simply feeling a part of the continuity of human society provides the same spiritual dimension.

Unfortunately, just as the emotional needs of mentally disordered people are often ignored, so too are their spiritual needs. Professionals and voluntary workers need to be aware of these needs, although equally they should be aware of the vulnerability of people with mental disorders and should resist any temptation to proselytize or advocate a particular religion or sect, no matter how strong their own spiritual beliefs.

Man is a gregarious animal. It is not enough to have relationships with only one or two other people who are very close. Most people have a circle of friends, acquaintances, neighbours and colleagues who provide a network, of contacts of varying closeness. For people who work outside the home, work provides the main opportunity to form this loose social network but for others the same support is provided by an extended family network of children, grandchildren, brothers and sisters and neighbours.

Just as the provision of work is not generally regarded by health and social service staff as their responsibility, so too it is easy to ignore those social aspects of life which mentally robust people organize so effectively for themselves. People who live alone, especially when they suffer from a serious disability, are particularly at risk of becoming isolated and friendless, and people with long-term mental disorder are often desperately lonely and socially isolated. While many are unable to tolerate a close, demanding, intimate relationship they nevertheless crave friendships and want to engage in normal social activities such as eating out and chatting over a drink in a club or pub. Mental disorder saps self-confidence and lack of practice at social gatherings leads to self-conscious awkwardness and a tense self-awareness which creates a barrier to relaxed conversation and the formation of friendships.

Services which promote occasions when long-term patients can develop leisure activities outside 'working hours' and with people outside the mental health system are also quite rare. While many day centres and day hospitals provide a 'social club' environment, the environment is highly segregated and normally provides little opportunity for mixing with other people outside the mental health system or at evenings or weekends. A welcome exception are the social clubs for former psychiatric patients run by voluntary organizations. They usually function one evening a week in a local church hall or community centre and can undoubtedly play a most valuable role. They are also much appreciated by members but tend to run the risk of segregating members from the activities of the normal community.

Befriending services are also now provided by some local voluntary organizations. A volunteer normally offers to spend two or three hours per week as a companion to a former patient and may go out with the person or help him with specific tasks. There is, of course, a difference between companionship and true mutual friendship and these schemes can be rather hit-and-miss in matching the 'befriender' and the target. Also, while unpaid volunteers have much to offer, and their work deserves to be commended, long-term commitment is sometimes improved if the befriender is paid for the hours of 'companionship' work as well as being reimbursed for travelling and related expenses. Statutory services have, however, done little so far to encourage the development of such services, even though they can bring very significant emotional benefits to individuals, particularly those living alone or who are estranged from their families. It should also be recognized that it is no easy task to spend several hours in the company of someone whose behaviour may be odd and conversation repetitive or bizarre. Therefore, the 'befrienders' or 'companions' need regular support and supervision to avoid becoming overstressed.

In the old large hospitals it was sometimes difficult to detect the strong mutual, informal relationships which developed amongst patients and provided a good deal of support, and, unfortunately, often little account was taken of these relationships when patients were moved from the hospitals into the community. When the first group homes of four or six former patients were established, it was quickly realized that old friendships and mutual dependencies could be a powerful influence on the successful functioning of the group. Community-based services should also be sensitive to emotional needs and can do much to foster the development of 'self-help' groups of service users.

8 From Principles to Practice II

An accessible service

In the old days of the large mental hospitals, all specialist treatment was either provided at the hospital or not at all. As outpatient clinics developed in local general hospitals, GPs started to refer patients to consultants in exactly the same way as they did for other medical specialties. While this suited some people with mild conditions, it became clear that those who attended as outpatients frequently had quite different characteristics from those who were admitted to the mental hospitals as in-patients. On the whole, outpatient clinics catered for a less severely ill group of patients and did not reach people with severe mental disorder. The clinics operated for short office hours on only one or two days a week and were not staffed to cope with disturbed and upset people who required help in a crisis. They were also staffed largely by doctors and had little input from other professional members of the team.

Outpatient clinics still operate widely and are convenient and comfortable for the doctor, provide a practical opportunity for training medical students and junior doctors and suit a minority of patients very well. Consequently, they have continued to dominate the style of psychiatric practice in many districts. However, in the past twenty years a variety of new approaches has evolved, beyond clinics on the one hand and mental hospitals on the other, to provide a more easily accessible 'user-friendly', informal 'open-door' facility. These can help patients with more serious crises and also meet the needs of the withdrawn, isolated or suspicious person who will not readily attend an outpatient clinic.

Community Mental Health Centres (CMHCs)

CMHCs developed in the United States and first appeared in Britain some twenty years ago. In 1990 there were about 150 centres across the country. A CMHC provides a physical base for the service team, often in a converted house or community-based clinic within easy walking distance of most of the local population, and usually has facilities for interviewing, counselling, family meetings and staff meetings. Such centres often welcome anyone who cares to 'drop in' to talk about a problem at any time of day or night but, in common with outpatient clinics, sufferers of severe mental disorder rarely turn up to CMHCs on their own initiative. Consequently some CMHC teams tend to focus on more articulate, well-organized, socially competent people in a transient state of distress and have less time for the more seriously disturbed and those with long-term disorders who are less readily engaged in treatment.

An effective CMHC is one which can provide a rapid professional response anywhere in the local community, either in the patient's own home, at work, in the street, at the police station or in court. Local GPs and social workers need to know that guaranteed specialist assistance is at hand both day and night and, as distress and despair do not conveniently confine themselves to the hours of nine to five, this means having experienced consultant psychiatrists and psychiatric nurses on call for community work at all times.

Teams working from CMHCs can provide a realistic alternative for most outpatient clinic work, although precisely where such services should be sited depends on the local geography, the social profile of the local population and the involvement of local GPs. While it may be possible to provide for most eventualities from a number of well-sited CMHCs within a district, a full community mental health service should offer a choice of convenient ways to get specialist help in addition to CMHCs, for example through the local GP health centre or surgery, at a local outpatient clinic or at home. Nowadays, many psychiatrists and psychiatric nurses visit GPs' surgeries regularly to discuss how the GP and his team can best help their own group of patients with mental disorder.

Support for long-term sufferers

It is extremely difficult for workers in Community Mental Health Centres to focus their efforts effectively for a dispersed community of people with long-term problems if their work is constantly being interrupted by crises and emergency work. The demands of people at risk of suicide or of harming others must always take precedence over the quietly distressed but passive long-term sufferer, and it is often better, therefore, to relieve mental health workers dedicated to the particular needs of people with long-term problems from having to cope with the emergency short-term demands of new patients.

The 'rehabilitation' or 'long-term support' team, as well as caring for a group of people with long-term problems, should also be responsible for maintaining a register of all people who should be receiving help in order to assist with monitoring their progress, ensuring that they receive the right care and treatment and that they do not get lost to the service. A computerized system is essential for accurate monitoring and follow-up. Such surveillance should not, of course, be thrust on unwilling recipients without good cause, but it is good practice to keep in touch and know how people are getting on.

Such specialist rehabilitation work is, however, demanding and stressful, and it is generally much easier to recruit professionals to work in what is perceived as the glamorous 'acute' sector of the mental health service than in the long-term support services. But experience has shown that it is possible to create elite, high-calibre long-term support teams if they are given the right leadership and training, an attractive physical environment to work from, good pay and conditions of service and, crucially, a set of realistic objectives about what they are trying to achieve. The phrase 'rehabilitation' denotes no more than the practice of helping individuals to function as well as they can in all areas of their daily life or, more simply, to be happier and more fulfilled people. In the early days, psychiatric rehabilitation services used to be based on the 'ladder' model where the idea was to assist all individuals inexorably upwards towards a progressively more independent life. Indeed, staff often felt themselves to have failed if patients could not attain an independent life-style. Gradually this approach is giving way to one of setting more realistic goals for each individual, allowing him or her to develop, or not, at his or her own speed. Staff need, however, to strike a delicate balance between giving optimistic support and encouragement on the one hand and accepting on the other that some individuals do not wish to, or cannot, change as a result of disability and may need to be helped, therefore, to cope with permanent social impairments and distressing symptoms.

In-patient beds and 24-hour asylum

The majority of people with acute mental disorder can be treated at home if sufficient staff are available to supervise medication and give adequate support. There are areas in Britain where very few patients are admitted, because of the wide availability of family and professional support – for example, a predominantly Asian suburb of Birmingham, and a prosperous south-west London suburb. But most families in Britain are familiar with using hospitals and demand in-patient care for their relatives when a crisis arises. There are also times when there may be no option but to admit someone to hospital for treatment when there is a serious risk that the person will harm him or herself or is becoming physically ill through inadequate nourishment and self-care. There are also occasions when someone may create such disturbance and disruption at home or in a public place that others are seriously overburdened by the symptoms and admission is necessary.

Under such circumstances, in-patient beds providing 24-hour asylum may be essential. Most such acute psychiatric wards are now sited in district general hospitals; and even though it is not essential for in-patient facilities of this type to be in the same place as other medical specialties, it is often helpful for elderly people, in particular, to be treated where specialist medical advice on physical illness and disability is readily available.

The numbers of acute beds that a service needs has long been a contentious issue. If there are too few to meet emergency treatment needs, there will be intolerable pressure on families and community services because people will be admitted only as a desperate last resort, treated rapidly and perhaps discharged too early. On the other hand, there should not too many beds as psychiatric wards are a very expensive part of the total cost of the service, and resources spent on acute beds will not be available for developing other parts of the service. Moreover, if there are too many beds people will inevitably stay too long, which increases the difficulties of resettling them back into normal life.

Also, as in-patient beds are much more plentiful than supported housing and hostels, they are often used as substitute accommodation because people have nowhere to live after hospital treatment has ended. Between a third and a half of all short-term in-patient beds are occupied by people with nowhere suitable to go, and it is not uncommon for patients to stay in an acute hospital bed for one or two years when they should have been discharged for continued treatment in a more appropriate domestic environment within three months of their admission. Indeed, conventional hospital wards are rarely designed with people with mental disorder in mind and, even when they are purpose-built, they do not provide a suitable environment for at least three groups of people listed below.

People who need intensive care in a secure environment Mental health services must be able to cope with individuals whose mental disorder is so severe that the person creates serious disturbance or threat to others. 'Raving madness' is rare, but severe episodes of manic disorder, acute schizophrenia and other delusional states are sometimes accompanied by hours or days of fluctuating distress, excitement, agitation or violent outbursts which require very close nursing supervision round the clock and very careful monitoring of medication. Many general hospital units find seriously disturbed people impossible to manage in an open ward; other patients are frightened and the whole ward may be disrupted. Moreover, the individuals themselves who are suffering these severe episodes need security and containment as well as space to move about, to feel unfettered and to retain some privacy. They are, most often, more frightened than anyone else about what is happening to them.

Staff with special training in dealing with distraught and potentially violent, disturbed people are needed in all acute in-patients services, as are specially designed areas comprising clusters of single rooms, each with its own sitting and dining areas and bathroom facilities. The smaller the unit, the shorter should be the stay inside it – there are very few patients who need to be contained within a locked unit of this kind for more than a few days. There are, however, some patients who, though not in an acutely disturbed state, will need extra security for a period because they have been a risk to the public at some time in the recent past or are considered to require special containment while assessment continues in conditions of moderate security. Mentally disordered offenders who have been admitted to ordinary hospitals from the courts, or from prison, or from the Special Hospitals such as Broadmoor may require such a period of care in conditions of medium security. The special needs of these individuals are covered separately in the next chapter.

People who need 'slow stream' treatment   The amazing improvements in symptoms which can be brought about by medication have created an expectation that most people treated in hospitals will be recovered from their acute episode of disorder and ready for discharge within a few weeks. But over the last twenty years a 'new long-stay' population has been accumulating on acute psychiatric wards. A third of this group, most of whom have schizophrenia, continue to experience symptoms which have responded poorly to treatment and remain quite disturbed for several months or years.

Many of these patients need close daily supervision because of a tendency to self-neglect and poor compliance with medication; they are often closely dependent on staff for day-to-day emotional support. The remainder of such 'long-stayers' are either those who simply have nowhere suitable to live where they can be adequately supervised or those who suffer from multiple physical and mental disabilities as a result of an accident or brain disease. Generally, such new 'long-stay' patients do not need a hospital ward; a closely supervised staffed house where medical and other treatments are readily available would be more suitable, but at present few appropriate facilities exist.

People who need asylum in a crisis   There are a surprising number of admissions to psychiatric beds of people who stay only two or three days. Hospitals provide emergency 'asylum' care for vulnerable people who find themselves in a personal emotional crisis and need to escape from a distressing family situation. They want a haven for a few days to talk to some neutral listener while they conquer an impending sense of 'going round the bend'. It has frequently been suggested that asylum of this kind could as easily be provided in a sheltered house or flat in the community as in a hospital ward. This interesting idea, which is being tried out in one or two districts at present, should be subject to research evaluation of the costs and benefits as no reliable data exist at present.

Staffing a service

It is easy to produce a list of all the professionals in health and social services who can play a part in a specialist 'mental health team'. Psychiatrists, psychologists, social workers, occupational therapists and psychiatric nurses all have a valuable role, and different educational backgrounds and training experiences bring a variety of perspectives to bear on mental health problems. Most professionals prefer now to work in a 'multidisciplinary' team where one or more of each profession is represented and where regular meetings of the team are held to discuss individuals' progress. Usually one member of the team is designated as 'key worker' and has a special responsibility to coordinate the efforts of the whole team for one person, and a social worker from the local authority is usually attached to the team.

Mental health teams are essential to the provision of a good service but on their own, without the back-up of others, health professionals may achieve little. These 'others' comprise housing workers, people skilled in developing and supervising work and other forms of daily occupation, welfare benefits negotiators, domestic care staff to provide help in the home and with personal care, teachers, counsellors and sympathetic listeners, people willing to act as befrienders and companions and, finally, responsive general practice services.

Overall, however, the single most critical role in the provision of a mental health service to an individual is, or should be, the case manager or care manager, as was discussed more fully in Chapter 6. This person should be the one who regularly assesses the individual's overall needs and is responsible for coordinating the efforts of health professionals responsible for treatment, social work and assistance with housing and other such problems. The case manager or care manager should be responsible for organizing a total care plan for each individual, spanning both 'ordinary' needs and 'special' needs, and for integrating the input of the NHS, local authority and voluntary organizations.

Unfortunately, there are drawbacks to any service staffed by professionals who work only within the confines of their traditional remit. Health professionals and social workers all have closely demarcated responsibilities which are impressed on them during training and they often bring to mental health services traditional attitudes and approaches which can act as a brake on the development of new ways of doing things. A little loosening of the reins of the professions and of their 'demarcation lines' would be no bad thing, and some fresh ideas on managing mental health problems might emerge, too, from widening the social and educational backgrounds from which mental health workers are recruited. Many nurses, for example, give injections, supervise medication, discuss problems and act as counsellors, but they do not usually negotiate welfare benefits, arrange outings, arrange for the gas board to read the meter, go shopping with a client, and so on. There are too many highly qualified, expensive professionals employed in mental health services who work within traditional professional roles, and too few general support workers or 'generic' mental health workers willing to turn their hands to a variety of practical and emotional support work.

The concept of the generic worker is still in its infancy, but some voluntary organizations and statutory services now favour this sort of employee and this may be a more satisfactory way to staff community services in future than by increasing the numbers of specialist professional posts. Naturally, such members of staff will need training, in-service educational programmes, close supervision and ready access to professional help, and many senior support workers will have specialist professional backgrounds. It is, however, also important to recognize the potential of other bright people who can be trained while in post, and the problems and inefficiencies which can arise from 'sectarian professionalism'.

The relatives' role

In considering mentally disordered people's needs, we have fo ~~~
so far on the individual rather than on the family. But the effect that
people with mental disorder and their relatives have on each other's
lives is a critical factor in community care. Now that large numbers
of people who would previously have been in asylums live in the
community, there are many thousands of relatives or close friends
bearing the brunt of providing daily care in their own homes, for
example, the parents of someone with schizophrenia, or the spouse,
daughter or daughter-in-law of a dementia sufferer. Relatives often
carry enormous personal burdens, for example, the grief of losing a
child's expected bright future, or the tragic decline into senility of a
loved companion. At the same time as coping with their own
emotional burdens, they may need to give practical, financial and
emotional support to someone with mental disorder and puzzle out
how best to manage the bizarre manifestations of that disorder.

Traditional services have in the past largely ignored the role and
needs of relatives, but there is now increasing recognition of the
vital part they play. Unfortunately, the government has not yet
backed up this realization with sufficient hard cash, and the benefits
available for supporting relatives are paltry compared to the costs
incurred by the state if someone is in long-term institutional care.
In theory, the Community Care Act of 1990 allows local authorities
to provide financial assistance to relatives but it remains to be seen
whether any will do so when the new system starts in 1993.

In the earliest phase of a mental disorder, relatives feel puzzled
and bewildered by what is happening, and it can take many months
or even years before deteriorating social function gives way to overt
symptoms which can be clearly interpreted as mental illness. From
the relatives' point of view, it is usually an enormous relief to be able
to label increasingly apparent peculiarities and emotional problems
as 'illness' because illness is no one's fault and families are, therefore, absolved from the guilt incurred by self-blame.

In the 1960s the writings of Laing and his followers were interpreted by some to mean that pressures inside the family drove
victims into madness. Oppressive parents, over-close siblings and a

stifling family atmosphere were regarded, for example, as causative factors in schizophrenia, and relatives – rightly – deeply resented a theory which never had any foundation in hard research evidence. The ideas of the Laingians in part struck a chord because someone with mental disorder causes enormous disruption and upset in a family – so it is no wonder that relatives appear deeply concerned and closely involved, a factor which professionals often forget. 'Over-involved' is a derogatory label still used by professionals to describe anxious, supportive relatives, yet it takes extraordinary judgment and sensitivity to manage a close relative's abnormal beliefs and behaviour in a way which neither colludes with pathological beliefs nor alienates the sufferer. And an additional problem for relatives is that while it may be a relief to designate mental disorder as 'illness', this may be deeply resented by the individual concerned.

In normal families, family members frequently do not like each other very much. Children often long to escape the parental home and a parent may be severely critical of one particular son or daughter. Mutual liking and respect prior to the onset of a mental disorder in one family member undoubtedly helps relationships afterwards, but families in this situation often stay together through loyalty and force of circumstances and sometimes they need practical help to develop their lives and put things in perspective. A further dilemma may arise when the individual whom professionals are trying to help has a very different interpretation of his or her circumstances, aspirations and prospects from those of relatives, or where the individual is suspicious and distrustful and does not want even close family to know what has happened to him or her.

Ultimately the individual receiving the service is the one whose wishes must be respected but, where that person depends on a relative for day-to-day care, it is only reasonable that the relative should be as fully involved as possible in decisions and become a full participating partner in the professional team, contributing to treatment and care plans.

It must be recognized that while relatives almost certainly do not cause mental disorder, the emotional atmosphere of the household certainly influences the course of the disorder. People with schizophrenia who are discharged from hospital to live with relatives who are over-critical, disapproving or who express a high level of anxiety and tension, are more likely to suffer early relapse than those returning to a neutral or tolerant atmosphere, and spending less time in daily contact with other members of the family, possibly by attending a day centre or going to work, seems to help some sufferers to cope with an emotionally charged home environment. Most relatives, however, develop an amazing degree of flexibility and over the years accommodate to eccentricity, peculiar behaviour, apathy and social withdrawal, though sometimes at a high cost to their own lives.

'Informal carers' is the term used in official documents to describe close supporting relatives though it is not a good term – 'informal' implies that the task is done by choice in a rather casual fashion, which is rarely the case, and 'carer' implies an embracing emotional commitment which may be wholly inaccurate. Most 'carers' simply happen to be those nearest relatives who find themselves in an unwanted, unsought and very stressful situation.

One relative, a 45-year-old divorced teacher caring at home for her 21-year-old unmarried son who had developed schizophrenia in his second year at university, wrote the following list of relatives' needs for the local mental health service. She is now the secretary of a local MIND group in a rural area in the south of England.

1. At the beginning I was very frightened. I had never met anyone with mental problems. The first thing you need is a sympathetic GP who will just listen and explain exactly what this illness is. GPs need to be better informed and realize how it affects the rest of the family. It would have helped to have had something to read in the quiet of my own home, so I could know what to expect in the future.

2. The consultant needs to see the relatives as well as the patient and take time to explain what the treatment is for, what its effects are and about the side-effects. How can I explain to my son why he should persevere with regular injections when I don't know myself?

3. Someone should have told me about the local MIND and the

National Schizophrenia Fellowship and what they could offer. The Citizens Advice Bureau gave me help with getting his benefits right but most people don't even know where to find the CAB. We need some solid practical advice on benefits and services.

4. Relatives want to be accepted as part of the caring team. We're doing the real work 90 per cent of the time. Often I feel the consultant listens more to what the nurse says than to me, but she only comes once a month; I'm here all the time.

5. It is very helpful to attend a relatives' group. I've learnt so much from other families in the same situation and it's helped me to accept the realities. This was particularly helpful in between his two breakdowns because relatives get even less attention when things seem to be sailing along all right on the surface. And we all enjoy 'having a go' at the rotten services we have to put up with.

6. One of the good things about the group is that they get lectures and talks from experts who know about recent research, progress in developments round the country, mental health law, what to do in a crisis. We want to improve our knowledge about the problems our relatives have.

7. It is vital that relatives are able to see the consultant, nurse or social worker on their *own* if we wish to. Although the issue of confidentiality is important, patients should be encouraged to agree to this. There are some things you just cannot say when the person is present. Relatives also need to know who to contact and how when an emergency arises.

8. Relatives often want to separate from the person for the sake of their own sanity. They need to know that it is possible to find alternative accommodation for the individual or themselves. Services shouldn't assume that because relatives cope silently they want to go on doing so for ever.

9. Relatives need a regular break. While I'm out at work during the week I get a break from my son's peculiarities. But in the long school holidays the tension between us rises to fever-pitch. He goes to a day centre three days a week but it would help if he could have a

two- or three-week holiday somewhere every now and again. Then I could take a break too.

10. Relatives want someone to take them seriously as individuals, not just treat them as 'appendages to a case'. Relatives are valuable and ought to be treated that way. Community care can't work without us.

11. All services should address relatives' needs seriously by giving information, ensuring they feel involved and above all by ensuring that they are given the support they need to carry on caring.

The contribution of voluntary agencies

Britain is fortunate in the diversity and breadth of the activities of 'not-for-profit' organizations. In the mental health field the voluntary sector is, on the whole, well organized and effective but it suffers from lower levels of charitable donations compared with more immediately appealing charities such as those for children, cancer research or research into heart disease. The fear and stigma of mental disorder deter a public which is ignorant of the pressing need and unclear as to what their gifts might be used for. In spite of this, MIND (the National Association for Mental Health) is one of the most effective campaigning and advocacy organizations in Britain and was largely instrumental in achieving the refinements in the law which enhance patients' rights and are embodied in the Mental Health Act of 1983. MIND has continued to play a strong public role in defending the civil liberties and rights to treatment and care of all mentally disordered people, and it has been particularly successful in supporting individuals who have been maltreated and neglected by the mental health service system. MIND's militant antipsychiatry stand in the 1960s and 1970s created a rift with professionals which has gradually healed, although there is still a healthy tension which is probably in service users' interests.

Like many voluntary organizations, MIND is composed of multiple autonomous local branches established by volunteers, often the relatives of patients or professionals. They run day centres, drop-in centres, social clubs, sheltered work programmes and befriending and counselling services. MIND is now a large 'direct-care' organization, that is, it receives money in grants from NHS and local authorities to provide some of the elements of the total service described in Chapters 7 and 8, and it employs a large number of staff to support and enhance the work of the volunteers.

The National Schizophrenia Fellowship focuses on one group of mentally disordered people, those with schizophrenia, and, in particular, their families, although local groups of NSF often operate in similar ways to local MIND groups. The NSF has the same broad objectives as MIND – it acts as an advocate for individuals, campaigns for better local services, organizes support groups for patients and their families and publishes some very helpful literature.

A third rapidly growing national and international organization is the Alzheimer's Disease Society, established in Britain in 1979 for dementia sufferers and their families. Largely a relatives' organization, it campaigns for better services, runs relative support groups and is beginning to consider providing more direct care services.

And, in addition, there are dozens of other autonomous voluntary groups, many operating only in one locality, launched by the enthusiasm of a single initiator, as well as certain quite large national organizations focusing on one type of disorder, such as Alcoholics Anonymous.

All voluntary organizations in the community care field face an uncertain though challenging future as a result of the government's encouragement to them in the 1990 Act to take a more active, participative role in providing services directly to clients in the community, with finance provided by the local authority or health authority. The dilemma for the voluntary sector is whether to expand their services and move to a more 'centre-stage' role in running and planning services or to remain as small, local, campaigning organizations. Many feel they run the risk of losing their ability to act as external advocates, campaigning for the needs of their local population. If they accept a contractual obligation to provide care, they may find that voluntary sector care increasingly substitutes for services which otherwise would have been provided by statutory agencies; they will thus become mainstream rather than supplying supplemental, additional services. They also perceive a danger that their skills in recruiting volunteers will be seen as a cheap way of providing care.

If, however, the voluntary organizations do choose to expand, they will need skilled professional help in becoming major employers, handling substantial finances and complex planning and management tasks. Sudden, over-ambitious expansion is certain to lead to disappointments all round.

A further major problem is that voluntary organizations have hitherto been able to choose the particular client group within the field on which they wish to focus. In mental health areas this has largely been the more articulate and less seriously disturbed group of sufferers. Voluntary organizations will need to demonstrate their willingness to work with people with severe long-term problems if they are going to contribute seriously to the real work of a service, and they will need professional support and training to do this more arduous work.

On balance it is well worthwhile for the voluntary organizations to seize this opportunity to play a fuller role. It provides them with the chance to be 'centre stage' and thus profoundly influence the delivery of care to mentally disordered people, and voluntary organizations have the additional advantage that they need only expand at their own pace, developing those areas which they know have the greatest need. They thus need only provide care to quality standards which they set for themselves when first agreeing a contract and they can avoid being drawn into the 'high volume/doubtful quality' trap. Overall, a healthy plurality of different initiatives is likely to arise if a strong voluntary sector grasps the opportunity with which it is currently presented and if it is actively supported by the statutory authorities. Most day care, work projects, respite care, befriending, counselling, advocacy and welfare benefits work, as well as some direct personal care services provided at home, could be done by 'not-for-profit' organizations, and focusing as they do on one client group's problems and having strong links with families, they are unlikely to lose their strong advocacy role.

Unfortunately, staff in the NHS rarely know much about how the voluntary sector operates or understand its potential. On the other hand, voluntary organizations are often small and too daunted by local bureaucracy to negotiate effectively with health and social services. A greater degree of interaction between the statutory and voluntary agencies could foster mutual education and understanding, and initiatives need to be undertaken by both sides.

Services provided by the private sector

Since the mid-1970s a growing number of privately owned small psychiatric hospitals has been established. They care for short-term patients who can afford to pay or who are privately insured. They serve a largely middle-class clientele and, for a small minority, provide a satisfactory option to NHS hospital care. However, since chronic mental disorder generally brings with it long-term unemployment or low income, the private sector psychiatric hospitals make an insignificant contribution to longer-term services. The private sector has, however, carved out a small specialist 'niche' in the provision of secure hospital accommodation for people with severe behaviour disorders, those who are considered beyond the care of a local psychiatric hospital. Health authorities and local authorities are sometimes willing to pay high prices to buy care for those one or two individuals who are felt to be unmanageable in their own services. In 1990 the fees charged by such hospitals were approximately £50–55,000 per person per year, and while one or two of these establishments provide excellent standards of care, others offer a poor-quality custodial environment very different from the care projected in the glossy brochures used to market their services. For the same or less costs, health authorities could combine their resources to purchase better care from within the NHS.

In addition to these hospital services for those with severe behaviour disorders, there is a huge, private 'cottage industry' of proprietors running nursing homes and residential care homes for elderly people with dementia. In 1990 half the residential care facilities provided for elderly people were owned privately and in most localities there are also increasing numbers of privately owned hostels, group homes and nursing homes, of widely variable quality, serving the needs of young clients. In some parts of the country a substantial part of residential services for adults with long-term mental illness, elderly or otherwise, is provided by private landlords who may employ one or two staff to assist with the care of a few residents. The future of these private establishments largely depends on whether, after April 1993, the local authority will agree to continue funding such residents; a decision which will be influenced, hopefully, by whether the quality of care provided in these establishments is acceptable to local authorities, and whether standards can be maintained and improved by local authority monitoring procedures.

In some prosperous areas of the country, too, specialist services providing domestic and personal care services direct to elderly people in their own homes have developed in response to local demand. There is clearly an opportunity for private entrepreneurial initiatives to provide a whole range of services for younger mentally disordered people, such as home care, day care and work projects. These would compete directly with voluntary agencies and health and social services' own provision and the quality and effectiveness of such services will depend on the contracting skills of purchasing agencies and on close quality-monitoring programmes. British people are, generally, deeply suspicious of 'with profit' companies who operate in the health and social care area and it remains to be seen whether free enterprise can win the hearts and minds of authority members and staff and make a profit at the same time.

Quality standards in mental health care

Most businesses rely on two complementary forces to ensure that they maintain and raise their standards. First, they take notice of what the customers want and incorporate their requirements into their products or services and, second, they have a quality-monitoring programme within the organization to ensure that agreed standards are being met. In businesses such as McDonalds where service provision is undertaken by relatively junior staff remote from the centre, very particular attention is paid to quality-control procedures as it is realized that lapses of quality or service may have a devastating effect on public confidence and attitudes.

Manufacturing businesses, on the other hand, where product quality is controlled in a central production unit, are much less vulnerable, though all successful businesses are meticulous about product quality.

Traditionally, health and social services have muddled along without paying much attention at all to what the recipients of services think, and only now, in the 1990s, are services beginning to consider developing quality assurance and quality-monitoring programmes. People with mental disorder cannot act like consumers in the ordinary sense of the word because of the nature of their problems – they cannot, for example, forsake the NHS for another service as they might McDonalds for Burger King – but we can, nevertheless, devise ways of listening to what they have to say and ensuring their voices are heard.

Advocacy – ensuring service users have a say

While writing this book I have tried to avoid, where possible, medical language that refers to people with mental disorder exclusively as 'patients', a race for whom doctors and other professionals make all the decisions, whether the 'patient' likes it or not. Some 'users' of the service are indeed patients in the conventional sense; they have entrusted their mental problems to a psychiatrist in the same way as one might entrust one's stomach problems to a gastroenterologist, but it is increasingly recognized that the model of conventional professional medicine is a poor framework for the provision of mental health services. It is thus important to use language which reflects a real change of attitude to people who for so long have been unwilling recipients of services designed largely for society's comfort and not theirs.

Some people prefer to be called 'clients', a term which suggests a rather more active participative role in a dialogue where the professional service provider negotiates an agreed course of action with the recipient of his services. The reality is that while the professional/client model is attractive, people who come into contact with mental health services often do not feel they exert the kind of influence that, for example, a person might have when he is instructing his solicitor.

Nor are mentally disordered people 'consumers' in the sense of the term used by retail and other service industries. They can rarely exercise real choice about what is provided for them, or decide to 'shop elsewhere', except by refusing to attend a clinic or hospital or by avoiding contact with local services completely. Moreover, people in personal crisis are not very effective at making their needs felt in socially acceptable ways; they do not organize themselves into consumer pressure groups to demand a better deal, not at least until they are recovered from their own crisis.

There are also a good many 'users' of the service who are treated involuntarily, where a family member, friend or professional has determined that he or she shall receive treatment and care whether it is wanted or not, because it is judged to be in the best interests of the individual's health or safety. And while a good many people subjected to compulsory hospital admission and treatment are grateful, in retrospect, for this enforced care, many continue deeply to resent the intrusion and to deny that it was either necessary or helpful. At times they are right to feel anger and resentment; at others such feelings are unjustified, though no less strongly felt.

For all these reasons, there are bound to be tensions in the relationship between mental health service providers and those on the receiving end. If we are genuinely to make the services more acceptable and enhance users' individual experiences we must take seriously the users' views about their own personal treatment and care. We must also involve all recipients of services in the planning and management of such services.

When professionals are trained in a philosophy of service which recognizes individuals' rights and entitlements, individuals participate in their own care and treatment. Regrettably, history suggests that people who are mentally vulnerable are consulted infrequently and in some cases are neglected, exploited and mistreated through either thoughtlessness or cruelty. A measure of protection is provided for patients detained in hospital under the Mental Health Act, but the vast majority of service users, both inside and outside hospitals, have no one fighting their corner or making sure their voice is heard.

Advocacy schemes have been developed to help people with

mental disorder assert their rights and make their own choices. 'Citizen advocacy' is a voluntary movement where coordinating staff train selected volunteers to represent the interests of specific individuals, and 'legal advocacy' is a specialized legal service directed at ensuring individuals exercise or defend their legal rights. But unfortunately, professionals are often deeply mistrustful of advocacy organizations and tend to see advocates as intruders creating a barrier to communication between the professional and the service-user. To an extent some such tension is inherent to the advocacy role: 'advocates' volunteer to get to know individuals using the service, set out the options for them and negotiate on their behalf with service providers. It is perhaps inevitable that professionals view advocates with a touch of apprehension and mistrust.

It is, however, encouraging that statutory authorities are beginning to see how helpful advocacy schemes can be in alerting them to easily ignored issues and in raising awareness of users' rights, particularly those focused on legal and civil liberties and welfare benefit entitlements. Some innovative health authorities have given financial assistance for the establishment of advocacy schemes, though such money must be provided as a 'donation' or 'gift' rather than as revenue with strings attached. For advocacy groups to work properly they must feel that they are truly independent of the influence of professionals employed by the authority, since any group will from time to time find itself challenging the advice of a consultant psychiatrist or service manager employed by the authority.

At present even those authorities who support the concept of advocacy tend to wait to be approached by a local voluntary group before initiating a project. They should perhaps look to take a more active role in initiating advocacy projects by funding development work with local users and with agencies such as the Citizens' Advice Bureau which have developed expertise in this area.

Advocacy schemes focus on the rights, entitlements and choices of individuals, but they do not generally much influence the wider issues of the way services are planned, shaped and managed. Most planners and managers, though they pay lip-service to the idea that users should have some influence on the way services develop, do not in fact involve users very much in the planing process, and there is no service in Britain to which I can point at present where users get anywhere near having a significant influence. One survey reported that a staggering 50 per cent of District Health Authorities, when asked about their plans to involve users in planning services, actually felt it was 'irrelevant' to involve users and had no plans to do so. Managers whose consciences tell them that service users ought to have a voice often choose just one articulate, recovered, temporary recipient of the service as a token single voice on the mental health planning committee, where this lone individual often feels at a serious disadvantage, confused by professional jargon and out of his or her depth in the complex and confusing world of statutory agency planning. Consequently, it is often impossible for token appointees to represent the views of users effectively and authorities must become more seriously committed to listening to service users' opinions and providing opportunities for them to exercise real influence. The initiatives which authorities should aim to develop include:

- *Service-users Councils* in hospitals, day centres, workshops, residential units and outpatients clinics, which are consulted on policies, plans and changes in the service
- *'Self-management' of facilities* by people who use these facilities either by having several user representatives on the management group or, where possible, by a user-only management group, supported if necessary by a professional administrator
- Encouragement, funding and practical support for *advocacy groups and user-only forums* so that they become active in monitoring local mental health services; formal channels of communication should be established from the users' group to health and local authorities

Community Health Councils, the health watchdog bodies now formally established in every area, and local voluntary organizations can play a key role in pressing for users' views to be heard.

Maintaining high-quality standards of care: quality assurance programmes

The horrors of eighteenth-century madhouses engender disbelieving revulsion in the twentieth century, yet throughout the last thirty years scandal after scandal has been reported in the press with depressing regularity and without the concern that might have been expected in an apparently liberal and caring society. Mentally disordered people are still subject to grossly inhuman, degrading or cruel practices, and serious problems have surfaced in large NHS mental hospitals, local authority-run residential homes, small, privately owned hostels and homes and units run by large profit-making corporations. No sector is immune from the problem although, fortunately, the reported scandals do appear to be relatively rare worst cases and are not the tip of some horrendous iceberg.

Nevertheless, developing and maintaining standards of high-quality practice in mental health services, especially those providing 'round the clock' care in hospitals and residential homes, is an uphill struggle and people who depend on others to provide the basic necessities of life for most of their lives are necessarily vulnerable as they are not in a position to complain effectively, 'vote with their feet' or refuse to be consumers of a bad service. Dr Douglas Bennett, a psychiatrist renowned for his commitment to rehabilitation services, remarked that 'dust will settle' in facilities for continuing care unless there is constant vigilance to maintain standards, and I have seen residential homes, established on the surest clinical foundations with excellent staff, deteriorate within a couple of years to become merely average.

It is possible to identify the characteristics of organizations and institutions where scandals arise. There are, usually: poor professional leadership; remote, ineffectual or invisible senior management; hazy systems of accountability; a high proportion of untrained and unsupervised staff; a poorly maintained physical environment; and, above all, a consequent low staff morale. As the situation within the institution worsens, staff develop their own ethos, practices and policies to make life easier and more bearable for themselves in an unpleasant and disheartening situation. Staff involved in scandals are nearly always the victims, too, of a system that has failed to recognize the needs of both users and providers.

When services were concentrated in large hospitals, it was possible for good managers to keep a watchful eye open for the danger signals, and although the physical and emotional environment may not have been of high quality, most residents would be properly fed and clothed and protected from abuse. Now that services are altogether more fragmented, it is very much more difficult for managers to keep a close eye on what is happening. It is therefore vital for services to have a formal system in place for monitoring the standards of care being provided. Moreover, this needs to be supplemented by the further safeguard of an external, independent monitoring system.

'*Quality assurance*' is the term used for a programme of activities instigated by service managers to ensure that certain standards are met. Any quality assurance programme should encompass the concepts of effectiveness in achieving the benefits desired and efficiency in reaching and giving priority to the people for whom the service is intended; it is also important to ensure that money is spent effectively and not expended on other less important areas of need. Managers responsible for assessing the quality of services need to compile a list of specific objectives for a service, such as those outlined in Chapter 7, and then establish a measurable set of criteria to assess whether the total service meets its objectives. It is, in fact, remarkably simple for managers to do this, though it is rarely done. Too often senior managers get carried away measuring features of the service system, for example, the numbers of doctors and nurses per head of population, rather than asking such questions as: 'Is the community team's service available twenty-four hours per day?' 'How long do people wait for a new outpatient appointment?' 'How many patients with a diagnosis of schizophrenia have been discharged in the last year to a hostel or shelter rather than to a home of their own?'

Mental health services and indeed all 'human care' services could learn a lot from the more successful service businesses on how to maintain quality of services in multiple remote locations. As we have seen , the franchised hamburger and fast food restaurants and hotel chains stand or fall on their ability to supply a reliable, predictable, high-quality product or service in a situation which is remote from the centre and where the actual provider is quite low down the corporate hierarchy. The most successful companies achieve success by:

- Defining very specific standards for the minutiae of every procedure and for the physical environment; rules are written in great detail and reminders are posted everywhere
- Ensuring that rules and standards are rigidly applied by intensive staff training on a continuing education and refresher course basis and by a 'fall-back' disciplinary or, even, dismissal procedure
- Imbuing staff with specific cultural attitudes which they must constantly rehearse; part of this consists of ensuring that staff are proud to be part of a highly elite team
- Having an absolute veto on local managers creating their own rules; local entrepreneurial activity is outlawed unless specifically agreed by senior management
- Clearly devolving responsibility for delivering the service locally by pushing such responsibility as far down the hierarchy to the point of delivery as is reasonably possible, and by ensuring that the local manager is placed in a hierarchy of managers, all with closely defined job descriptions from top to bottom of the organization
- Encouraging local managers to use their entrepreneurial and leadership qualities by contributing to the *corporate* planning and decision-making structure; in other words, they can influence the future of services if they can convince colleagues and seniors that such change is justified across the organization, but they cannot do whatever they want without authority
- Ensuring that services stay up to set standards by employing a team of inspectors to monitor the service in detail
- Seeking the opinions of customers and adapting their services according to changing customer demands
- Monitoring rivals closely to copy good ideas and ensure that they are keeping their service in the forefront of developments

- Rewarding successful managers according to clearly agreed quality and performance criteria

All these features are as relevant to running a high-quality home for mentally disordered people as they are to selling hamburgers, and many services are now devising rules for 'human' care which can be monitored in exactly the same way, covering aspects of the physical environment, care practices and procedures and 'customer satisfaction' with the service.

It is important to realize, of course, that while the *system* protecting care standards may be rigid and incapable of local, independent relaxation, the creative diversity of care activities and freedoms of choice for the individual can be endlessly varied. Thus the quality of the environment which is required to provide autonomy of action and personal freedoms has to be rigidly defined in the care system, but within this system the care provider has considerable freedom and responsibility. The two apparently opposing concepts of tight systems on the one hand, and considerable managerial authority and responsibility on the other are by no means incompatible.

There are four key areas that any quality assurance programme should cover in its detailed schedules:

- Human and physical resources and the physical environment
- External links and the relationship of the unit to the community
- Management procedures and policies and how residents spend their working, leisure and social lives
- Specific treatment and rehabilitation practices and how individual needs are met

A key feature of any quality assurance programme should be a system whereby managers regularly review different aspects of the service and provide feedback to staff about their performance and the performance of the unit so that new objectives can be set for the next assessment period. Feedback is crucial, otherwise staff feel uninvolved and unable to participate in improving service standards.

Arm's-length monitoring

Service managers in public sector services usually both hold the purse-strings and are responsible for quality standards, and the tensions implicit in having this dual responsibility should be recognized. Where such a dual management function exists, an external group of people should be appointed to evaluate the performance of the service against agreed criteria. Public authorities refer to this kind of 'almost independent' quality-monitoring system as 'arm's-length' monitoring, and local authorities are now required by statute to establish 'arms-length' monitoring of their own residential care homes.

Establishing nationwide standards of care

Nationally, at present, there are several quality-monitoring inspectorates with well-defined but overlapping remits. First, the Social Services Inspectorate is concerned with quality standards in services provided or contracted by local authority social services departments. Second, the Health Advisory Service visits hospitals and health services to advise on improving the current quality of service and to examine and advise on development plans for mental health. Third, the Mental Health Act Commission has a specific and quite narrow remit to protect the rights of detained patients, to ensure that the provisions of the Mental Health Act of 1983 for consent to treatment are followed, and to investigate individual complaints. In addition to these three, there are a number of professional bodies concerned with maintaining standards of professional training, such as the English National Board for nursing, and the Royal College of Psychiatrists for doctors.

There are probably too many official visiting bodies concerned with external monitoring of standards of service. Inevitably they sometimes give conflicting advice and although, in some areas, the inevitable overlaps provide 'belt-and-braces' security, in others problems may be overlooked altogether. As services move to multiple locations in the community, the need for a unified approach to establishing and monitoring standards on a national scale becomes even more pressing.

The government should seriously consider creating one national quality-monitoring commission for mental health services with a remit to cover all aspects of hospital and community care. Such a body would be able to set nationally agreed standards and ensure that local quality-assurance programmes are working effectively.

9 Some Special Topics

Most of this book has been about mainstream mental health care of adult people. The problems of children and adolescents have not been discussed here because this group requires a network of specialist medical, social and educational services which are very different from those required for adults. Elderly people have not been singled out for special consideration either, but for quite a different reason: their needs are broadly the same as those of younger adults, and specialist mental health services for elderly people are now developing all over the country as a direct response to the enormous growth in the numbers of people with dementia. Such services should be based on the same broad principles as those outlined for other adults.

There are, however, some special problem areas that mental health services have in the past tackled very poorly. Indeed, the enthusiasm and effectiveness with which statutory authorities have addressed these areas is often a good 'litmus test' of the overall quality and commitment of local services. In this chapter we consider the special problems of mentally disordered offenders, problem drinkers, drug misusers and homeless people with mental disorder. Finally, the difficulties of devising appropriate services in a multiracial society are also considered.

Mentally disordered offenders

The majority of mentally disordered people never get into trouble with the law. They are inclined to be retiring, anxious and solitary and are far more likely to be victims of crime than perpetrators. The minority who do find themselves embroiled in the criminal justice system are usually involved in petty crime such as shoplifting, casual theft, prostitution and minor public order offences rather than violent crime, and may become frequent offenders – magistrates complain that they see a procession of recidivist minor offenders in whom unemployment, poverty, poor intellect, long-standing emotional and social difficulties and a wide range of mental health problems are compounded. While most magistrates are keen to prevent people from serving custodial sentences for minor offences, inevitably some such offenders do end up in prison and the probation service, which has a responsibility to assist and supervise many of these individuals after their discharge from prison, is usually unable to do its job properly because of a lack of appropriate accommodation, and an inability to provide close personal supervision. The community could cope with this group of minor offenders better through the provision of special hostels and supervisory care staff but, at present, few initiatives are planned in this area.

There is, however, a minority of people coming to the notice of the police or courts in whom mental disorder has played a direct causal role in the offence. The offences committed by such people are at times of a rather bizarre nature and may be trivial or serious. Three typical examples will give a flavour of the nature and range of such problems.

1. A woman in her eighties was plagued by hallucinations of loud machinery noises coming from her neighbours' houses, noises which she believed were deliberately made to disrupt her sleep. After many weeks of trying to persuade puzzled neighbours to 'stop the machines', one night, in desperation, she hurled empty milk bottles through the windows of the terraced houses on either side. Fortunately the police did not prosecute and she was very successfully treated with medication. She was also fitted with a hearing-aid and conciliation with the neighbours was engineered by a community psychiatric nurse. The 'machinery' noises faded to an irritating occasional 'shushing' noise in one ear.

2. A 40-year-old man with a long history of schizophrenia was arrested in a public car park while attempting to break into a car to

steal a blanket off the back seat. When stopped by the car park attendant, the disturbed man shoved the attendant aside, causing him to fall and break his wrist. Frightened by the collecting crowd, the man lashed out at several others until he was finally arrested by the police. It transpired that he had been sleeping rough for weeks and that his last known address was a Salvation Army hostel 100 miles away. He was remanded in custody and remained in prison for six weeks, unwilling to be treated for his distressing voices and persecutory beliefs and unable to give a clear account of himself as a result of his jumbled thinking and speech. Psychiatric reports were eventually obtained and recommended that he should be detained in hospital for treatment, not in prison. He was transferred after waiting a further month for a bed to become vacant. Within six weeks he was improved mentally and fit for discharge but remained a further three months on the ward while a suitable home and day centre were found for him.

This unfortunate man exemplifies many of the problems of mentally disordered offenders. He was held in a wretchedly depressing and isolating prison environment for many weeks while the legal process ground slowly on. He waited an excessive length of time for a psychiatrist to examine him and make a report. And he waited far too long in prison for a place to be made available in hospital. His distress could have been alleviated with treatment far earlier if he had been diverted into the hospital system straight from the police station, or direct from the court, rather than via prison. Finally, he remained in hospital months longer than he needed to.

3. The third example is a young man who falls into the rare category of those who pose a serious threat to public safety, a threat which in some instances exists for only weeks or months, although occasionally a person may remain potentially dangerous for some years. This tall, well-built 19-year-old came from a large, chaotic household in a north-west dockland town. He was a poor performer at school, often in trouble for truanting, and by the time he was 16 he had had several appearances in the juvenile court for stealing and 'joy-riding'. On three occasions he was referred by the court for a psychiatric report on account of his oddness, lack of sociability,

occasional outbursts of violence and a suspicion that he was taking illegal drugs. As he grew older he became preoccupied with becoming physically fit, collected body building magazines and spent many hours practising on an assortment of home 'fitness' machinery. He never found work, made no male friends and had only a passing acquaintance with people in a local pub, including the 20-year-old barmaid. He began to tell his family she was his girlfriend although in reality she had rejected his overtures. However, he persisted, following her home in the evenings and continuing to press his suit with increasing, insistent agitation. One evening, after threatening her with a knife, he raped and then stabbed her. She was severely injured but made a full recovery. Throughout his remand and trial he denied that he had injured her and appeared to be in a fantasy world, convinced of his own merits and powers. He was without remorse, seemingly unable to understand the gravity of the offence. However, he was found fit to plead, found guilty and detained under an order of the Mental Health Act in one of the Special Hospitals which provide care and treatment in conditions of close security.

As the years went by this young man matured and developed. He trained as an electrician while in hospital and formed several friendships with other patients. Five years later he was judged by the hospital staff and by the Home Secretary, who has to agree to the fitness of certain patients held for indeterminate periods, to be discharged on trial leave. It was, unfortunately, a further year before a suitable hostel place could be found where he could undergo further rehabilitation before finally being released into the external world again.

Offenders who are mentally disordered suffer the stigma of being labelled as both 'mad' and 'bad', although for centuries it has been recognized that some people have diminished responsibility for their actions as a result of mental abnormality and that punishment and retribution, usually demanded by society of someone who has committed a crime, should be dispensed with in favour of providing humane care and treatment. Madness, in fact, carries far greater stigma than simple criminality; society fears people who are unpredictable or incomprehensible far more than those who are simply dishonest career villains. It is understandable that society should demand to be protected from the risk of recurrence of a violent or sexual offence, but at present society's response to even modest degrees of risk tends to be overly repressive and restrictive. Services have thus frequently emphasized the need for custody, punishment and control rather than for rehabilitation and rein-tegration.

The time has come for a radical re-examination of the provision of services for this particularly disadvantaged group of people. The greatest challenge is public education in order to reduce fear and to promote a better understanding of the aims of services. The degree to which such fear exists can be judged by the ease with which the gutter press froths up public agitation over stories concerning dis-charged former offenders. People need to understand that it is possible to promote the welfare of mentally abnormal offenders while at the same time protecting the public at large.

Coordinating the efforts of the NHS, local authority services and the criminal justice system is, however, formidably difficult. The system should enable offenders with mental disorder to move quickly out of the courts and prison system to the most appropriate place for treatment, but in reality the system moves grudgingly slowly and in some parts is at a virtual standstill, leaving disturbed people in restrictive, unsuitable environments which are almost guaranteed to worsen their condition.

Over recent decades, too, as psychiatric units have promoted a more 'open' and liberal attitude, NHS hospitals have become increasingly reluctant to accept patients who need a degree of security. Many psychiatric units now have no lockable wards at all and while this may be admirable for most in-patients, it has inevitably led to the rejection of mentally disordered offenders who require a modest degree of security and who could benefit from assessment and treatment in an ordinary hospital. Such individuals may wait many weeks on remand in a prison hospital wing, some-times even in a cell in a local police station, before they are assessed by the local service. Many will be rejected outright by the NHS hospital staff and remain in the prison system, inadequately treated.

One significant advance in the last ten years is that there are now specialist forensic psychiatry services in most Health Service Regions, and most Regions have constructed special Regional Secure Units (RSUs) where mentally disturbed offenders can be assessed. But there is a desperate shortage of places and the expertise and facilities of these units is best concentrated on the more difficult or seriously dangerous offender. Most offenders do not require this degree of security and could be managed in ordinary NHS hospital units, provided there was a simple lock on the external ward door, the right internal architectural design and a team of nurses and therapists trained to manage menacing or aggressive behaviour with confidence. Mental disturbance requiring such security is often short-lived and within a week or two the person may be well enough to enjoy the normal freedoms accorded other patients.

The few 'intensive care' or 'medium-secure' units in ordinary NHS hospitals which accept mentally disordered offenders are nearly all sited in badly designed old wards in large hospitals. The high capital costs of building a good 'medium-secure' unit on a general hospital site with other admission beds has been a deterrent to developing more suitable facilities.

A further potent factor working against improving care for these patients is their rejection by local mental health professionals who regrettably often share the public's negative and fearful attitudes. With the right training and commitment by senior managers and doctors, the care of this particularly disadvantaged group could be significantly improved.

A number of recently developed innovative schemes encourage early diversion of mentally disturbed people out of the courts and into the care of the mental health services before they reach prison. For example, there are 'court liaison' services where a specialist forensic psychiatrist is available on call for magistrates and crown courts so that 'on-the-spot' rapid assessment can be made and recommendations delivered for the court's instant consideration. Some courts have a specialist probation officer who promptly channels those suspected of having mental health problems into the local service. More such schemes would be welcome. The courts would also be able to keep many more people out of custody if there were more bail hostels, where defendants could reside in a sheltered environment while receiving assessment from local services, and more sheltered hostels for sentenced offenders who require supervision by probation officers but not the restrictions of a prison.

Mental disorder in prisons

In recent years prisons have accumulated increasing numbers of mentally disordered people who at one time would probably have been cared for in the old asylums. A Home Office study in 1990 found that 20 per cent of sentenced prisoners have serious mental disorders and that among women the figure rose to 35 per cent. It is estimated that there are 7,000 inmates in Britain's prisons requiring specific help for mental disorder, and while it is possible for prisoners to receive psychiatric treatment from visiting consultants while in prison, facilities on the whole are poor and the environment is far from conducive to improving a person's mental state.

Recently great concern has been expressed about the high suicide rates of young offenders and adult prisoners held on remand in prison or after sentencing. Of the forty-eight people in prisons who killed themselves in 1989, 40 per cent had a history of previous mental disorder. Such suicides are nearly always preventable and many of those in despair should have been moved to hospital for treatment or received active medical help while in prison. Whether or not people who feel suicidal require specialist mental health services – and many do not – the criminal justice system should be able to provide protection, care and support for those in its charge. Bullying, boredom, fear, hopelessness about the future and lengthy hours of isolation lie behind many prison suicides, factors which are all amenable to management changes in the prison service.

Seriously mentally disordered people should not be put in prison. Ordinary NHS hospitals must recognize their responsibilities for taking over the care of offenders misplaced in prisons, and to encourage this, 'carrots' and 'sticks', probably of a financial nature, need to be devised by the Home Office and the Department of Health to ensure that local psychiatric services cannot ignore their responsibilities. However, there will always be a need for specialist mental health services to be readily available for offenders in prison who do not need to be admitted to hospital. A government review of the Prison Health Service was undertaken in 1990 and recommendations may emerge which will eventually improve the care which is provided in prisons.

The Special Hospitals

Broadmoor, Rampton and Ashworth Hospitals provide care for 1,700 mentally abnormal people who are judged to require high conditions of security. A relatively small number of people, about 180 to 200, are admitted or discharged each year, compared with the 200,000 or so people admitted to ordinary Health Service psychiatric units.

In 1990 staff in the Special Hospitals estimated that approximately half their patients no longer required maximum security and remained in their charge simply because there was nowhere suitable for them to go. The three 'exit routes' from the Special Hospitals, at least for those who do not die there, should be via the Regional Secure Units, local psychiatric hospitals or directly into hostels or flats, usually under some form of supervision. The RSUs provide some former Special Hospital patients with further assessment and rehabilitation to enable eventual resettlement in the community, but at present there are insufficient places to take the large numbers who could benefit. Some patients in the Special Hospitals could be moved directly to ordinary NHS units if local services were prepared to bear even minimal risks. Often they are not. But many Special Hospital patients could move straight into independent living in hostels or flats of their own with the right professional support from local services. Accommodation is, however, desperately hard to find. So for one reason or another, people stay on for years in Special Hospitals, sometimes hundreds of miles from their home area, denied the opportunity to develope a normal life for themselves again.

Moreover, when Special Hospital patients stay too long, places do not become available for others who might benefit from a place and the result is large numbers of seriously mentally ill long-term prisoners held in maximum security jails.

Unblocking the system

It will not be easy to speed up the system by which mentally disordered people are moved through the courts, prisons, NHS hospitals, Special Hospitals and, eventually, back into the normal community. Local health and social services, for example, are unlikely to develop better care for mentally disordered offenders within their own home districts unless financial incentives encourage them to do so. At present local NHS services do not have to pay for the care of individuals in Regional Secure Units or Special Hospitals; they can shuffle off their responsibilities by claiming to have no suitable facilities and, in any case, such people receive little public support or sympathy. Positive financial incentives in the form of specific grants from a specially established Department of Health Fund would certainly help. Extra financial resources might also be needed in the short term to establish a workable transfer system, though in the longer term a fast transfer system could work out far cheaper than the existing system: a Special Hospital or Regional Secure Unit place costs double that of a place in an ordinary mental health unit and quadruple the cost of a hostel place.

It will be rather more difficult to create incentives to move people out of the prison system into hospitals and instead a fundamental policy change by those who are responsible for planning local mental health services will be required. This will involve an acceptance of the problem and reality of these offenders and a determination, particularly on the part of the Home Office and Department of Health, to consider how they could create policies and incentives, financial and otherwise, to encourage a shift in the right direction. Senior civil servants and ministers must themselves take initiatives to put right the current barbarities.

Problem drinkers and drug misusers

Services for people who drink alcohol to excess or who misuse drugs have long suffered from a lack of clarity about what the exact nature of the problem is. The terms 'alcoholism' and 'drug addiction' are still in common usage but conjure up stereotyped images of ageing drunken derelicts and feckless 'mainlining' delinquents.

In reality heavy drinking is far more pervasive than is commonly realized and most drugs which are consumed to excess are prescribed by a GP rather than bought illegally.

Problem drinkers

While writing this book I surveyed the alcohol policies of a number of health and social services organizations, talked to experts at the forefront of innovations in the field and read numerous descriptions of services. I was struck by the fact that no one referred to how enjoyable it is to drink alcohol and that no one mentioned that in our culture it is absolutely normal to consume alcohol to excess on some occasions and that most people will have experienced the effects of over-indulgence at some time. While there is some evidence that awareness and concern about the adverse social and health effects of alcohol are spreading among young, better-off people, daily consumption of alcohol in the home is now a commonplace occurrence in most families.

Drinking too much therefore is 'normal', and is not a disease or mental 'disorder', although in rare cases very severe mental illness may be the result of years of alcohol abuse. Under such circumstances it is more helpful to view services as needing to be 'problem-oriented' rather than 'illness-focused'. Thus every individual needs to be regarded as having a unique set of problems, some of which may have encouraged him or her to drink too much, and some of which may be the outcome of the drinking, rather than being thought of as an 'alcoholic' or an 'addict'. The problem drinker in our society can be defined as any person who experiences social, psychological or physical problems as a consequence of his or her own repeated drinking, and services should not only be aimed at the individuals themselves but also at family members who suffer as a result of someone else's drinking.

The scale of the problem has been estimated by a variety of different surveys. Ninety adults in 1,000 drink more than 35 units of alcohol a week (men) or 20 units a week (women). One unit is a glass of wine, a measure of spirits or half a pint of beer. In the 1980s in a household survey, thirty adults in 1,000 admitted to problems with drink and five in 1,000 are known to at least one agency as having problems associated with drinking. In Britain there are 100,000 convictions annually for driving under the influence of drink and it has been estimated that 20 per cent of all hospital admissions are associated with alcohol in some way. Diseases of the liver and digestive system, motor vehicle accidents, accidents in the home and mental disorders are all commonly related to alcohol, and drinking also impinges powerfully on the work of social services, where child abuse is often related to parental drinking, and on the work of police and probation services. The economic burden of alcohol abuse falls not only on the individual and on the public purse, but also on employers: it is estimated that over £600 million is lost annually by employers through absenteeism, lateness, sickness, accidents and reduced efficiency resulting from excessive drinking.

Services for problem drinkers must focus on both the individual and his or her environment. They should aim to enable individuals to use their personal emotional and intellectual resources to modify their attitudes and behaviour and to learn new social skills so as to achieve a stable way of life with diminished or no use of alcohol. Effective agencies working in this area also provide a socially supportive environment so that the person can develop a more fulfilling life-style than the one which promoted drinking – often the work, social and family life-styles of the problem drinker revolve around opportunities for drinking, which makes developing a satisfactory role in life without drink extremely difficult.

Alcohol consumption and the number of problem drinkers in a community are largely governed by the cost and availability of alcohol, and while public education about alcohol problems and a vigorous promotion of the dangers of drink are all very laudable, investment in health education schemes aimed at prevention are largely wasted in the face of cheap, readily available alcoholic beverages, attractive marketing and agreeable social environments where alcohol is served. If the community really wants to tackle the problems of alcohol abuse it merely has to encourage the government to push up the cost of alcohol beyond the point of everyday affordability. At present the evidence suggests that society would prefer to tolerate the adverse consequences of ready consumption than curtail the enjoyment of the majority.

However, there are two worthwhile targets for health education; employers and primary care workers such as GPs, nurses, social workers and probation officers. These groups need to be able to recognize problem drinking and its causes and effects, have a knowledge of the help required, be able to provide counselling and know when to seek more expert help. Most specialist agencies find that a good deal of the counselling and practical advice they give could as easily be provided by someone with less specialist knowledge. Employers could also help themselves and many of their staff by banning lunchtime drinking and all consumption of alcohol during working hours.

Services for problem drinkers are very fragmented at present. Some districts have traditional NHS inpatient units and outpatient clinics, but these fell out of favour when studies of outcome revealed that they were not particularly effective and were not reaching a sufficiently wide range of drinkers who might benefit from the service. It is now recognized that a 'multi-agency' approach in which the NHS, local authority and voluntary agencies cooperate is more successful at reaching potential service-users. Voluntary agencies have played a very important role in developing local services suited to their own area and providing an access point for information and individual counselling. They often provide a drop-in centre and sometimes they provide group counselling as well as a link to appropriate specialist health services. In all instances it is important for services to offer choice – some people need individual counselling or family work; others merely want to talk to someone when they get desperate or need practical advice but are not yet ready to contemplate altering their habits.

Getting started on a rehabilitation regime sometimes requires help with detoxification, a process to remove excess chemicals from the body. The process can be unpleasant and dangerous if unsupervised, but with medical, nursing and family help most people can 'detox' surprisingly easily within a few days at home or, if necessary, in hospital, without untoward symptoms. Following 'detox', most people can be helped as day attenders at a special centre but some benefit from getting right away from their old life by entering a residential unit for some weeks or months. This gives a breathing space for people to establish a sense of their capacity to live without drink. The danger is that once they leave this sheltered environment, resolve may slip away. There is therefore no point in providing residential care unless this is followed by an intensive discharge rehabilitation programme. This can be provided by Community Alcohol Teams of specialist social workers, nurses and psychologists who provide support to people at home as well as information, education and guidance to other agencies handling drinkers.

Drug misusers

Public concern about 'the drug problem' has broadened with each new wave of publicity about a new drug allegedly sweeping Britain. In reality the impact of illicit drug misuse on the rest of society is fairly minor compared with the effect of alcohol, and is far less of a public health hazard than that commonest of all drugs, tobacco, a legal substance which kills about 100,000 in Britain every year. Illicit drug use also has to be set against the context of prescribed drug-taking. In the late 1980s nearly 40 million prescriptions for psychotropic drugs were issued every year, of which 40 per cent were minor tranquillizers such as Valium. Twelve per cent of women and 5 per cent of men regularly consume tranquillizers, and there is now a growing awareness of the addictive nature of these drugs; numerous self-help groups have been established to assist people who want to stop taking them. In large part the misuse of tranquillizers was directly created by doctors and indirectly by the pharmaceutical manufacturers; both were insufficiently aware of the dangers and over-enthusiastic about the real but limited benefits that these drugs can bring to a tiny number of people.

To most people, however, 'drugs' do not mean tranquillizers but, rather, cannabis, heroin, cocaine or a variant of one of these. The illicit drug in commonest use is cannabis and the majority of low or moderate users of this drug rarely experience adverse effects on their health although they may, of course, find themselves at odds with the law. The commonest drug problem encountered by specialist services is multiple drug use; a person may be using alcohol, tobacco, cannabis, hard drugs and 'pills'. Indeed, he or she will use whatever is available locally at the time.

The principles for the provision of services for drug misusers are exactly the same as those for heavy drinkers, with the proviso that services have to accept that many service users are initially very reluctant attenders and are sent by the courts, police, school or parents. Often the continuing desire to use drugs is only marginally tempered by the impact of the heavy cost of drugs and regular brushes with the law. Nor is there a typical 'addict', although in some areas there may be a particular local problem – a school where solvent abuse has become a minority craze, for example, or a housing estate where crack (a form of cocaine) is readily available for sale. Providing a service often requires a thorough local knowledge of the culture and mores of small areas of the community.

Preventing substance misuse is largely a matter of controlling the availability of drugs and this involves controlling the cultivation and processing of drugs, preventing their import through ports and airports, and ensuring tight pharmacy security and controls on prescribing. All these approaches have had a degree of success, but the drug scene is a dynamic, creative one where just as one drug seems to be under control, a new threat emerges. Controlling production by massive 'bribes' in the form of aid to Third World drug-producing countries in exchange for specific measurable target reductions in production and controls on local drug merchants requires major intergovernmental agreements and even so will not prevent the illicit manufacture close to the point of consumption of man-made 'designer drugs'. Local education and information campaigns, though well-meaning, have proved of dubious value in prevention terms, although it is sensible to educate local youth workers, school teachers, probation officers and the primary care team to recognize the problem and be able to tackle it in an informed way.

Drug misusers who particularly want to reduce their usage of drugs can, however, be helped. The outlook is not entirely bleak and it is reckoned that of those who enrol at a clinic, for whatever reason, about 40 per cent will be drug-free within ten years, although within that time, too, 15 per cent of opiate addicts may well be dead. Many people seem simply to grow out of heavy drug use, rather as many young drinkers mature out of heavy drinking.

Services are best organized along multi-agency lines, with a range of detoxification facilities, drop-in clinics and day care and residential units. Some agencies combine services for drinkers and drug-takers into one 'substance misuse service' and this may well be the right approach in a rural area or country town where opiate use is minimal.

An important feature of all good alcohol and drug services is instant accessibility. People should be able to walk in off the street when the mood takes them. They should thus be open in the evenings and at weekends as well as during ordinary office hours so that working people can attend without having to take time off work. They must also offer confidentiality and staff need to be non-judgmental and ready to offer help, whether or not the individual is ready to 'kick the habit'. New-style services of this type are usually less expensive to run than traditional Drug Dependence Clinics and the in-patient beds provided in some areas by the National Health Service; money spent on establishing local voluntary organization action and a professional back-up service will usually reach a far wider group of people. Community care services in this area offer much better value for money than the traditional NHS approach.

Services for homeless people

The major problem faced by homeless people is that of not having a home. Most homeless people are not 'social problems' in any other respect than that they need a roof over their head. The stereotyped view of a homeless person used to be of a drunkard who has slipped into the gutter as a result of a lifetime's fecklessness and, more recently, the visible evidence of frankly mentally disordered people on city streets, the phenomenon of 'Cardboard City' and the increasing numbers of people sleeping rough has merely added to the belief that most homeless people are destitute wrecks or foolish youths. In reality, however, the majority of the homeless are families, particularly single-parent families, living in bed and breakfast lodgings or cheap hotels while they wait to be rehoused by the local council. The physical conditions in which many of these families live are extremely seedy, with seriously inadequate sanitary and cooking facilities and little privacy or space. As a result, life in such temporary accommodation can be extremely stressful and can serve to add markedly to the stresses which gave rise to homelessness in the first place.

Homelessness is a social phenomenon, not part of the human condition, and has been created in part by economic policies which have deterred local councils, housing associations and private property owners from maintaining or developing low rental housing. The sale of council houses and flats, the soaring costs of capital projects in the 1980s, the loss of accommodation provided directly by employers (for example, farmers and hoteliers), the increasing need for single-person or small-number occupancy dwellings for young people and small family units, have all added to the numbers of people without a home of their own. The blame does not, however, lie at the feet of only one government but is the result of a succession of employment, social security and housing policies over the past twenty years. Large numbers of people have benefited from the positive aspects of many of these policies but the casualty list has also been appalling. Only coordination at Cabinet level will make a significant impact on the problem.

The provision of health services for homeless families living in lodgings or hotel accommodation is a task for local GPs, health visitors and other members of the primary care team, and while depression, anxiety and emotional disorders are common, few require the services of the specialist mental health services. Where they do, these services are best provided in the least stigmatizing way possible, from the local community mental health service.

The majority of people in need of a home do not, then, have severe mental health problems. However, there is no escaping the fact that fifteen years ago it was rare to see wildly deranged people on the streets of London and other major cities. Now it is all too commonplace and scarcely commented on.

There is a popular misconception that long-stay patients were dumped straight out of mental hospitals on the streets when they were abandoned. In fact the sequence of events was much more complex than that, although, as discussed earlier, many former patients were discharged to inadequate accommodation without aftercare, and progressive reduction of psychiatric beds over the past thirty years has contributed significantly to the problem.

In the 1930s, twenty years or so before the hospital bed reductions began, a period of economic standstill and high unemployment drove many single, unemployed, poorly educated young men from, mainly, depressed areas in the north of England, Scotland and Ireland to more prosperous areas in the south in the vain hope of finding work. City centre lodging houses and 'casual wards' run by local authorities housed many thousands of vagrants at night, but during the Second World War, when work became plentiful, the numbers dropped to a few thousand.

After the war, as numbers began to climb again, the government established Reception Centres where 'persons without a settled way of life' were provided with temporary accommodation. But the problem continued to get worse and a series of surveys in the 1950s, 1960s and 1970s established the main characteristics of these single, homeless people. These men – and overwhelmingly they were men – came from large, poor families, moved from job to job in catering and manual work and were unable to save out of their meagre earnings. They lived as cheaply as possible, permanently on the brink of destitution, and were often withdrawn, self-isolating personalities with few friends and no contact with their families. Perhaps 10 per cent misused alcohol and were in persistent trouble for minor breaches of the peace and alcohol-related crimes, a smaller percentage than is commonly thought. Their health tended to be extremely poor; tuberculosis, chronic bronchitis, malignant disease and infections were common. A survey in one Edinburgh hostel found a high rate of mental disorders; schizophrenia was diagnosed in 26 per cent, organic brain disease or lifelong mental handicap in a further 15 per cent, serious alcohol abuse in 9 per cent. Fourteen per cent of the sample had been in a mental hospital at some point. A further survey of men in the Camberwell Reception Centre one night in 1965 found that a quarter of them had at one time been in mental hospitals and a further quarter were heavily dependent on alcohol.

As the years passed, surveys have shown that the proportions of mentally disordered people in single homeless hostel populations have grown, while the number of hostel places available has diminished. In the 1980s most surveys found that 30–40 per cent had overt psychiatric disorder. In November 1988 there were over 3,000 places in twenty 'direct access' hostels in London run by the Department of Social Security, the Salvation Army, local authorities and private proprietors. Around Britain it is estimated that there are now 180,000 single people without a permanent home who live in temporary shelters, hostels or on the streets. The number of destitute people with serious mental disorder now living more or less permanently in this way is reckoned to be 60–90,000, but no one knows for sure: a large number of people but still a quite small proportion of the total number of people in our society in need of a home.

Hostel dwellers do not move around from place to place as much as many people think. Over half live for many years in one hostel. But those who stay only for short periods of weeks or months are much more likely to be suffering from serious mental disorder than long term residents. A survey in a Southwark Salvation Army hostel in 1987 found that nearly 40 per cent of men who had recently moved in had symptoms which pointed to a diagnosis of schizophrenia. Almost all of these men had been in psychiatric hospitals at some time in their lives, especially the younger ones. Half had been discharged quite recently from an acute psychiatric admission ward – hostels provide a cheap and available alternative to a permanent home and avoid the mental health teams having to plan a more satisfactory discharge. The other half had been discharged from the large hospitals years earlier, after many years as in-patients. Originally most had been placed satisfactorily but they had not been followed up and had drifted away two or three years later as circumstances changed.

From the men's point of view hostels offer a tolerant, undemanding atmosphere where they can live in 'a world of their own' without being 'social-worked' or 'assessed' or 'treated' unless they expressly desire it. But they live in a physically impoverished environment which provides far fewer amenities than the average long-stay ward – the cost is often less than a third that of a hospital bed. Many, too, live desperately unhappy lives and want help to achieve a better quality of existence. And it *is* possible to help by a low-key, unthreatening, gradual approach, building trust over a number of months. Many men will accept medication to help distressing symptoms but they also, of course, need help with accommodation, often requiring highly staffed housing which is not readily available.

There needs to be a two-pronged strategy to deal with the problems of the minority of homeless people with mental disorder. The first is to provide *now* a mental health service specifically for hostel dwellers or those living on the streets. That will require significant investment in specialized accommodation, social work input and health care. Voluntary organizations already play a major role in providing day centres, lunch clubs, advice and pastoral counselling, and probably the most effective way of providing an acceptable mental health service is by attaching professional workers to the places where homeless people already go willingly for help.

The second tactic is to ensure that we stop adding more people to the numbers of tragic people on our streets as a result of years of social and self-neglect. We must ensure that hospitals have well thought out discharge plans for every individual, whether he or she has been in hospital for five years or just five days, and that follow-up and after-care services are available for a lifetime if necessary. We know that people do not drift away from their main sources of financial help, social support and continuing treatment, particularly if they have built up a relationship with someone in the service they trust.

Mental health services in a multiracial society

Existing mental health services in Britain have developed within a largely white, Westernized culture with its own characteristic notions of health and disease. We have expectations of the way people relate to each other and of the roles they play within families. Traditional attitudes about the value of autonomy and independence and notions of personal responsibility and duty may, however, be quite different in other cultural groups. As a result puzzling misunderstandings sometimes arise even between British-born professionals and other Europeans, and cultural differences can create a chasm of incomprehension between Britons and members of some non-European societies.

The barriers are not, however, insurmountable, provided that professionals take time to listen to individuals and their relatives. Cultural barriers have been cited rather too glibly to explain the serious difficulties which exist in providing acceptable services for ethnic minority populations. A much more important factor is, to put it bluntly, racism. Though sometimes overt, racism is usually covert, but is deeply ingrained in professional and institutional practices. Most often it is totally unconscious and goes unrecognized by staff and service users.

A second factor of importance is the very real differences which exist between the prevalence of certain types of mental disorder, particularly schizophrenia, in different ethnic groups. Certain immigrant communities have been documented for many years as having higher mental hospital admission rates. In England and Wales people from Poland, Ireland, Scotland and the West Indies all have higher rates of admission than native English and Welsh, whereas admission rates for Asian immigrants are low. The multiple causes of migration and the problems which individuals have are so diverse that it is impossible to generalize about the reasons for these differences. Migration, for example, may be an enforced personal tragedy following persecution or a voluntary choice for a more prosperous life. Much will depend, therefore, on the person's abilities and aptitudes, knowledge of English, family and cultural background, financial and educational status and ability to come to terms with enormous personal upheavals. All individuals' circumstances must be considered separately in the light of their former and current lifestyle and beliefs.

Accurate diagnosis and treatment rely on effective communication through discussion of personal experiences, emotions and ideas expressed in an individual's own language. Good interpreters can aid communication but professionals must be trained to use interpreters properly or, ideally, should have fluency themselves in an individual's native language. At present hospitals and community services often use the translation services of a relative who is bilingual, or of a kitchen porter or nurse who may know nothing of mental health problems, or of anyone in the vicinity who happens to speak the language. Such expedient solutions are, however, often demeaning and worrying for the patient and ineffective and frustrating for the staff, and professional interpreters, though expensive, are essential in localities where a substantial minority speaks a language other than English. In some parts of London where there are forty or more languages in common use, local authorities should establish a panel of professional interpreters who are available for hire at short notice by all local statutory and voluntary agencies providing personal services to the public.

It must also be recognized that hospital admission can prove a particularly daunting experience for someone whose basic life-style is totally different from the British one. British food, for example, may be unfamiliar or not uncommonly, unacceptable on religious grounds, but it is very easy to get diet right if catering staff ask individuals or their relatives about their dietary habits.

But most members of ethnic communities in Britain are not migrants, they are British-born and bred. One group in particular seems greatly disadvantaged by the current system and ill-served by current mental health services – service-planning for the Afro-Caribbean population often creates a great deal of dissent and anxiety amongst both service managers and service-users. For many years it has been known that black people are more likely than whites to be admitted to hospital for treatment of mental disorder, more likely to be admitted compulsorily following being arrested in a public place by the police and far more likely to be diagnosed as having schizophrenia than white people. In one London area where 15 per cent of the general population is black, black people make up a third of all psychiatric admissions under the age of 65 years. Why? The following reasons have been suggested:

1. Black people find the existing services difficult to approach, hard to get access to and overwhelmingly dominated by middle-class

white professionals who know little of black culture. When distressed, black people naturally resist accepting help in frightening institutional settings from people they do not trust. Consequently they attend for treatment late, reluctantly, often unwillingly, and are more likely to be treated in locked or secure settings as their fear leads to aggression, violence and a cycle of anxiety and rejection by staff.

2. Treatments offered to black people are more likely to be physical, such as drugs and ECT, rather than counselling and psychotherapy options. Professionals respond to reluctant, uncooperative or culturally different patients by unconsciously spending less time with them. Many Community Mental Health Centres treat a smaller number of black clients than would be expected. Drug doses also tend to be higher and given for longer periods. Professionals feel ignorant and at a disadvantage working with patients they feel they do not understand and who, in turn, do not trust them.

3. The unhealthy relationship between the police and the Afro-Caribbean population has its roots both in white racism towards blacks and the historically high crime rates in black areas. Minor public order incidents can be treated less sympathetically than for white people and can lead in turn to confrontation and serious disorder warranting emergency admission.

4. The high rates of diagnosis of schizophrenia among black people were at one time thought to be due to widespread misdiagnosis of bizarre behaviour and transient hallucinatory experiences by white psychiatrists unfamiliar with normal Afro-Caribbean cultural expressions of severe distress. It is now clear that this is no longer an adequate explanation and that the rates of schizophrenia in British black young people are worryingly high. We do not know if the cause is genetic, the result of physical or mental antecedents such as infection or early childhood experiences or, as has been suggested by some observers, the outcome of growing up feeling disaffected and disenfranchised in a rejecting society which offers black people few prospects of work, wealth and the good things in

life to which white people aspire. The reasons have been insufficiently studied because of the reluctance of the ethnic communities themselves to examine the issues dispassionately and because service planners and managers dance nervously round 'the problem', hoping that the differences can all be explained away by a statistical artefact such as the ways people are brought to the attention of the services, by claims of racial prejudice in the ways staff handle patients, or by simple misdiagnosis. But these explanations are insufficient on their own. The roots of the differences may be cultural, but if so, they are deeply embedded in the current disadvantaged position of non-white populations in Britain. If the situation is to be changed, then society has to change fundamentally the educational and employment opportunities for black and non-white communities.

Ultimately, the aim should be to provide fully integrated services for people of all races and cultures which are designed to respond appropriately to individual differences. But as an interim solution it may be advisable to develop specialist services for ethnic groups where the ethnic community asks for them. Specialist day centres, advice centres, and advisory services staffed largely by professionals and volunteers from the community can successfully bridge the cultural divide and also link individuals into mainstream services when these are required. Statutory agencies can encourage the establishment of local ethnically focused voluntary organizations by targeting specific grant aid. Indeed, Asian communities in the London area, parts of the Midlands, and in West Yorkshire are now served by specialist services, a development which has been much helped by the availability of trained Asian health care professionals and a strong community infrastructure.

But specialist services can make only a fairly modest contribution to an overall plan for services in a multiracial society unless mainstream services are also radically overhauled in those areas with substantial ethnic populations. Service planners should actively consider the specific needs of their local ethnic populations for mental health services, and consult users, their families, local community leaders and organizations about the way services are organized.

Services should also affirm their policies on equal opportunities by ensuring that they monitor the use of their services by specific ethnic groups, test that the information they make available for the public is comprehensible and accessible, canvass users' views of the current services, recruit staff of different ethnic backgrounds, at all levels in the organization (although, in the case of Afro-Caribbeans in particular, this can be difficult due to the lower educational opportunities of this group and, in consequence, a paucity of suitable candidates for posts), and institute a programme of training for staff of all grades and backgrounds to understand their own conscious and unconscious prejudices about race and culture.

Finally, senior members of ethnic communities should take the lead in initiating research in conjunction with academic and professional organizations into the causes and consequences of mental disorder characteristic of their populations.

10 Community Care Works

Nearly thirty years have passed since the government gave official backing to community care policies but there is still nowhere in Britain where I can point to an excellent comprehensive service built broadly on the principles which have been outlined in this book. There are of course many first-rate 'acute' psychiatric services, where teams of doctors, nurses and other professionals respond quickly to the needs of people requiring urgent, short-term help, backed up by good admission wards where the best sort of hospital care is available for people while they are in-patients. Furthermore, there now exist hundreds of examples of small 'homely' homes which provide continuing care in domestic environments and which have helped to replace old 'back' wards in long-stay hospitals. And scattered all over the country there are multitudes of projects run by the statutory, voluntary and private sectors which provide work, day care, leisure and social opportunities. There are now, therefore, many good local schemes providing help for thousands of people, but what is lacking is a comprehensive, failsafe system in all areas of the country with adequate provision of all the individual elements brought together into one single well-managed mental health service.

Recommendations about what needs to be done to draw all the threads together have been made throughout the second half of this book, but two important questions remain. The first is whether, after a hospital closes, a satisfactory life can be provided outside it for all those whose home it had become. The second is whether mental health services can provide comprehensive care and treatment in the community for all the mentally disordered people who would formerly have been cared for in the asylum.

The outcome of hospital closure for resident patients

Very few large mental hospitals have closed completely, although many are scheduled for closure by 1995 and are only part-used. Surprisingly, there have been few objective research evaluations of the outcome of closure from the former resident patients' point of view or enquiries into what professional staff, local GPs and patients' relatives think about the results. Only in the 1980s, when Regional Health Authorities began to target one or two hospitals in their area for planned closure, was a little money invested in prospective research.

It is often implicitly assumed by service managers and planners hoping to close the large institutions that patients who have been living there in the bleak conditions of a long-stay ward will automatically respond positively to the prospect of leaving. A thoughtful layman, however, when considering the same question, may make the opposite assumption and consider it cruel to move out of hospital people who have lived for up to thirty years in a place they now regard as home. Dr David Abrahamson's studies of patients' attitudes at Goodmayes Hospital, Ilford, suggested that they are initially very reluctant indeed to consider moving out of hospital, not because they like institutional life, but because they have realistic concerns about financial resources, their continuing need for treatment and how they would cope outside. The desire to move out becomes much stronger, however, as information is acquired about what can be provided, and even after decades in hospital patients are willing to consider alternatives if provided with realistic information, an opportunity to develop the necessary skills and the reassurance that they will be able to maintain important friendships. In fact, patients inevitably hear on the hospital 'grapevine' about the likely closure of their hospital, whether anyone tells them or not, and they are generally willing to look realistically at alternative options. An opportunity to visit homes where other former patients have made a successful transition to the community undoubtedly helps to develop a positive attitude.

But having taken the plunge and moved out into a supported house, group home or sheltered flat complex, what do former patients think about how life turned out for them? Does community care deliver the promises that were made?

In the early 1980s North-East Thames Regional Health Authority decided to close two of its major hospitals – Friern Hospital, formerly Colney Hatch Asylum, in North London and Claybury Hospital, a large old hospital in suburban Woodford, East London. A research unit was established under the direction of Professor Julian Leff to study the effect of the closures on patients' mental and physical health, social relationships, living environment and quality of life and, perhaps most importantly, to seek former patients' opinions about their new home and life outside hospital. In addition, the costs of providing homes and care in the community were analysed and compared with the costs of keeping the hospitals open.

The study will continue for some years and, as I write, only early results are available for the first 278 patients who left the hospitals between 1985 and 1988. Early leavers in most closure programmes tend to be the less disabled ones who are easier to settle at lower cost than more disabled patients, but this does not seem to have been the case for the Friern and Claybury 'leavers' who spanned a range of disabilities; most were categorized as moderately disabled. The majority were settled into purpose-built, planned, staffed, supported accommodation, but some went to flats of their own, others to hostels, a few were 'fostered' with families and a small number went to private residential care homes. At follow-up in 1989 only six people had 'slipped through the net' and lost contact with services. Three of these six had returned to a life of vagrancy, a life-style which they had adopted before admission, two people had disappeared before being resettled and one person who was resettled into a private residential home later drifted off into vagrancy. It is worrying that even after several years in hospital a minority of patients had failed to become sufficiently engaged with the services or even with one member of staff to stay in their new homes.

One person was imprisoned briefly as a result of an offence arising from his disorder and was returned to hospital by a court order. Thirty patients were readmitted for a period of treatment because of a deterioration in their health, showing how important it is to offer continuing professional expertise to discharged patients; only three patients were readmitted because of their dissatisfaction with their placement outside hospital. The overwhelming opinion of leavers was that they had a strong preference for their new accommodation and for their new life over their previous hospital existence. They had gained in independence and were more likely than patients who had stayed behind to be occupied in purposeful daytime activity on a regular basis. The second year's assessment after discharge suggested a slight improvement in patients' social behaviour. Finally, the death rate of leavers in the study was the same as for similar patients remaining in hospital.

It is important to note that the 'leaver' patients, when assessed one year after leaving hospital, were not better mentally, in the sense that their psychiatric symptoms remained more or less as troublesome or otherwise as the symptoms of patients who remained behind; nor had their social networks of friends and acquaintances increased much either. However, by the second-year follow-up study there were encouraging signs that former patients were beginning to show an improvement in their psychiatric symptoms and had fewer readmissions for further treatment. One unpredicted finding was that 'leavers' developed a rather more critical attitude to their medication; whereas over half had felt their medication was helpful before they left hospital, less than a fifth claimed it was helpful when they were asked at follow-up. Perhaps this is a sign of healthy questioning independence developing in a group formerly accustomed to doing what doctors and nurses told them.

Cautious optimism is warranted by the early results of the Friern and Claybury closure programmes. It is also worth noting that these were carefully planned discharges, every individual having received a period of preparation, a full assessment of their aftercare needs and good follow-up. It will be interesting to see if the momentum of commitment to follow-up and lifetime supervision is maintained over the next few years, particularly two to three years after discharge, a critical period when patients are most likely to drift away from the service if inadequately supervised.

A much smaller study of the views of seventeen former patients from Saxondale Hospital in Nottinghamshire who moved back to their original home district, Bassetlaw, also reported very heartening results. These patients all moved into 'hospital hostels' in the community, highly staffed, small, homely units closely linked to a well-developed community mental health service. Twelve of the fifteen who were able to respond to questions expressed great satisfaction with their new homes and the three who were discontented with their new situation did not want to return to the hospital but wanted to move on to homes of their own. The relatives of the Bassetlaw patients were equally enthusiastic. Without exception relatives who had retained regular contact with former patients and now continued to visit them in their new homes were satisfied with the prospect of their relatives staying there permanently.

Reading the results of research studies is never, however, as convincing as witnessing in person the impact of good community care on former patients. While preparing this book I visited a group of sheltered flats in East Ham, in East London. The flats were in a new and indistinguishable terraced addition to a Victorian tree-lined terraced street. Many of the residents of these new flats were known to me personally as ten years earlier they had occupied an old long-stay ward at Goodmayes Hospital which was near my own admission ward. I remembered them, in the main, as a seriously disturbed, difficult group of people, peculiarly dressed in assorted hospital garb, behaving in an irksome and irritating manner. One would loiter outside my ward door, constantly begging for cigarettes and shouting obscenities if his request was refused; another used to lie for hours on the floor across the ward entrance. Could these people really live outside the sheltered protective environment of a hospital? After long months of preparation by the hospital rehabilitation team these most difficult long-term patients had been settled into their individual personal homes. The flats had communal dining and sitting room facilities for those who wanted them and there were daytime activities for those who wished to participate.

Most, however, went out regularly to day care centres. The flats were staffed round the clock, the role of staff being to help people improve at their own pace their daily living skills and independence.

I saw a real transformation in these former patients. They were still shy and inarticulate but they clearly took pride and delight in their new homes. They were better dressed and seemed less 'peculiar' in their behaviour. Many had begun regularly to visit pubs, shops and cafés in the vicinity and it was for me a most convincing demonstration that the most severely mentally disabled people have a capacity for developing a better quality of life if they are provided with the right environment and skilled help.

Can a comprehensive mental health service be provided without a mental hospital?

There are now many districts in Britain where patients are no longer admitted to large psychiatric hospitals far away from the catchment area. Generally, these services manage as best they can with inadequate facilities, often complaining that a lack of resources prevents them from providing an adequate service. But, as we have seen, financial resources are only one factor; organizational factors are of greater importance and setting the right priorities for a service most important of all.

There are some districts where professionals claim that they offer a comprehensive community care service but such districts are usually in less disadvantaged areas and such claims must always be viewed in the context of the locality where the service is based. Inner-city areas which have much poverty, poor housing, unemployment, social deprivation and a relatively poor ethnic minority community generate much higher rates of mental disorder than less disadvantaged areas. Indeed, admissions to hospital for treatment for mental disorder may be two or three times higher in such areas, both because of the high rate of serious disorders but also because in such areas there are many socially isolated individuals living alone in substandard housing, which makes it very difficult for treatment to be supervised adequately at home. Inner cities also act as magnets for mentally disturbed individuals seeking anonymity and privacy. Inner London, in particular, attracts many long-term sufferers who cluster in lodging houses and hostels around the main line railway and bus stations. It is no accident that Victoria, Waterloo, King's Cross and Paddington are districts where people with overt untreated mental disorder are distressingly visible to passersby. When judging the success of community services in rural or suburban areas, it is important to know whether the services are catering for all the potential users of the service or whether the most difficult people have been conveniently displaced to other areas by allowing people with long-term mental disorder to drift elsewhere.

Nevertheless, in spite of such difficulties of assessment, it is clear that some District Health Authorities in England are developing services where a great deal of thought, time and effort have been put into developing a total 'community care' service, often in conjunction with the local authority and the independent and voluntary sectors. I have chosen three services as examples and these cover a fairly wide cross-section of typical localities – Torbay in Devon, Kidderminster in Worcestershire and the London Borough of Hackney. They highlight the very wide-ranging challenges which face different geographical areas and the difficulties in providing effective community care everywhere. But they also demonstrate a degree of success in meeting many of the goals of community care.

Torbay

South-East Devon is one of the prettiest corners of England, a fairly sparsely populated rural area of rolling farmland fringed by a cluster of former fishing ports whose main industry now is tourism. Torquay, Paignton and Brixham, collectively called Torbay, all attract large numbers of summer visitors, some of whom return permanently in retirement – the Torbay area has a higher than average population of elderly people. But tourism waned in the 1970s and early 1980s when Britons began to seek guaranteed sunshine abroad. Since then unemployment has been higher than elsewhere in the South of England, added to by a migrant drifting population of young unemployed people attracted to the coastal towns from Midland and Northern cities by the availability of cheap lodgings. Nevertheless, Torbay is a relatively prosperous area of small, cohesive communities with lower than average rates of mental disorder.

For over 140 years the area's mental health service was centred on Exminster Hospital, a large hospital near Exeter, forty miles from parts of the Torbay district. In 1983 a decision was made jointly by the health authority and Devon County Council to close the crumbling old hospital and provide instead a totally locally based service. Central to the plan was the objective to establish a comprehensive hospital, domiciliary and community service. The notion was that each town or locality would have as its central service base a Community Mental Health Centre (CMHC) staffed by a multidisciplinary team of health professionals and social workers. The centres were to be conveniently situated for easy access, open for 'walk-in' referrals and informally welcoming to all comers. In addition staff would provide an 'outreach' service to people with longterm mental illness by assisting with the rehabilitation needs of patients discharged from hospitals and providing support to people living in a network of houses, group homes and hostels. Staff were also meant to play a role in developing further sheltered housing, employment opportunities and day care.

Even though the heart of the service was to be based at the CMHCs, acutely ill patients could be admitted to a small psychiatric unit built on the Torquay District General Hospital site. Consultants would provide a link between the wards and the locality team but their focus and base were with the multidisciplinary teams in the CMHCs.

The bridging capital for building and converting houses and hostels to replace Exminster was provided in advance of the closure by the Regional Health Authority, and the finance needed to expand and develop the new service outside the hospital was provided by a substantial commitment from the local Torbay District Health Authority. As the health authority was keen not to lose the valuable talents of existing hospital staff, wherever feasible staff were encouraged to move from Exminster to new posts in the community. The basic elements of the service were in place by the end of 1986 and from then on no new patients were sent to Exminster and the old hospital finally closed in July 1987 when the last group of patients was resettled.

Inevitably the new service had teething problems; some staff found it hard to adapt to new ways of working; a minority of local GPs regretted losing the possibility of instant admission to Exminster and found it difficult to adjust to working with a team of professionals rather than dealing only with consultant colleagues, as they had previously.

In 1988 the World Federation of Mental Health sponsored a review of progress, focusing on the crucial issue of how the services were perceived and experienced by the people who used them. They found that on the whole both staff and users regarded the new service as a vast improvement over the old hospital, and former doubters were, in the main, enthusiastic converts. But there were shortcomings in the service, too, which were noted in a later report by the Regional Health Authority. Limited help was available, for example, out of ordinary office hours, CMHC teams had less involvement with long-term patients than had been planned and carers still experienced burden and distress. Sheltered work and leisure opportunities were also sparse and needed further development, while many patients lived in private lodgings and residential care homes of questionable suitability. In addition, elderly people with dementia had few options but to enter private residential homes because of the inadequate provision of the right support to remain in their own homes, and the hostel which had been provided for seriously disturbed long-term patients from Exminster was isolated and difficult to integrate into other services, an important observation because Torbay has only a tiny number of these individuals compared with many urban districts.

The number of acute admission beds was also too small, thus creating a pressure for early discharge and a reluctance to admit. Nor was there a system in place to ensure that former patients maintained contact with the service and did not just 'disappear'. The good early links with social services also did not stand the test of time – Devon County Council contributed less money and staff to the development of the service than had been hoped originally. Links to education, housing, leisure departments and local employers were also poorly established while, on the other hand, the private sector played a more important, if unplanned, role than originally predicted, and local voluntary organizations, especially MIND, were providing a substantial proportion of day care and informal support to individuals. Finally, the management of the service was poor and fragmented, the new teams and units were not properly controlled and the organizational structure fostered professional dissent. Unfortunately, no proper system was put in place for monitoring quality standards.

Although it is important to highlight the less successful parts of the service and, clearly, mistakes were made in planning and managing the service in its early days, this should not detract from the service's very positive achievements. Furthermore, Torbay has courageously submitted its service to external appraisal and has been willing to learn from its own mistakes. The original strategy was for a ten-year programme of development. Torbay is still improving and developing the programme to address the deficiencies. In spite of the fact that the involvement of service users in planning and managing the service was fairly minor, patients and their families expressed far greater satisfaction with the new style of service than with the old. For the vast majority of people in Torbay with mental disorder community care, for all its early problems, worked far better than the old hospital system.

Kidderminster

Consultant psychiatrist Dr Sandy Robertson calls his Kidderminster catchment area 'middle England'. Kidderminster is a prosperous, if architecturally undistinguished, town of 100,000 people, which flourished in the nineteenth century with the growth of the woven carpet industry, and carpet manufacture and other light industry still dominates the town's economy.

On a map the town looks almost to be part of the industrial conurbation of Greater Birmingham but in fact it is separated by strikingly pretty countryside and has retained its own settled character. There is little movement in and out of the town, social deprivation is rare, unemployment low and homelessness almost non-existent. There is also a surprisingly small ethnic minority population compared with other West Midlands towns and in many respects, though it may feel like an average, ordinary place to those who live there, in reality it is probably closer to a 'disappearing' England than to 'middle England'.

Following the publication in 1975 of the White Paper, *Better Services for the Mentally Ill*, the Department of Health decided to fund a project to demonstrate that the White Paper's plan could work in practice. It wanted to show that districts could provide adequate community mental health services without a mental hospital, and the aim of the Worcester Development Project was to create local services in two health districts, Worcester and Kidderminster, to replace the old asylum, Powick Hospital. In 1978 Powick stopped taking admissions and it closed completely a few years later.

Central government provided funding to build a new district general hospital psychiatric unit, a day hospital, a social services day centre, a small hostel for 'new long-stay patients', a hostel run by social services for medium-term rehabilitation and a small group home. In addition to generous provision of capital for the necessary building developments, central government money was also made available for a well-staffed NHS team of professionals and for good social work back-up, although in fact local social services had already provided a relatively good service before the project began. The local housing department had also, historically, taken a sympathetic attitude to the special needs of people with mental disorder.

Kidderminster is a clear demonstration that Powell's 1962 Hospital Plan and the 1975 White Paper scheme really can work – at least in prosperous areas like Kidderminster. In some ways the service, as it is described in official documents, appears curiously old-fashioned, caught in the 'time warp' of a model of care created in the mid-1970s. It is hospital-focused, in that the consultants, their teams and all their facilities are on one general hospital site, and continuing care facilities are run by the NHS rather than by social services, voluntary organizations or housing associations, as they increasingly will be in the future. But in reality the service is more impressive than the research papers convey. For example, multidisciplinary team work was clearly functioning well – all the professions seem to take an important role in the service and when I visited in 1990, the current chairman of the hospital 'psychiatric division', the administrative forum for the service, was a psychologist, not a psychiatrist. The hospital itself was also acting rather like a Community Mental Health Centre for the locality, not as an aloof general hospital, and was able to respond rapidly to local GPs' needs and to crises in the local community, a situation much helped by the fact that 90 per cent of the local population live within four miles of the hospital and relationships between professionals, senior officers and members of authorities and voluntary agencies are fostered through personal links formed outside working hours. Kidderminster is a small, close-knit community.

For the first eight years, the new service provided all the supported accommodation that long-term service users required, but in the late 1980s, as council property became less available as a result of cutbacks and council house sales, and as staffing of the hostels came under increasing financial pressure, more long-term disabled people accumulated in the general hospital unit. However, the need was relatively small compared with elsewhere and the service has gradually been able to respond to such problems. Moreover, while in inner London it has been estimated that the number of supported sheltered places for people with mental disorder should be one place per 1,000 of the local population, in Kidderminster the figure is probably rather less than half this, a massive difference in terms of the need for long-term supported housing, which may reflect very low rates of new cases of schizophrenia in Kidderminster compared with an average district and the apparent fact that fewer people with schizophrenia require long-term care in Kidderminster than is usual elsewhere. Such differences in prevalence are puzzling, particularly as there is no evidence that people leave the town to be treated elsewhere, and it seems that Kidderminster is not only a 'nice' place to live and work, but has blessedly low rates of mental distress too.

The Kidderminster mental health service, like many others, lacks sheltered work, and social and leisure facilities are also inevitably restricted in a small town. Staff complain further that while it is possible in such a small place to follow up all their clients by using simple manual registers and check-lists, their work would be a lot easier if they had a computerized information system to assist them with their day-to-day work and the evaluation of the service's effectiveness for long-term users.

Fifteen years on from the White Paper which conceived the future shape of local services, Kidderminster has demonstrated that the principles of community care are workable given the right financial arrangements, a population with relatively few problems and the willing commitment of both the local health authority and local government. But Kidderminster is an unusual place and what works in Kidderminster would probably not work elsewhere where communities are more geographically and socially fragmented.

Hackney

Staff working in health and social services in Hackney would be the first to admit that many parts of their service fall far short of what is desirable. If Kidderminster is a mental health worker's paradise, the inner London Borough of Hackney is a kind of hell. It is a depressingly ugly place, comprising in the main poor-quality housing estates of medium- and high-rise concrete flats alongside decaying Victorian terrace houses. It has a few tiny pockets of 'gentrification' around the parks but key measurements of social deprivation such as unemployment, poverty and crime rates all put Hackney near the top of the list of the least desirable places to live in Britain. It also has one of the highest prevalence rates of mental disorder in the country, generates more than its fair share of mentally abnormal offenders and has a high rate of homelessness. Problems are compounded by a lack of family cohesion; large numbers of young people live alone or in single-parent households and many old people are isolated and living in substandard accommodation. Service provision is also made more difficult by the multi-ethnic nature of the population. All these factors impact adversely on staff in the mental health services who feel constantly that they are just 'on the edge' of coping with the stressful level of demand. The badly maintained, decaying psychiatric admission wards at Hackney Hospital feel like a temporary staging-post providing transient care for desperate people.

It is, therefore, remarkable to find that Hackney leads the field in addressing the needs of people with long-term mental disorder. The Community Psychiatry Research Unit (CPRU) in Hackney was established with charitable funds in 1979 to act as 'catalyst, instigator, helper, coordinator in developing local projects to improve the housing, employment, occupation and social support of people with long-term mental disorder'. Dr John Reed, the initiator and first director, had worked for over a decade in Hackney, attempting to establish a locally based service. In 1974 he and his colleagues 'declared UDI' (as he described it) from the old asylum, Long Grove Hospital, many miles away in Epsom, a difficult two-hour journey across London, where long-stay patients from Hackney had previously been reluctantly consigned. Dr Reed and his staff decided to try to run a local service within the borough and to manage without a large, distant psychiatric hospital.

Since 1979 an expanding number of projects have concentrated on three areas of work; first, development of a wide range of housing options; second, long-term support in the community to individuals with serious mental disorder; and third, the coordination and monitoring of local services by developing computerized information systems based on a register of all those in contact with the service.

Finance has been forthcoming from agencies such as the King's Fund, the Department of Health, Inner City Partnership, Hackney Social Services, the Housing Corporation and Hackney Housing Department as well as the private charitable foundation, a Sainsbury Family Trust, that originally helped to get the project launched, and City and Hackney Health Authority.

As in other inner-city health districts, financial constraints in the 1980s had a serious adverse effect on progress. Nevertheless, the achievements of the Unit are outstanding. There is now a range of flats, hostels and staffed homes that, by the end of 1991, will be providing care for ninety or so very dependent people. Most of these developments are staffed round the clock. The housing provision is managed by an independent, charitable limited company established for the purpose, with strong representation on its board from both statutory and voluntary agencies. There are a further thirty-seven single flats and five family flats where residents are supported by CPRU staff on a non-residential basis.

Dr Niall Moore, the current director of the service, stresses the need for housing developments to be highly adaptable so that the same facilities can be used by future generations as well as current service users. He estimates that because of the very high prevalence of serious mental disorder and the characteristics of the local population, a total of 300 residential places are needed in total. This excludes the provision required for dementia sufferers. This number of places would replace all conventional hospital long-stay provision for people with long-term mental disorder and ensure that the acute psychiatric wards did not 'silt up', as they do now, with people waiting to be rehoused. A half of all the in-patients on acute wards in Hackney are waiting for a home of their own. The figure of 300 places, which represents approximately 1.6 places per 1,000 of the population, would also include provision for the twenty or so seriously disturbed mentally abnormal offenders who need long-term care. Clearly, Hackney is a long way off meeting their own accommodation targets but they have gone further than any other inner-city service to meet the need locally. Their need for accommodation is approximately three times that of Kidderminster.

Perhaps the most impressive development in Hackney is their long-term support team of generic mental health workers, a team of highly skilled people from a variety of professional backgrounds who each work with twenty to twenty-five seriously disabled people, most of whom live alone. 'We keep a tenacious grip on the needs of the most disabled people in the community – we are there to aid their survival,' one team member said. The team has a very clear mission – its job is to do any work which will assist their clients to live independent lives. 'Our clients often have nothing left but their independence to keep them going, to feel like other people'.

The team can be distinguished from many other multidisciplinary teams of traditional professionals by the following key features:

- The team has a very high community profile; they use local, ordinary community resources with their clients and involve clients in local activities

- They do things 'alongside' rather than 'opposite' a client
- They will commit themselves to working with a client indefinitely
- No job is 'beneath their skills'; no task is so difficult that the right kind of assistance cannot be summoned
- Team members play a strong advocacy role for their clients

One interesting team initiative is the 'concerned neighbour' scheme. Through close links with local authority tenants' associations, local people are identified who, in exchange for a small sum of money (£6 per week in 1990), agree to 'keep an eye on' neighbours who are clients of the long-term support scheme. The concerned neighbour will 'pop in' regularly, sort out minor problems and keep in close touch with the team key worker when necessary. The social services department pays for this service.

The team's work will be helped considerably by the computer-based case register system which should be fully operational in 1991; they currently use a manual system of follow-up. Their chaotic office, with wall charts, flagged maps and lists on boards with notes pinned all over, evokes films of a wartime operations room under enemy attack and perhaps the battle analogy is a good one. The team has the unmistakable aura of an elite cadre tackling some of the most difficult human problems at the front line of the war against social disadvantage.

Hackney does not yet have a comprehensive community mental health service, simply because the extent of local need is phenomenally large compared with more prosperous areas. But Hackney is demonstrating how real community care can be done, using scarce resources to tackle priorities in ways which more prosperous localities have not. If it can be done in Hackney, it can be done anywhere.

*

These three examples demonstrate that some areas have progressed a good way towards providing what is required for a comprehensive service. There are many other districts where substantial progress has been achieved in spite of local bureaucratic and organizational difficulties. Community mental health services are no longer a pipe-dream but a realistic target to set our sights on.

The costs of community care

It is often claimed that 'community care is not a cheap option' and that is undoubtedly true. No new style of service is going to be as cheap as warehousing large numbers of people in bare buildings staffed by a minimum of poorly paid nurses. But good community-based services may not be an excessively expensive option either.

When hospitals close large amounts of money can be generated, but is this enough to fund a good alternative programme covering all the components of a new service? Can we really afford good community care of the kind outlined in this book? The new styles of service impose costs not only on the NHS but on authorities, the Department of Social Security and, of course, often on relatives. Moreover, these new costs arise before monies are released by the closure of the old hospitals.

In the late 1980s the cost of caring for someone in a large psychiatric hospital worked out at between £10,000 and £25,000 per annum, depending on the location of the hospital and the number of skilled and unskilled staff employed. These sums may seem large compared with the income of an average family but they are modest when compared with the costs of a bed in a general hospital which are approximately double or treble that amount, although of course a general hospital bed may be used to treat many people in a year whereas only one person occupies a long-stay ward place. The sums quoted reflect the high costs of maintaining large old buildings and the large numbers of staff that are involved in the mental health services. There is, however, enormous variation in the costs of caring for individual patients, depending on their need for personal care and supervision, and these costs are not accurately reflected in average figures; when considering any cost studies it is important to know the extent of the disablement of the group being studied.

Economists working on the Friern/Claybury research group compared the costs of the new community services for discharged patients with the costs of the old services provided at Friern and Claybury Hospitals. Surprisingly they found that for these moderately disabled people the costs under the community care system were slightly lower than those of providing the old hospital service. The average cost of caring for a person in hospital (at 1986/7 prices) was about £17,000 per annum whereas the average cost for a person discharged from the hospital was about £14,000. The range of costs under the new system was also greater; the most expensive person cared for in the community cost nearly £30,000 per annum but the cheapest cost only £2,000 per annum. It is also salutary to note that nearly 80 per cent of the costs of reprovision could be attributed to accommodation and living expenses and only 13 per cent to services provided by the NHS. The reprovision service to former Friern and Claybury patients did not, however, include work opportunities, social or leisure facilities. These were not specifically planned for as day care services were expected to cover these needs. Had these services been provided in full, the overall costs of the service might well have been slightly more expensive than the hospital service, though it is possible, too, that the costs of day care might have been reduced.

In the past costs have usually been calculated on the basis of how much money is required to provide current residents of the old hospital with a new service and the calculations have not included the costs of providing for the thousands of mentally disordered people already living in the community at present and receiving no service. There have, therefore, been no accurate costings for a total, fully comprehensive community service. However, the Friern/Claybury group attempted to predict the costs, both in capital and revenue terms, of such a total service, and their estimates suggest that it would indeed be possible to meet the total needs of a community service for all-comers from the resources which would be released by the eventual closure of the old hospitals.

The costs of services will, of course, vary widely from one district to another, first because of marked differences in the prevalence of mental disorder, and second, because the cost of buildings, land and wages varies markedly between the north and south and between cities and rural areas. The areas which have most mental disorder, especially inner-city districts, tend to be those where it is most expensive to provide services. Unfortunately, government funding has never taken proper account of these very real differences and, as a consequence, services in some prosperous county areas are gradually improving while in many inner city areas services are deteriorating. But the Friern/Claybury figures suggest that community care is not beyond our aspirations. Nor is there a bottomless pit of need; the numbers of people affected can be calculated. Community care for people with mental disorder is both affordable and practicable.

Concluding remarks

One winter's evening in 1989 I was walking back to the City from Guy's Hospital, over London Bridge. I was startled by a filthy, smelly woman, perhaps in her forties, shouting obscenities to an unseen tormenter, oblivious to passers-by. People like her are a common enough sight now in London near any station, but I recognized this woman from her short stay in Guy's a week or two earlier. I recalled the scene in Dickens' *Little Dorrit* where Amy was similarly startled one evening in the very same spot by a deranged lunatic while walking back across the old Iron Bridge to the Marshalsea prison. The scene made me feel that little had changed since Dickens exposed the nastiness of the life of London paupers and the hypocrisy of its forbidding institutions. We must make community care work if we are to avoid slipping yet further back to the pre-Dickensian era of neglect. The vision of real community care needs a united effort to push it back on to the political agenda. Better mental health services are clearly within our grasp now.

Useful Addresses

Alzheimer's Disease Society
158–160 Balham High Road, London SW12
Tel: 081-675 6557

MIND (National Association for Mental Health)
22 Harley Street, London, W1
Tel: 071-637 0741

Good Practices in Mental Health
380–384 Harrow Road, London W9 2HU
Tel: 071-289 2034

National Schizophrenia Fellowship
28 Castle Street, Kingston upon Thames, Surrey KT1 1SS
Tel: 081-547 3937

Mental Health Foundation
8 Hallam Street, London W1N 6DH
Tel: 071-580 0145

Peter Bedford Trust
Legard Works, 17a Legard Road, Highbury, London N5 1DE
Tel: 071-226 6074

Index